Reflections on Philosophy and Religion

Reflections on Philosophy and Religion

Alan Donagan

Edited with an Introduction by
Anthony N. Perovich Jr.

New York   Oxford   Oxford University Press   1999

Oxford University Press

Oxford   New York

Athens   Auckland   Bangkok   Bogotá   Buenos Aires   Calcutta
Chennai   Cape Town   Dar es Salaam   Delhi   Florence   Hong Kong   Istanbul
Karachi   Kuala Lumpur   Madrid   Melbourne   Mexico City   Mumbai
Nairobi   Paris   São Paulo   Singapore   Taipei   Tokyo   Toronto   Warsaw

and associated companies in
Berlin   Ibadan

Published by Oxford University Press, Inc.
198 Madison Avenue, New York, New York 10016

Library of Congress Cataloging-in-Publication Data
Donagan, Alan.
Reflections on philosophy and religion / Alan Donagan
edited with an introduction by Anthony N. Perovich Jr.
p. cm.
Book is based on papers presented at various symposiums and
colloquiums at different times.
Includes index.
ISBN 0-19-512132-5
1. Philosophy and religion.   2. Christianity—Philosophy.
3. Christian ethics.   I. Perovich, Anthony N. (Anthony Novak),
1951–   .   II. Title.
B945.D621 1998
191—dc21   98-20754

1 3 5 7 9 8 6 4 2

Printed in the United States of America
on acid-free paper

For Henry Veatch
Alan's friend and guide

Preface

This volume brings together Alan Donagan's most important writings about religion. Several of these papers are explicitly about religion, and the Christian faith in particular. Others deal with philosophical topics that provide the context within which his ideas about religion need to be understood. These essays and lectures, while conceived independently, have a systematic interconnection with one another and with Donagan's work in ethics and action theory that I try to bring out in the Introduction and in their organization. This systematic viewpoint would surely have been more fully developed had he lived longer, but the outlines are sufficiently clear, I think, to offer inspiration and guidance to all those inclined to pursue their thinking in similar directions.

I have personal reasons for being grateful for being able to prepare this collection. Toward the end of my years at the University of Chicago, where I had studied under Alan Donagan during the mid-1970s, I began to think more seriously about issues of religious faith than I had up to that point. Shortly before I left I visited Alan to discuss some of my questions with him; without being at all sure of the precise nature of his views, I knew enough to expect a sympathetic hearing and a thoughtful reply, and of course I received both. Although I was much too shy to ask him directly about his own beliefs, the tenor of his response was such that I was not surprised to learn a short time afterward that he had himself become a Christian. In the following years I did not hesitate to consult him in regard to religious matters that perplexed or intrigued me, and I never failed to receive a response that was illuminating, or encouraging, or both. It was thus not only an honor but an opportunity to take a small step toward the discharge of spiritual and intellectual debts when, after Alan's death, Barbara Donagan sent me the following papers and asked, after we had agreed that they would constitute a valuable collection, if I would undertake their editing. I am very glad to have done so, for it was only as the result of my protracted acquaintance with them that I came to appreciate the very definite place they occupied in the systematic structure of his thought.

My indebtedness extends in many directions. Above all I should like to thank Barbara Donagan for asking me to undertake this volume, for her patience and support once it was under way, and not least for her transcription of some passages and more lengthy sections left in Alan's rather crabbed handwriting. She also furnished the dedication to Henry Veatch, who was kind enough to supply me with the comments he made at the memorial service for Alan at the University of Chicago and to give me permission to quote from them. Sander deHaan, Don Garrett, Arthur Holmes, Richard Mouw, Kelly Osborne, Allen Roth, and Peter Schakel replied to specific questions that arose along the way. (Professor Garrett, in addition to responding most patiently to a large number of questions, also helpfully supplied me with the proofs of Alan's article on "Spinoza's Theology.") Andrew Dell'Olio, Bobby Fong, Carol Simon, Henry Veatch, and Alan Verhey read an earlier draft of the Introduction and greatly improved it through their suggestions. My editor at Oxford, Cynthia A. Read, offered very helpful advice at several key junctures. Sally Smith prepared typescripts of most of the articles and did much else to ready the collection for publication. Troy Suess and Jeremy Van Ek worked very hard making sure that the typescript of this volume differed from its sources only in intended ways. Hope College, in particular through the Willard Wichers Fund for Faculty Development, a Third Reformed Church Faculty Development Grant, and part of a sabbatical leave, generously supported work on this volume. My wife, Nancy, has not only been an interested and supportive observer of my efforts but also provides the context in which any such efforts seem worthwhile. My gratitude to all the above is most deeply felt.

A. N. P.
Hope College
1998

Contents

Editor's Introduction:
Alan Donagan's Papers on Philosophy and Religion

*A*t a memorial service held for Alan Donagan at the University of Chicago, Henry Veatch, after recalling some of the administrative accomplishments of Donagan's career and the personal qualities for which he was so well loved, remarked on the place religion had come to occupy in his philosophical thinking:

> Indeed, what many may not have realized was that in these latter years he had become a convert to Christianity, with the result that his philosophic enterprise tended quietly, but increasingly, to become one of "faith seeking understanding" (*fides quaerens intellectum*). True, his death came too soon for him to have been able to work out just how it was that his faith might be made to contribute to his understanding, and yet without at the same time adulterating that understanding; or his understanding be made to contribute to his faith, without becoming a mere crutch for that faith to lean on. And what a tragic loss this has accordingly meant for those of his friends who, like him, were seeking to be Christians as well as philosophers. For with his remarkable learning and insight as regards the entire history of Western philosophy and theology—an insight and a learning that were focused particularly on the figures of both St. Thomas Aquinas and Immanuel Kant—Alan Donagan could have been "a true light to lighten the Gentiles," as it were—which is to say, those others of us who, as his friends, might hope to become, if not actual philosopher kings of the stature of Alan Donagan, then at least more truly Christian philosophers, following in his footsteps.[1]

Professor Veatch is unquestionably right to point out that it was a concern with Christianity[2] in particular and not simply with religion in general—moreover, a concern rooted in active adherence rather than merely academic curiosity—that stimulated much of Donagan's philosophical reflection during the last dozen years of his life. Veatch is also right to identify St. Thomas and Kant as the two figures most central to Donagan's effort to think through the relation of the Christian faith to philosophy. But while Veatch is justified in lamenting the fact that death prevented Donagan from bringing that project to completion, this collection shows that he had carried that undertaking further than might have been suspected: some writings in which he explored that relation most fully were not published by him, and, when taken together with those that were, a well-integrated conception emerges—more what might be called a Christian-philosophical worldview than a philosophy of religion in the ordinary sense—in which faith is exhibited as coherent with and indeed as a needed supplement to an independently defensible philosophical core.

The papers in this collection, taken in conjunction with Donagan's writings on the theory of action and on moral philosophy, suggest a straightforward argument that leads from his action theory through his moral philosophy to his reflections on Christianity. I shall first present that argument in summary fashion and then proceed to relate the following papers to it by commenting on the three most significant issues it raises: (i) naturalism, antinaturalism, and the identification of *praeambula fidei*; (ii) Kant, Aquinas, and the integration of the end in itself with the image of God, and (iii) Christianity, philosophy, and the criteria for a satisfactory religion.

The Argument in Brief

St. Thomas Aquinas speaks of God's existence and some other like truths not as articles of faith, but as *praeambula*, preambles to or presuppositions of those articles, because he believes that they can be established by philosophical argument and yet concern matters about which further, revealed truths have been presented in the Christian faith.[3] Donagan believes that no such attempted proofs of God's existence are successful, and that in any case the identification of the object of a philosophically established thesis with the object of a revealed truth is never assured and is always open to challenge. This does not, however, lead him to dismiss the idea of a *praeambulum fidei*, but rather to locate it elsewhere, in metaphysical claims that can be established philosophically but that do not concern matters about which revelation is typically thought to speak: the preambles of faith are to be found, according to Donagan, in the theory of action rather than in natural theology. A passage from section 5 of "Can Anybody in a Post-Christian Culture Rationally Believe the Nicene Creed?" viewed and expanded in the light of remarks found elsewhere in his writings, makes clear the interlocking relations among action theory, moral theory, and Christianity in his comprehensive viewpoint, and outlines the argument central to his conception of philosophy and religion.

> If philosophy provides any *praeambula fidei* it is in the theory of human action, and in particular in that part of it sometimes called "moral psychology." In conceiving human beings as creatures of will as well as of desire, and in refusing to think of their actions as predetermined outcomes of their desires and beliefs, Christianity presents naturalism with the task either of giving a naturalist account of the will, so understood, or of showing that it is a chimaera. The poverty of existing naturalist accounts of the human psyche, and in particular of the phenomena of special interest to Christianity—those of a will that is free (in each individual case, there are options between which it can choose), and which nevertheless predictably will not in all cases make the right choice it can make—should be better recognized than they are. These phenomena point to the unique status of human beings among known animals: they alone can recognize the difference between moral good and evil, and act on it; and yet they are compelled to judge themselves evil by virtue of the ways they in fact choose to act.

This paragraph provides an epitome of Donagan's worldview, a view from which Christianity and philosophy are seen to be mutually supportive. On the one hand, particular convictions about our nature as agents (and the moral philosophy that those convictions undergird) are presupposed by Christianity but are independently defensible by philosophy. On the other hand, the combined theories of action and morality stand in need of supplementation and generate a need for the explanation of certain recognizable patterns of human behavior that seem puzzling when taken in conjunction with those theories.

The argument that this passage suggests begins with a conception of human beings as possessed of a will, that is, a power (of a sort Donagan, following the Aristotelian tradition, calls a "rational appetite") to choose or not to choose what they do. He believes we are entitled to attribute such a power to ourselves because his theory of action, and our culture's traditional concepts and beliefs about human action (with which he regards his theory as consistent), both presuppose that we have a will and because, contrary to what many naturalists think, no objections have succeeded in showing either that we do not have such a power or that possession of it is incompatible with current scientific knowledge.[4]

Second, common morality, of which the Kantian principle of respect provides the foundation, finds in precisely such a power of willing its best support. For the ability rationally to decide what to do independently of what our beliefs and desires would by themselves dictate makes human beings—for a variety of direct and indirect reasons to be discussed below—ends in themselves, bestowing on them a dignity not shared by nonrational creatures and entitling them to respect in consequence of this dignity. Hence the fundamental moral principle from which all further moral precepts are to be deduced: every human being is to be respected as being a rational creature; one must never use another rational being merely as a means.[5]

Finally, the combination of theory of action and morality sketched here is inadequate, not because it is unsound but because it is insufficiently explanatory and comprehensive. Taken together, the theory of action and morality suggest that human beings know what is right and have a capacity by which, apparently, they can choose to do what they know to be right; nevertheless, what we observe is that human beings all too often choose what is wrong instead. Furthermore, morality provides only a partial account of what a good life involves; in particular, it tells us nothing about the purpose of life. For Donagan, it is at this point that the philosophical relevance of Christianity becomes apparent: it is a doctrine that is consistent with the philosophical theories regarding action and morality that he believes to be true,[6] it explains and offers a remedy for the human predicament of knowing good and doing evil, and it offers a vision of what life is for. It is clearly Donagan's conviction that Christianity satisfies these needs, generated but unattended to by the theories of action and morality, and satisfies them better than any other view, even if establishing this latter claim requires more than the papers left to us provide. Nevertheless, the outlines of his conception are clear and offer a novel conception of how philosophy and Christianity can be integrated into a mutually reinforcing whole, one in which philosophy defends what Christianity presupposes and in which Christianity supplies the sort of complement that philosophy needs but evidently lacks.

Naturalism, Antinaturalism, and the Identification of Praeambula Fidei

Philosophy as Donagan sees it does not merely defend what Christianity presupposes. The defense at the same time challenges the naturalism that is perhaps contemporary Christianity's most dangerous intellectual threat. Donagan's description (from "Philosophy and the Possibility of Religious Orthodoxy") of the background assumption of much scientific work by the end of the nineteenth century—"that there [is] nothing but nature, and that ideally everything that happens, if it has an explanation at all, has an explanation in terms of one or more of the natural sciences"—could serve as a working definition of what he means by the term "naturalism." His opposition to naturalism emerges in several of the essays below but is especially evident in the first two. He was particularly severe in his criticisms of contemporary versions of naturalism, not merely because he thought many of their claims false but also because he found a number of the drawbacks that he identified to consist of unnecessary, self-inflicted defects. For example, while contemporary naturalisms are flawed insofar as they tend to be materialistic[7] and to be incapable of telling us anything about what makes life meaningful, such failings are avoided by the naturalism of Spinoza; in fact, he remarked that he wrote his book on Spinoza "to help philosophers who aspire to work out an adequate naturalism to learn from the greatest of their naturalist predecessors."[8] (Spinoza, by the way, might well be added to Professor Veatch's list of the philosophers who did the most to shape Donagan's conception of what an adequate philosophy looks like.[9] One might say that Spinoza offered the most successful naturalist counterpart to the antinaturalist philosophy that Donagan was himself developing, a counterpart from which even the antinaturalist could learn.) In his deep concern with the purpose of life—with human blessedness, with the intellectual love of God, with the acceptance of nature—Spinoza is seen to have been possessed of a profoundly religious nature, albeit one compatible with his naturalism.[10] The failure of contemporary naturalism here lies in its inability to tell us anything about what life is for; the failure of the better sorts of naturalism must be that they do not provide as satisfying accounts of the purpose of life as supernaturalism (and, in particular, Christianity) does.

While what Donagan has to say about the question "What is life for?" will be considered below, there are other defects of naturalism to be addressed. From his Christian perspective, naturalism is unavoidably and obviously flawed because it denies the existence of God, a supernatural being who created, sustains, and on occasion intervenes in the natural world. Consequently, the unacceptability of naturalism would be most adequately demonstrated if one were able to establish philosophically the truth of these supernaturalist claims. However, according to Donagan, the philosopher is in fact unable to prove that God exists or that God created and intervenes in the world. While it can be shown that such beliefs are possibly true in the sense of being neither self-contradictory nor reported only in patently fabricated documents, and so on, the frontal assault of philosophical theology does not achieve its goal of conclusively establishing the truth of such claims and thus the inadequacy of naturalism. His view is here closer to that of Spinoza than to that of many of Spinoza's theistic contemporaries, for although nature is, according to Donagan, the creation of supernature, it nevertheless appears (at least to the scientifically oriented investigator) as if it were not so dependent. Thus there is nothing in the ordinary course of nature that can successfully be shown to provide a basis for establishing the existence and characteristics of nature's Author. Such beliefs, if they come, come as the acceptance of a revelation, not as the result of a philosophical demonstration: they are *de fide*, not *praeambula fidei*.

Contemporary naturalism, however, also treats another subject area central to the foundation of Donagan's philosophico-religious enterprise, namely the proper way to understand human action and the beings who produce it. Unlike the existence of God, this topic *is* amenable to philosophical treatment, so that any inadequacies of naturalism that emerge here do not require the eyes of faith in order to be perceived. While the philosophical consequences here reach beyond issues of causality, that is perhaps the best place to begin.

Naturalist philosophers who regard the natural sciences as providing the prototype for all satisfactory descriptions and explanations of observable phenomena will plainly not hesitate to insist that human action be accounted for in the same terms used in more fundamental, "better understood" scientific contexts. (The most basic context is typically thought to be provided by physics.) In particular, such naturalist views imply that human action is to be explained by reference to the same conception of causality as is adequate for the investigation of nature. Donagan, on the other hand, tries to develop a theory of action that defends the need for and the legitimacy of an alternative type of causality. Explanations employing this alternative causality he holds to be more adequate than the explanations of human action that, while appealing to the everyday concepts of desire and belief, do not employ this alternative, and by far preferable to those views that, by not availing themselves of everyday concepts at all, are unable to explain or even to make sense of the ordinary phenomena connected with human action.

In his book on the theory of action he asks about the account developed there, "What does it imply about who and what we are?" The answer is in two parts and draws on a distinction among intellectual cognitive attitudes such as believing, felt appetites such as desiring, and intellectual appetites such as wishing:

> First of all, [it implies] that we are creatures not merely of desire, but also of will.... [A]n acceptable theory of intention must show that human action can[not] be explained ... in terms of beliefs and felt desires alone (a view which allows human beings intellectual cognitive attitudes, but not intellectual appetites).... And secondly, it implies that will is a general power to choose intellectual appetitive attitudes, whether they be choices to do now what you believe to be in your power, or wishes, or intentions. In addition, ... this general power is of a kind which its possessors may exercise or not, unlike the power of fire to burn or of water to quench.[11]

These implications constitute suitable *praeambula fidei*.[12] They provide the basis of a philosophical picture of ourselves that is not only consistent with and indeed presupposed by Christianity but that also—at least from the perspective of faith—is "completed" by the picture Christianity offers. How this is so will be explored more fully below, but here it is the antinaturalist character of these implications that needs to be explained.

Donagan's account of human capacities stands opposed to naturalism by employing a conception of causality different from the standard one employed by naturalists. Cause and effect is most often understood as a relation between two events such that the first is (part of) a sufficient condition for bringing about the second. If this is the only way in which the idea of causality is to be understood, it would seem to be impossible for humans to possess a power such as Donagan takes the will to be, namely, a capacity exercised by the agent. The cause in this latter case is not an event but a substance, and, insofar as the will is a power to choose or not to choose, the effects that it produces would thereby have no (logically) sufficient conditions.

The first sort of causation, held by the typical philosophical naturalist to be the only variety, is often called "event-causation," the second "agent-causation." While some contemporaries hold this latter variety to be unintelligible, Donagan approvingly and repeatedly quotes J. L. Austin's claim that it is in fact the root idea of causation[13] and notes that it has a long and distinguished pedigree:

> Not only uninstructed common opinion, but a venerable philosophical tradition, holds that human actions are not mere links in chains of event-causation. Ac-

cording to the position in question, human actions are not, strictly speaking, caused by other events at all, although they may be reactions or responses to them. Rather, they are caused by agents. Aristotle drew the distinction between event-causation and what may be called "agent-causation" by an example: "The stick moves the stone and is moved by the hand, which again is moved by the man: in the man, however, we have reached a mover that is not so in virtue of being moved by something else" [*Physics* VIII, 256ᵃ6–8]. Whereas the three events—the movement of the hand, the movement of the stick, and the movement of the stone—form a chain of event-causes and effects, the cause of the movement of the hand is not another event but a substance—a man.[14]

Donagan frequently distinguishes between the genuine constraints on our beliefs imposed by the actual developments of the sciences and those imposed by a too-ready acceptance of the predictions regarding the future developments of the sciences made by naturalist philosophers. Singling out the former for our respect is more sober and a good deal less limiting than attending unduly to the latter. And in Donagan's view there are no well-established scientific or philosophical results with which agent-causation is incompatible, and this conception of causality is therefore available to us if we find it philosophically superior to any of its rivals.

One rival account undertakes to explain actions as the results of our beliefs and felt desires. Now, while beliefs and felt desires are propositional attitudes and not events, explanations that appeal to them are nevertheless explanations by way of events.[15] Hence, such an account is compatible with a naturalism committed only to event-causation. However, according to Donagan, appeals merely to beliefs and felt desires are insufficient for the adequate explanation of human action: sometimes we choose not to gratify our strongest desire even though we believe we know how to do so, and this fact introduces an element into agency, viz., the will, that as noted will not sanction explanations merely by way of events.

A more radical rival account would be offered by a cognitive science that jettisoned all explanations in terms of beliefs, desires (and, for that matter, the will) as a primitive—and false—"folk psychology." But Donagan points out that history depends on such "folk psychology" and recalls Collingwood's observation that natural science exists in the context of history: until a plausible successor discipline to history emerges, a cognitive science that would jettison propositional attitudes will exhibit an incoherence between its psychological claims and its historical understanding of its own motivation:

> The [psychological] thesis that there are no beliefs is perfectly intelligible; and so is the [historical] thesis that the belief that there are beliefs underlies a stagnant research program. Both Churchland and Stich, in their different ways, assert the latter in arguing for the former. The objection is that it is inconsistent to do so. This objection may be unsound, but it begs no question. And on its face it is sound.[16]

Such a successor discipline would need to provide a naturalist substitute not only for explanations now given in terms of belief and desire but also for phenomena involving the will. While such a naturalist successor to history may appear, it is not in the offing, and Donagan sees no reason to be sanguine that it will ever arrive.

Praeambula fidei, then, are located in the antinaturalist foundations of Donagan's viewpoint. They are located not in supernaturalist claims, philosophically established, about God's existence, but in antinaturalist claims, philosophically established, about human agency. As already indicated, understanding how such claims function as *praeambula fidei* requires that we follow a route through moral philosophy.

Kant, Aquinas, and the Integration of the End in Itself with the Image of God

The fundamental principle of morality does not, according to Donagan, require or permit a merely theological foundation. On this, as on many other points, he agrees with Kant. However, while insisting on the autonomy of morality, Kant nevertheless did acknowledge that moral precepts are also properly viewed from the religious perspective as divine commands.[17] Donagan believes as well that moral rules are correctly regarded as divine commands, but only derivatively, insofar as they issue from reason, and insofar as God is recognized as the exemplar of the reason that is realized, albeit less perfectly, in human beings. And he believes, moreover, that the code of morality that can be discovered by unaided practical reason has also been revealed by God. But the interconnection—a connection that is theological, not logical—between autonomous morality and Christian faith goes even further. In Donagan's view the Aristotelian-Thomistic idea of an agent-cause, the Kantian conception of the end in itself, and the Christian doctrine of the image of God are all interwoven. The last-named, however, is not essential for understanding or justifying either what the demands of morality are or the claim that one is bound by them. The central idea connecting these is the second of the two sorts of teleology to the exposition of which Donagan returned again and again.

The point on which his nontheological and Christian views about morality converge—the second sort of teleology—is the idea of a pre-existent end for which an agent acts.[18] Because the main writings where Donagan distinguished between two teleologies are contained in this volume,[19] there is little need to discuss them at length. His thinking on this matter is already implicit in "The Scholastic Theory of Moral Law in the Modern World," the earliest of the essays printed here and the only one written before he became a Christian. It is explicitly discussed in several of the other essays included here and is perhaps most thoroughly expounded in his Aquinas Lecture "Human Ends and Human Actions." In their common recognition of this second sort of teleology Donagan seeks to display an underlying affinity between the moral views of Aquinas and Kant.

Not all ends are brought about, although of course some are. Those that are—ends that are producible—represent the first sort of teleology. Misguided views of some modern philosophers to the contrary, Aristotle and the Scholastics had already recognized the idea, central to Kant's moral philosophy, that in addition to "producible" ends there are "self-existent" ends: the worker on the "Habitat for Humanity" house labors not only to build the structure but also for the sake of the family who will, at least in part by his or her efforts, be able to afford a home.[20] Nor should "for this or that person's sake" in contexts like this be taken to mean merely "for his or her own pleasure or use," as may be seen from the fact that actions can be undertaken for God's sake without anyone thereby intending that God be benefited in any way. Thus, Donagan considers it perfectly intelligible to recognize ends of actions that are prior rather than subsequent to those actions ("pre-existent" ends), ends that, while not being themselves producible by the actions done for their sake, are nevertheless that for the sake of which producible ends are ultimately produced ("self-existent" ends): such ends are called by Kant "ends in themselves." Any action, then, that fails to treat a being as something that actions are ultimately *for* fails to treat it as an end in itself, and hence it is reasonable to treat with respect and never as a mere means to another's ends any being that is an end in itself. Donagan believes that human beings are such ends, and, indeed, the only such ends among animals with which we are acquainted (although as with Kant the key characteristic possessed by humans that is relevant here is rationality, and thus there is no suggestion that only human beings could be such ends). There are philosophical as well as religious grounds for this last belief, involving in both cases Donagan's conception of human beings as creatures possessed of a will.

First, the philosophical grounds. Donagan acknowledged that the case for regarding humans as ends in themselves could be made in a variety of ways, and in fact he made it differently in different places. Each argument, however, seems to me to employ or to presuppose our status as willing beings.

For example, Donagan sometimes argues quite directly that our will (and the higher type of causality—agent-causality—that it involves) provides the basis for regarding rational agents like us as ends in themselves. Unlike animals, who direct themselves only to producible ends dictated by their nature, human beings have the power to deliberate about whether, for *any* producible end, natural or not, they will pursue it and the power to make a choice based on this deliberation, free (that is, negatively free) from causes external to reason. A being's possession of such a power justifies its being regarded as an end in itself:[21]

> Since they are negatively free, the actions of a rational being have a causality higher than those of a brute animal; and it is because of that higher kind of causality that rational beings are ends in themselves—ends which are not producible but which exist independently of the actions done for their sake. It is as ends in themselves that rational beings find in their own natures a ground for the law they lay down to themselves.

Sometimes the involvement of the will is less direct. In "Common Morality and Kant's Enlightenment Project" Donagan argues that rational agents should recognize one another as ends in themselves because only by doing so can they live "full human lives." Living such lives is possible only in communities where the behavior of rational agents is regulated by mutually accepted laws, and such communities are precisely the ones whose members are recognized by one another as ends in themselves. Yet governing one's behavior by rules that one decides to accept is possible only for a being possessed of capacities for deliberation and choice, so will here becomes the precondition for treating others as ends in themselves.

In "The Irrelevance of Theology to Ethics" Donagan tries to establish the claim that humans should be regarded as ends in themselves by appealing to the centrality of happiness for any acceptable morality. A plausible moral code must both allow and set limits on the pursuit of happiness, and the most satisfactory candidate here enjoins us in its fundamental principle to treat beings capable of happiness as ends in themselves. As only rational beings are capable of happiness in a fully fledged sense, human beings should, in light of their rationality, be regarded as ends in themselves. While the will is not explicitly mentioned in this brief argument, I believe it is doubly implicit. Donagan regularly maintains that our happiness matters only because we are the types of beings we are, viz., beings possessed of will. I also think it likely that his apportioning to animals only a "secondary" sort of happiness would derive from his distinction between a brute's life spent pursuing producible ends determined by an animal's nature and a truly human life (cf. the "full human life" referred to above) that involves judging which ends are to be pursued and which not, and even when happiness itself is to be sacrificed for the sake of some nonproducible end. All three of these arguments support the view that human beings are to be regarded as ends in themselves because they possess a will: this power affords them a dignity worthy of respect and alone makes possible a fully human and genuinely happy life.

Second, the religious grounds for believing that human beings are ends in themselves. We have seen above that a clear case of acting for the sake of some being without intending to benefit it is afforded by actions done for the sake of God, and Donagan believes that we show love of God by regarding Him as the ultimate self-existent end toward which all our actions are ultimately directed. (For Donagan God, not the beatific vision of God but God Himself, is the ultimate end of all human action.) But we are taught to love not only God but also our neighbor, and Donagan believes that this is because our neighbor is in the image of God. Now St. Irenaeus had already remarked that "Man is rational and therefore like God; he is created with free will and is master over his action,"[22] and St. Thomas wrote in regard to the image of God in us:

> Now since the rational creature also exhibits a word procession as regards the intelligence and a love procession as regards the will, it can be said to contain an image of the uncreated Trinity by a sort of portraiture in kind.... Thus God's likeness in the manner of an image is to be found in man as regards his mind....[23]

Donagan similarly thinks that, because our neighbors share with God in the capacities of rationality and agency, of deliberation and choice, they are said to be in the image of God and therefore also deserving of the respect due to those who because of this resemblance are to be considered self-existent ends. Thus, the powers of reason and will form the image of God in us and the basis for loving our neighbor as we love Him of Whom our neighbor is the image; hence, they provide the religious basis for regarding human beings as ends in themselves.[24]

From a certain point of view it is correct to say that Donagan subsumes the natural law theory of Aquinas under the viewpoint of Kantian moral philosophy, although it would be more accurate to say that he discovers that Thomistic theory anticipates the Kantian. The peculiar character of Kant's teleology—that there are ends that are not produced but that are independent "ends in themselves"—is, in Donagan's view, already present in Aquinas's thought. On Donagan's reading of Thomas, the fundamental principle of the natural law states that (along with loving God) we are to love our neighbor, and Thomistic love of one's neighbor must be understood not as promoting our neighbor's flourishing but as treating our neighbor, that is, any rational being we encounter, as a self-existent end. The fundamental principle of the natural law is therefore equivalent to the fundamental principle of Kantian morality as stated in the formula of the end in itself.

It is, however, worth noting that, while Kant enables us to make explicit what is already present but not perhaps readily apparent in St. Thomas's natural law theory, Aquinas enables us to correct the excesses of Kant's account of agency. For although Kant correctly sought to recognize the activity of the agent as different from that encountered in nonhuman behavior, he found himself compelled to locate that activity in a noumenal realm outside of space and time. For Kant held that the phenomenal realm was a determinist world accessible to and describable (so far as it can be described) by the natural sciences, and the First Critique suggests that the conception of causality that those sciences employ is that of naturalist event-causation. He concluded from this (and from other considerations) that the realm of freedom, of agent-causation, must then lie outside the phenomenal world. Donagan finds Kant's noumenal realm implausible, but this does not produce the philosophical problems for him that it would have for Kant. Donagan, like Aquinas, sees no reason to accept the view that the world we encounter in our experience is a deterministic system or that the only causation to be found there is event-causation. The Aristotelian/Thomistic account of agent-causes capable of deliberation and choice provides a compelling description of human action and avoids locating the agent in a mysterious noumenal realm. And when disentangled from its transcendental idealist trappings, the Kantian view of agency is in fact seen to accord entirely with its predecessor.[25] Thus Professor Veatch was quite right to link the names of St. Thomas and Kant: not only are they individually influential on Donagan's views, but each at some point serves to clarify and illuminate what can be perceived only more obscurely in the other.

Christianity, Philosophy, and the Criteria for a Satisfactory Religion

To recapitulate: being an agent-cause and having a free will (the *praeambulum fidei*) grounds one's status as an end in itself, from which the content of morality is in turn derived. This explains our knowledge of right and wrong, but Donagan does not stop at attributing such knowledge to us. He goes on to remark on our subsequent behavior (in a passage already cited more fully above): among the animals known to us only human beings "can recognize the difference between moral good and evil, and act on it; and yet they are compelled to judge themselves evil by virtue of the ways they in fact choose to act." It is this last-mentioned, melancholy fact of which we must try to make sense and which provides in the argument the point of transition to revealed religion: morality by itself enables us to recognize when our lives have gone bad; the appeal of Christianity is found in the help it offers in understanding why this so often happens and what the cure for it might be. People are drawn to revealed religion because they see in it a remedy for their condition, and (apart from historical plausibility and whatever compatibility it might exhibit with various intellectual domains) it is because of religion's success in making sense of our lives and giving them purpose that those who accept a revealed faith rationally are led to do so. As Donagan says at the end of "Philosophy and the Possibility of Religious Orthodoxy," "those who accept a revealed religion do so because they believe that it makes sense of human life in a way that no other putative revealed religion does, and that no view of things that does not claim to be revealed does." In Donagan's view it is Christianity—to which the making of free choices and the consequences of them (particularly those that represent a turning away from God) are so central—that makes the best sense of our lives, that makes the most plausible promises to correct their defects, and that most persuasively gives them meaning and purpose.

In Donagan's view any satisfactory religion must meet three criteria: (i) it must meet negative rational tests of validity; (ii) it must make sense of life; and (iii) it must offer a purpose for living beyond the guidance in decency that morality provides.[26] It is worthwhile to comment on each of these, although in some cases one wishes that Donagan had had the opportunity to expand and develop the ideas that he was able only to sketch.

Donagan would consider meeting the "negative rational tests of validity" a matter of establishing consistency: are the doctrines of Christianity consistent among themselves, with history, with science and metaphysics, and with morality? He gives, of course, affirmative answers to all these questions, and for most he would assume those responses or develop them along lines already discussed. Thus, I think he takes it for granted that Christianity is internally coherent and not implausible on purely historical grounds. Nor do any actually established results of natural science or metaphysics rule out, for example, the possibility of interventions into the series of event-causes by either Divine or human agents.

Finally, the large areas of coincidence between rationally established and Divinely revealed moral codes not only establish consistency but also show what Donagan regards as the true philosophy and religion to be to some degree mutually reinforcing. Of course, even here there are some discrepancies, leading one, on being faced with incompatible precepts,[27] to look for errors in the ways that either rational or Hebrew-Christian theistic systems of morality have been articulated. The case is rather different when one considers systems of morality based on happiness, be they eudaimonistic or utilitarian.[28] Both of these latter systems assume that our happiness matters, as does the "common morality" represented by both the philosophical and religious traditions to which Donagan subscribes. But these traditions explain further that human happiness counts because humans are the sorts of beings (viz., rational) who count, beings for whose sake alone it makes sense to act. Thus, while acting for the sake of some rational being or beings will typically involve pursuing happiness, there can arise cases where acting for some rational being's sake requires the agent to act so as not to pursue it. The fact that some theories of morality fail to acknowledge the rationality of such behavior[29] suggests to Donagan that compatibility between moral theories and Christianity is by no means a foregone conclusion. In general, then, it may be said that Donagan considers Christianity to be consistent with the results of historical and textual research, scientific investigation, and metaphysical and moral philosophy, or at least with those results that he believes there are serious, independent grounds for accepting. This is a fact about Christianity that, while far from conclusive in establishing its truth, is by no means trivial.

With regard to the second criterion, he points out in "Philosophy and the Possibility of Religious Orthodoxy" that neither philosophy nor theology has explained what it is to "make sense of life" and proceeds to use this as an undefined expression. From his practice (both here and in essays written later), however, we can identify two elements that might plausibly be regarded as involved in making sense of life. Pascal said of a true religion, "it ought to be so much the goal and center towards which all things tend that anyone knowing its principles would be able to explain the whole nature of man in particular and the whole conduct of the world in general."[30] So stated this is an impossibly ambitious claim, but in Pascal's practice it comes most interestingly to showing how ordinary but puzzling features of human life (for example, our need for diversion) can be seen to be just what one would expect if Christianity were true. And this I think is part of what Donagan means when he speaks of making sense of life. The features of human life about which Donagan was primarily thinking in this connection are those involving human failings.[31] He calls attention to the contrast between our ability to distinguish right from wrong (and to act accordingly) and the choices we in fact make. This discrepancy between what we know and can do, on the one hand, and what we in fact choose to do, on the other, is surely intended to recall St. Paul's description of his own condition, "For the good that I would I do not: but the evil which I would not, that I do" (*Rom.* 7:19). Now a view that not only identifies the diseases infecting our lives but also explains their cause and shows the availability of a cure makes better sense of our condition than another that merely achieves the former. Morality is sufficient only for the former, but morality, according to Donagan, is only one part of ethics, the part that concerns basic standards of decency. Ethics includes this, but is also concerned with whatever else pertains to the good life of rational beings. And because only religion (and, in particular, Christianity) makes sense of our condition in the more comprehensive way described above, it is fundamental to the ethical life, as Donagan notes at the end of "Common Morality and Kant's Enlightenment Project": "what any acceptable religion offers is not a distinctive morality but a remedy for the state of those who already have a more or less adequate conception of the morality common to all such religions, but who flout it in practice." Christianity, insofar as it incorporates the correct morality, can be said to make sense of our lives in all these ways: its morality shows where our lives go wrong, its doctrine of sin explains why that happens (and with such alarming regularity), and its teachings regarding justification offer release and show beings like us how we might come to a fully good life.

What he has to say about the third criterion (explaining what life is for)—as well as his reasons about why it is difficult to say anything at all about it—can be found in the last of the essays in this collection, "The Relevance of Theology to Ethics." Unfortunately, in its final, most relevant passages, it is less fully developed than one might like. What life is for cannot be discovered from morality, which sets limits to how we may go about living our lives but gives us no guidance as to its ultimate purpose. It is a question that in Donagan's view requires a response that involves what he calls supernature. Thus he quotes with approval a formulation of the traditional Christian answer—"Man's chief end is to glorify God and to enjoy him forever"—and notes that a life achieving such an end begins in this world through membership in the Church and brings with it a new motive, that of expressing the love of God, capable in its fullest development of displacing not only our attention to happiness but to morality (which becomes superfluous) as well.

What marks this love of God? I suggested above that Donagan could be regarded as viewing Spinoza's philosophy as the naturalist counterpart of his own, and the conclusion of his work on this philosopher offers a contrasting account of this love:

> To love God is [according to Spinoza] to accept what nature is, because nature cannot be otherwise. God's or nature's love of itself is the fullness of that acceptance, and is without any passive affect whatever towards its modes. It cannot be said of Spinoza's God: "herein is love, not that we love God, but that he first loved us" [*I John,* 4:10]. Yet if God is what Spinoza believed he is, there is nothing greater to which human beings can aspire than to love him without desiring that he should love them in return (E5p19). For that is "the very Love with which God loves himself, not insofar as he is infinite, but insofar as he can be explicated by the human Mind's essence, considered *sub specie aeternitatis*" (E5p36). "*Acquiescentia*" is a fitting name for it.[32]

Yet if God is not what Spinoza believed he is—if not naturalism but the supernaturalism represented by Christianity is true—then the purpose of life is to be found not in acquiescing in the natural course of things, let alone in any ways and goals of living suggested to us by naturalist cultural assumptions, nor merely in following the precepts of morality, but rather (as Donagan writes at the end of "The Relevance of Theology to Ethics") in finding "reasons for living [that] are not in the world at all."

Organization and Origins of the Papers

Most but not all of the papers included in this collection were written during the last dozen years of Donagan's life, after he had converted to Christianity. (It may be useful to remark explicitly, as there has been misapprehension about this matter, that *The Theory of Morality* was written by Donagan *before* he became a Christian.) As is to be expected from papers that, while written on related topics, were not intended to be gathered together, the themes identified above recur throughout, and a good many other topics of interest are also treated. I have tried to arrange them based on what I took to be the philosophical "center of gravity" of each; read from beginning to end, the outlines of a comprehensive, Christian, and philosophically defensible viewpoint and also an argument whose structure reflects that order emerge.

I have made the spelling and punctuation of the papers conform to contemporary American usage, have standardized the style of the citations, and have silently corrected obvious misprints. In some cases I have been able to compare Donagan's typescript with the published versions of his articles, and in the very small handful of cases where I found that the sense was clearer in the typescript I have silently incorporated the original into the text. Except as noted, quotations from the Bible come from the Authorized Version. The words supplied to fill out the sense of sketchy sentences are enclosed in single diamond brackets [< >]; substitutes for words in manuscripts that are missing or illegible are enclosed in double diamond brackets [<< >>]. Further editing decisions are discussed below.

The first three papers all cast light on the relation of naturalism and antinaturalism to religion. The first two offer a helpful general orientation as well. "Philosophy and the Possibility of Religious Orthodoxy" was Donagan's John Neveen Lecture delivered under the sponsorship of the Baptist Theological Union on April 15, 1981. It has not been published, and indeed the manuscript heading reads "not for quotation or ascription." It is included because it contains a helpful discussion of Donagan's views on naturalism, and it treats subjects only adverted to in passing elsewhere. "Can Anybody in a Post-Christian Culture Rationally Believe in the Nicene Creed?" first appeared in *Christian Philosophy*, ed. Thomas P. Flint, Notre Dame Studies in the Philosophy of Religion, No. 6 (Notre Dame, Indiana: University of Notre Dame Press, 1990), pp. 92–117. "Spinoza's Theology" is chapter 8 of the *Cambridge Companion to Spinoza*, ed. Don Garrett (Cambridge: Cambridge University Press, 1995), and appears on pp. 343–82.

The next several papers deal with themes in the philosophy of St. Thomas Aquinas and in Thomism more generally. The first two focus on Donagan's interpretation of Thomas's theory of human action, the next two on natural law, and the last on the theory of double effect.

The fourth paper, "St. Thomas Aquinas on the Analysis of Human Action," provides an account of the traditional theory of action on which Donagan draws throughout. An abbreviated version appeared as "Thomas Aquinas on Human Action" in *The Cambridge History of Later Medieval Philosophy*, ed. N. Kretzmann, A. Kenny, and J. Pinborg (Cambridge: Cambridge University Press, 1982), pp. 642–54. The original version is printed here, incorporating only those few changes that in the Cambridge version represent stylistic improvements rather than alterations made to accommodate cuts. "Human Ends and Human Actions: An Exploration in St. Thomas's Treatment" was given as the 1985 Aquinas Lecture at Marquette University under the auspices of the Wisconsin-Alpha Chapter of Phi Sigma Tau and was published that same year as a separate volume: *The Aquinas Lecture, 1985: Human Ends and Human Actions: An Exploration in St. Thomas's Treatment* (Milwaukee: Marquette University Press, 1985).

"The Scholastic Theory of Moral Law in the Modern World" appeared in the *Proceedings of the American Catholic Philosophical Association*, 1966, pp. 29–40, and was reprinted with revisions in *Aquinas: A Collection of Critical Essays*, ed. Anthony Kenny (Garden City, N.Y.: Doubleday and Co., 1969), pp. 325–39. While this revised version has been followed here, some remarks of interest, omitted in the revision presumably because of the difference in audience, have been reintroduced in the notes. "Teleology and Consistency in Theories of Morality as Natural Law" was first published in *The Georgetown Symposium on Ethics: Essays in Honor of Henry Babcock Veatch*, ed. Rocco E. Porreco (Lanham, Md.: University Press of America, 1984), pp. 91–108. "Moral Absolutism and the Double Effect Exception: Reflections on Joseph Boyle's 'Who is Entitled to Double Effect?'" follows naturally on section III of the preceding paper, which discusses the conditions under which Thomas considered the taking of human life permissible. It was published in the *Journal of Medicine and Philosophy*, vol. 16 (1991), pp. 495–509.

Several of the preceding papers discuss and support Donagan's characteristic claim that a Kantian principle of respect was already acknowledged by St. Thomas. "Common Morality and Kant's Enlightenment Project" is devoted to presenting and defending Kant's moral theory itself and to discussing its relation to "any acceptable" religion. It first appeared in *Prospects for a Common Morality*, ed. G. Outka and J. P. Reeder (Princeton: Princeton University Press, 1993), pp. 53–72.

The next three papers show Donagan responding or offering qualifications to alternatives to the morality based on respect for ends in themselves. "On Developing a Contemporary Theistic Ethics" was a reply to Robert M. Adams, "Platonism and Naturalism: Options for a Theocentric Ethics." Both were published in *Ethics, Religion, and the Good Society*, ed. Joseph Runzo (Louisville: Westminster/John Knox Press, 1992); Donagan's paper is found on pp. 43–52. The reviews of the first and second editions of Alasdair MacIntyre's *After Virtue* have not been previously published: the first was delivered at a meeting of the Society of Christian Philosophers at the Western (now Central) Division Meetings of the American Philosophical Association in Cincinnati on April 26, 1984; the second was presented at a colloquium at California State University, Los Angeles, on June 3, 1985.

The last two papers on ethics and theology were delivered at the 26th Annual Philosophy Conference at Wheaton College on October 18 and 19, 1979, and have not been published before. While clearly among the most interesting of those collected here, they also present the most editorial problems. The first ("The Irrelevance of Theology to Ethics") is in a largely finished state, with only the concluding paragraph left in manuscript. The second ("The Relevance of Theology to Ethics"), on the other hand, exists in typescript only through the opening line of the paragraph beginning "If the philosophical assumption which all demythologizing scholarship brings...." The remainder exists only in manuscript,[33] often difficult to read and becoming somewhat sketchy near the conclusion. While Donagan would surely have filled out what he says here about what life is for if he had been able to put this essay into a more finished form, the direction and character of the argument are nevertheless clear regarding a topic that is often mentioned elsewhere in his writings but never so explicitly addressed.

Notes

1. Unpublished remarks made in Bond Chapel on October 4, 1991.

2. Although Donagan states at the outset of "Can Anybody Rationally Believe the Nicene Creed?" that "the Christian religion" means too many things for useful philosophical questions to be raised in terms of it, I shall nevertheless for the sake of simplicity refer throughout the introduction to "Christianity," and mean by it Christianity as Donagan understood it. The evidence of the papers that follow is that his understanding was quite traditional (with an evident lack of sympathy for demythologizing undertaken in order to square it with a contemporary naturalist viewpoint) and true to the straightforward sense of Scripture and traditional creeds, while acknowledging the genuine cultural limitations of such documents (which most emphatically do not include their supernaturalist commitments).

3. St. Thomas Aquinas, *Summa theologiae* I, 2, 2 ad 1.

4. This paragraph draws on Donagan's discussion in *Choice: The Essential Element in Human Action* (London: Routledge and Kegan Paul, 1987), pp. 182–88.

5. This paragraph draws on Donagan's discussion in *The Theory of Morality* (Chicago: The University of Chicago Press, 1977), pp. 224–33.

6. This is not a trivial claim, for as will be discussed more fully below and in the papers themselves, many widely held beliefs about action and morality are in Donagan's view inconsistent with Christianity.

7. Unlike the Cartesian view, the antinaturalist conception of a world containing free will and immaterial, mental phenomena requires according to Donagan two divisions: free will is found only in rational beings, whereas many of the higher but nonrational animals exhibit intentionality, the essence of consciousness. On this latter point, see "The Worst Excess of Cartesian Dualism," in *Human Nature and Natural Knowledge: Essays Presented to Marjorie Grene on the Occasion of Her Seventy-fifth Birthday*, ed. Alan Donagan, Anthony N.

Perovich Jr., and Michael V. Wedin, Boston Studies in the Philosophy of Science, vol. 89 (Dordrecht: D. Reidel Publishing Co., 1986), p. 323.

8. *Spinoza* (Chicago: The University of Chicago Press, 1988), p. xiv.

9. Cf., e.g., *Spinoza*, p. xi, a passage revealing for the light it sheds on Donagan's view of a satisfactory and complete philosophy: "Spinoza was the first major modern philosopher to believe that nature exists in its own right, and needs no supernatural being to create or to sustain it. In his own day, to the applause of natural scientists, his fellow philosophers competed in supplying new versions of the scholastic proofs that nature depends on supernature. In our day, those who believe that nature depends on supernature do not believe it to be philosophically demonstrable that it does. What was last has become first. However, Spinoza's seventeenth-century form of naturalism does not fall short philosophically as today's varieties of it do. Today's naturalism is materialist; his is not. Yet the research program of materialism—either to analyze thinking, the distinctive human activity, in terms of the concepts of the physical sciences, or to replace the concept of thinking with those of activities that can be so analyzed—has led nowhere. More important, except in treating the discoveries of modern natural science, perhaps the greatest of the achievements of the human mind, today's naturalism is culturally barren. To questions about why human life matters and how it should be lived its answers are either evasive or contemptible."

10. The chapter in Donagan's book on Spinoza that covers some of the same ground as "Spinoza's Theology" is in fact titled "Judaism Naturalized."

11. *Choice*, p. 21.

12. The lengthy passage quoted above from "Can Anybody in a Post-Christian Culture Rationally Believe in the Nicene Creed?" suggests as much both by clearly echoing these remarks and also by introducing the theory of human action as the proper source for *praeambula fidei*.

13. "'Causing,' I suppose, was a notion taken from a man's own experience of doing simple actions, and by primitive man every event was construed in terms of this model: every event has a cause, that is, every event is an action done by somebody—if not by a man, then by a quasi-man, a spirit." J. L. Austin, "A Plea for Excuses," in *Philosophical Papers*, 2d ed. (Oxford: Clarendon Press, 1970), p. 202. (Quoted in Alan Donagan, "Chisholm's Theory of Agency," in *Essays on the Philosophy of Roderick M. Chisholm*, ed. Ernest Sosa [Amsterdam: Rodopi, 1979], p. 218, and in *Choice*, p. 167.)

14. *The Theory of Morality*, p. 45. For the development of the ideas of agent-causation, the writings of Chisholm are important: see Roderick Chisholm, "Freedom and Action," in *Freedom and Determinism*, ed. Keith Lehrer (New York: Random House, 1966), pp. 11–44 (where the passage from Aristotle appears as an epigraph); *Person and Object: A Metaphysical Study* (La Salle, Illinois: Open Court Publishing Company, 1976), chap. 2 ("Agency"), pp. 53–88; and "The Agent as Cause," in *Action Theory*, ed. Myles Brand and Douglas Walton (Dordrecht, Holland: D. Reidel Publishing Company, 1980), pp. 199–211. See also Alan Donagan, "Chisholm's Theory of Agency," pp. 215–19.

15. See *Choice*, p. 39.

16. For Donagan's discussion of the question, "Should the Socratic Tradition be Jettisoned as Folk Psychology?" see ibid., pp. 10–18; the quotation appears on p. 16.

17. "Religion is the recognition of all duties as divine commands, not as sanctions, i.e., arbitrary and contingent ordinances of a foreign will, but as essential laws of any free will as such." Immanuel Kant, *Critique of Practical Reason and Other Writings in Moral Philosophy*,

trans. and ed. Lewis White Beck (Chicago: The University of Chicago Press, 1949), p. 212. (The passage comes from the *Critique of Practical Reason* and is found on p. 129 of vol. 5 of the Prussian Academy edition.)

18. His (to an important extent Christian) views about *ethics*, or the good life for human beings, need to be distinguished from his views about *morality*, or the (minimally) decent life for human beings, and will be discussed in the following section. Morality constitutes only one part of ethics.

19. The two teleologies are also discussed in *The Theory of Morality*, chap. 2, sec. 4 ("The Fundamental Principle"), esp. pp. 63–64, and chap. 7, sec. 3 ("The Limits of Purpose"), pp. 224–29.

20. Although Donagan quotes with approval Aquinas's statement, "the ultimate end of any maker, as a maker, is himself..." (*Summa contra gentiles* III, 17, 8), he immediately goes on in this passage to discuss ways in which actions are done for the sake of others as well; see *The Theory of Morality*, pp. 63–64.

21. This paragraph draws on Donagan's discussion in *The Theory of Morality*, pp. 227–33. The following quotation appears on p. 233.

22. *Adv. haeres.*, 4,4,3; PG 7/1, 983.

23. *Summa theologiae* I, 93, 6 (Blackfriars ed.). Edmund Hill O.P. remarks in a note to this section that the love under discussion here is of "an activity of the rational appetite, that is the will."

24. See "Teleology and Consistency in the Theories of Morality as Natural Law" and "On Developing a Contemporary Theistic Ethics."

25. "Kant's moral theory can be detached from the transcendental idealism by which he offered to show how natural science is possible, and should be. When it is thus detached, the theory of action it incorporates can be seen as what it is: a revival of the traditional pre-Humean one" (*Choice*, p. 140).

26. Cf. the end of "Philosophy and the Possibility of Religious Orthodoxy." In this passage Donagan includes the provision of a supermoral purpose for life as a main part of "making sense of human life." I prefer to employ this expression for Donagan's use of Christianity to explain puzzling features of human behavior, in contrast to his discussion of Christianity's answer to the question of what life is for, though it will be seen that these two elements cannot be wholly kept apart.

27. In "The Relevance of Theology to Ethics" Donagan offers, among others, the contemporary example of a Roman Catholic moralist committed both to the view that certain forms of contraception are permissible and also to the acceptance of the Church's magisterium, and hence of its teachings that deny the permissibility of these forms.

28. For eudaimonism, see *The Theory of Morality*, p. 225; for utilitarianism, see "The Irrelevance of Theology to Ethics" below. (Donagan devotes chap. 6 of *The Theory of Morality* to a critical discussion of utilitarianism.)

29. Mill writes, "The utilitarian morality does recognize in human beings the power of sacrificing their own greatest good for the good of others. It only refuses to admit that the sacrifice is itself a good. A sacrifice which does not increase or tend to increase the sum total of happiness, it considers as wasted" (*Utilitarianism*, ed. George Sher [Indianapolis: Hackett Publishing Co., 1979], p. 16). Mill himself, to be sure, sees no incompatibility between Christianity and utilitarianism and indeed finds in the golden rule "the complete spirit of the ethics of utility" (ibid.).

30. Blaise Pascal, *Pensées*, trans. A. J. Krailsheimer (London: Penguin Books, 1966), p. 168.

31. See in particular "Can Anybody in a Post-Christian Culture Rationally Believe the Nicene Creed?" and "Common Morality and Kant's Enlightenment Project."

32. *Spinoza*, p. 206.

33. As does a large section of the first paragraph, which addresses an objection raised the morning the paper was delivered by Professor Richard Purtill. See note 1 to that essay.

Reflections on Philosophy and Religion

Philosophy and the Possibility of Religious Orthodoxy

itles of philosophical lectures, like those of sermons, are apt to mislead. I hope mine has not misled you. I propose to examine whether the kind of position that is referred to as "orthodoxy" in certain religions is compatible with commitment to philosophy as an intellectual enterprise. The question, of course, is an old one. In the form "*Quid Athenae Hierosolymis?*" it was a weapon with which the Christians of the late Roman Empire attacked philosophy. The boot is on the other leg now. Philosophy, or perhaps I should say what is widely taken to be its legitimate—and better—successor, natural science, is accepted by the vast majority of the educated as the sole legitimate source of respectable intellectual opinion about the origin, nature, and destiny of man; and the old religious orthodoxies, which are correctly perceived to deny that claim, are therefore dismissed as superstitious survivals.

I shall not waste my time and yours by discussing at length what philosophy is, and denouncing in the name of pluralism and open-mindedness those whose view of it differs from mine. Perhaps the best delineation of philosophy is that it is a subject with unlimited intellectual pretensions whose practitioners have always quarreled about its nature. I believe that it can be demonstrated that if this were not so its pretensions would be invalid. But I prefer to confine myself to the remark that I conceive philosophy to be the investigation of nature and man by way of free reflection on the existing sciences of nature and man, both theoretical and practical. That accords with the practice of all the major philosophers from Plato to the recent past; and I do not think that philosophy has been on the wrong track since Plato, as some recent philosophers have maintained: for example, Heidegger, perhaps Wittgenstein, and certainly contemporary French deconstructionists. What more specifically I take philosophy to be, you may infer from my practice.

Unfortunately, I cannot avoid saying more than I wish about what I mean by religious orthodoxy. First, "religious." There are religions that do not admit of orthodoxy in the sense I have in mind: the polytheism of the ancient Greeks and Romans did not, and I doubt whether Hinduism does. There are others that do, and of them, those I have in mind are Judaism and its descendants, Christianity and Islam. Being a Christian myself, I do not use "descendant" as a term of disparagement: I refer to the fact that both Christianity and Islam accept the Jewish revelation as genuine, and incorporate it into their own doctrines, sometimes interpreting it differently from the Jewish tradition, and sometimes not. In all three religions it is believed that various truths about God, about man, and about their relations, and various commands of God to men (some to all men, some to a particular people—the family of Abraham—and some to individuals) were directly revealed to individual human beings, and that means were provided for securing the transmission both of these truths and of information about these commands to those to whom they were not directly revealed. In all three religions, those means have included the production of certain written texts, and their authorization as canonical.

That both Judaism and Christianity existed before the Scriptures they recognize as canonical were so recognized—and even before they were written—shows that you cannot identify either with the acceptance of these Scriptures as canonical. In addition, the Scriptures themselves are not fully intelligible except by reference to traditions of interpretation for which, within the religions in question, authority is claimed.

Second, "orthodoxy." Religious orthodoxy, as I conceive it, is accepting as genuine what is claimed within a religious tradition to be a revelation from God to somebody, authoritatively interpreted. As the tradition of all three religions attests, two human beings may share the same religious orthodoxy, and yet disagree about what it is. Even authoritatively interpreted scriptures may give rise to further, and divergent, interpretations. Within a tradition of religious orthodoxy the answering of new questions brings what Cardinal Newman called doctrinal "development." But, to the orthodox, development cannot annul what was authoritatively taught before, nor can it add anything not in some sense implicit in what was so taught. An orthodox believer (whether Jew, Christian, Moslem, or adherent of any other faith admitting of an orthodoxy) must therefore be committed to some form of the canon of St. Vincent of Lérins: nothing is a genuine part of what has been revealed unless those who have accepted that revelation have believed it everywhere, always, and without exception: it is *quod ubique quod semper quod ab omnibus* is received among the faithful. When two orthodox believers differ, either it must be about something not determined by revelation, or at least one of them must have failed to grasp something in some sense implicit in what he already believes.

Until fairly recently, the bearing of philosophy upon religious orthodoxy was presumed to be a matter of the conclusions of each. First, are there conclusions of philosophy that contradict doctrines allegedly revealed as true? If so, to adapt the title of a famous book, there is warfare between philosophy (science) and religion. Suppose, however, there is no such conflict. Then a more hopeful question arises: Are there any revealed doctrines which can be shown by philosophy (science) to be true?

The medieval Arab, Jewish, and Christian philosophers certainly believed that there are. The philosopher who supplied most of their proofs was Aristotle. He was rightly judged preeminent as a philosopher of nature; and yet not only did his physics require one and only one God as the final cause of nature, but his ethics and politics were taken to have shown that gentile nations ignorant of the revealed law of Moses could nevertheless work out for themselves those parts of it having to do with a decent human life on earth. I agree with Étienne Gilson that something of the kind is inevitable whenever human beings committed to a religious orthodoxy in which doctrines about nature and the good life on earth are revealed discover a philosophy which appears to demonstrate some of those doctrines. As Gilson put it, with reference to Christianity, "The inevitability does not flow from the essence of Christianity, which is grace, but arises from the very nature of the recipient of the grace. The recipient is a nature, and nature is the proper object of philosophy. As soon as a Christian begins to reflect on the subject that carries grace, he becomes at once a philosopher."[1]

Unfortunately, Gilson did not apply to medieval Christian philosophy a lesson he vigorously taught about the Christian philosophical systems of the seventeenth and eighteenth centuries. Aristotle was not to remain pre-eminent as a philosopher of nature: there were to be (to mention only professed Christians) Descartes, and Leibniz, and Newton, each of whom had a system of nature that was widely accepted as fundamentally true, and each system required one and only one God to create (and in Newton's case to intervene in) nature. Just as it was inevitable that medieval Aristotelian Moslems, Jews, and Christians should construct systems of Moslem, Jewish, and Christian Aristotelianism, so it was inevitable that seventeenth- and eighteenth-century Christians who accepted Cartesian, Leibnizian, or Newtonian physics should construct Cartesian, Leibnizian, or Newtonian systems of Christian philosophy.

Since the deficiencies of the Cartesian, Leibnizian, and Newtonian systems of nature are now familiar, nobody has any difficulty in perceiving that it would be dangerous for advocates of a religious orthodoxy to construct a religious philosophy in terms of any of them. However, presumably because he imagined that he could separate Aristotle's philosophy of nature from his science of it, Gilson imagined that Christian Aristotelianism, at least as exemplified in Aquinas, remained safe. He was wrong. For, at least from the time of Boethius, Christian philosophy had accepted the Platonic-Aristotelian doctrine that the eternity of God was identical with time-lessness—and it was good scholastic doctrine (Aquinas's, for example) that Boethius had satisfactorily solved the problem of reconciling divine foreknowledge with human freedom by supposing that, from the point of view of a timeless God, foreknowledge is not knowledge in advance. The defect of this, as the so-called process theologians have pointed out, is that it reduces time to a mere appearance. Things are as God knows them to be; and if God knows them only in a timeless present, then the passage of time as human beings experience it can only be an appearance.

The lesson to be drawn by defenders of any religious orthodoxy is, I submit, this: that no matter how tempting it may be to identify an entity asserted as part of religious revelation with an entity asserted by philosophy (or science), their identity should always be regarded as disputable philosophical doctrine, and not as part of the deposit of faith. With the criticisms made by process philosophers and theologians before us, the deficiencies of the Boethian conception of God's eternity, as an elucidation of Christian—or Jewish or Moslem—doctrine are plain. But even if they were not, the identification of Boethius's philosophical eternal being with the creator of *Genesis* should be regarded as a philosophical matter, and under no circumstances as *de fide*.

Those who will not learn from history are condemned to repeat it. It is proper and indeed, as Gilson saw, inevitable that whenever religious believers encounter what appear to be philosophical proofs of theses bearing upon what they take to be revealed doctrine, they will investigate that doctrine philosophically. This holds for the proofs in process philosophy by which Boethius's doctrine of divine eternity has been criticized as it did for the Platonic and Aristotelian proofs that prompted Boethius to construct his philosophical theology. And some of the investigations arising from process philosophy have had results that are persuasive both from the philosophical and the religious points of view. For example, Peter Geach and Nicholas Wolterstorff have persuasively argued that God's eternity should be analyzed in terms of everlastingness and changelessness rather than of timelessness, and have drawn attention to our need for an adequate philosophical analysis of change. Again, Charles Hartshorne has persuasively argued that divine omniscience is better analyzed as knowing all that is knowable than as knowing all that is true—an analysis which, as Richard Taylor has pointed out, has parallels in Aquinas. However, instead of confining themselves to modest results of this nature, accompanied by warnings that they are philosophical speculations, and not *de fide*, many theologians have constructed a new conception of God in terms of the philosophy of Alfred North Whitehead, and then proceeded to identify that God with the God of Abraham with the same assurance as Boethius in the sixth century performed the same feat for his Platonic-Aristotelian God. From the point of view of religious orthodoxy their errors are opposite, and yet fundamentally the same.

Is it not possible that God, as conceived by some system of philosophy, may be identical with the God of Abraham? Certainly it is possible. What I am urging is: first, that such an identity should never be asserted as a matter of religious faith; and second, that history suggests that such assertions are unlikely to be true. Concepts worked out in purely philosophical theology may turn out to be adaptable to the God of a religious revelation, but it is to be expected that adaptation will be necessary.

But if that is how it turns out, does it not follow that philosophical theology and revealed theology are incompatible: that the ancient choice between Athens and Jerusalem still confronts us? And if so, philosophers are committed to Athens.

This is, I believe, the assumption of most contemporary philosophers and theologians. Here is an example, from a paper by Manfred Mezger, dedicated to Rudolf Bultmann on his seventy-fifth birthday. He is explaining the concept of "freedom of the text" in preaching, by means of two horrible examples of its absence. This is one.

> First, Acts 1:9—"As they were looking on, he was lifted up, and a cloud took him out of their sight." One may, of course, if he so desires (but we would rather not), speak on that text as a 1959 Ascension Day essay (from a Catholic pen) has:
>
> "... Christ is now trans-spatial. This concept of trans-spatiality is well known to modern science. In simple words, the report of the ascension expresses nothing more and nothing less than this when it speaks of the glorified body of the resurrected Lord. The Lord elevates himself slightly from the earth, as though he were exhibiting to his Apostles his freedom from the powers of nature. [Mezger inserts a note of exclamation here.] Then a cloud envelopes him, providing a visible means for the astonished Apostles to understand that the body of their Master still remains in existence, but has been removed from their sight and touch—and indeed, from the grasp of every material power whatever. He is no longer spatial, but trans-spatial; he is no longer on the earth, no longer in this world, but in heaven."
>
> This sort of translation really is passé, although it seems to remain close to the text throughout.[2]

Certainly the passage Mezger quotes has a radically objectionable feature: the obfuscating falsehood that there is a well-known *scientific* concept of transspatiality by means of which the text from *Acts* may be elucidated. Whether there is a scientific concept of transspatiality or not I have no idea; one need not have one in order to know that even if it should make sense in physics to speak of a body being no longer spatial but transspatial, it is *not* part of what the Apostle's Creed means when it speaks of Jesus ascending into heaven—it being understood that the ascension was from earth. For a preacher to have spoken in that way was scandalous. But remove the two sentences in which that false and scandalous idea is expressed, and the passage becomes routine orthodox exposition, which, despite Mezger's insinuation to the contrary, remains close to the text throughout. Why is it contemptuously dismissed? Because it is "passé."

I assume that Mezger chose the word "passé" deliberately, knowing that those of orthodox mind would be shocked by the evaluation of a piece of scriptural interpretation by a criterion usually reserved for the criticism of style and fashion, and intending to shock them. In implying that there is an analogy between judging scriptural interpretations and judging fashions he is perfectly serious. He presupposes that human beings of a given culture conceive the world and their place in it in a characteristic way, which they are utterly unable to escape—and that if they live in a period of transition between cultures, or in circumstances in which they are open to many cultural influences, without having a coherent one that is theirs, they will be confused, and unable to classify their confusion except by finding a coherent culture and embracing it. And from this presupposition he concludes: first, that the canonical Scriptures of any religion with an orthodox tradition will be expressed in terms of the culture to which its writers belong (I think he quietly assumes that canonical Scriptures could not be culturally confused); and second, that adherents of that religion whose culture is other than that of the writers of its canonical Scriptures will not be able to take seriously some of the concepts in terms of which it is expressed. There is an example in my quotation from Mezger. The text from *Acts* describes Jesus as "lifted up," that is, as the essay criticized expressed it, he "elevate[d] himself slightly from the earth"; and that, to the Apostolic writers, would have implied that he was not subject to the normal natural limitations upon human bodily movement. But the concept of any human being, even the God-man, being free from the powers of nature, although acceptable to first-century Jews and to superstitious Greeks (not to the nonsuperstitious ones), is not acceptable to anybody caught up in twentieth-century scientific culture. It is passé.

It follows that religious orthodoxy, as I have described it, is philosophically unattainable. The history of any religion that persists through cultural change will be one in which, adopting Rudolf Bultmann's words, as traditional ecclesiastical images cease to be credible to those whose culture is different, new images of God are required, the old having become obsolete.[3] The application of the Vincentian canon will merely insure that religion dies; and it was Christianity as conceived by its orthodox adherents that Nietzsche pronounced dead. But is what has died really Christianity? What if you are convinced that all sorts of valuable things have been transmitted by Christianity, and that transmitting those things has been what is essential to it? Obviously, you will do what Bultmann and his associates and followers have done: you will declare that what has died is not Christianity, but only the images or myths by means of which essential Christianity was expressed in a culture that has passed, and you will attempt to "demythologize" it: that is, to separate it from those passé images and express it in terms of others through which it can be communicated to contemporary human beings. You will not, of course, claim that the expressions suitable for the late twentieth century will necessarily be those needed in the twenty-fifth. We have our cultural images and myths, just as the first century had its. The point is to distinguish essential Christianity from the cultural form in which it is expressed in any given time and place. And a similar view can be taken of other religions.

The great difficulty with such programs is that, when we try to distinguish between essential Christianity and the images and myths by means of which it is presented, remembering, of course, that a "pure" imageless statement is not to be looked for, it is difficult to give any reason for describing it as a religion at all. When Mezger writes, for example, that "when we allow for complete and unreconstructed recognition of the text's complexity and of its freedom, the assertion which the text is making is *only* translatable for us today if we adopt a mode of assertion the movement of which is *radically contrary* to the text," and adds "It is precisely because of the message, which in this text has such an overwhelmingly miraculous form, that every attempt at illustrating Easter falls short"[4]—the only thing I can find to say is that the text is no longer exerting any real control on him at all: it has become merely the occasion for existential free association. And, if that is so, he cannot claim the authority of a preacher: that he is expounding a revealed text.

If radically demythologized orthodoxy is vacuous as religion (it may have all kinds of merits of other kinds) is there any *religious* response to the presumed death of orthodoxy? Of course there is. It is what may be called "liberal" theology, without implying any necessary connection with political liberalism. The fundamental principle of liberal theology, as I understand it, is that theological systems are analogous with philosophical and scientific ones in this respect: each is an attempt to answer certain fundamental questions, each has before it the answers given in the past, and each must try to reach its own conclusions by reflecting, not only on these past answers, but on everything it can find that is pertinent. Nor must it be forgotten that the very questions theology sets out to answer, like those of philosophy and science, are not fixed: the questions of theology in the twentieth century are not identical with those of the thirteenth, even when they are expressed in the same words.

So expressed, the philosophical legitimacy of liberal theology is unquestionable. And its religious character is equally unquestionable. There can be no reason to deny that such philosophers as Spinoza, or William James, or Whitehead were in a straight-forward sense deeply religious: they did care about what human life is for, and passionately sought the truth about it. What liberal religion lacks is neither religious seriousness nor moral character—it is religious *authority*. Moses and the Jewish prophets, Jesus and St. Paul, and Mohammed all have this in common: that they do not offer us theses to be discussed and investigated. And although orthodox theologians in the Jewish, Christian, and Moslem traditions do offer us theses to be investigated, they are theses about an alleged deposit of faith that is not so offered. This is not necessarily an objection. Adherents of liberal forms of religion may well reply that there is no religious authority in the sense in which those who accept the various varieties of religious orthodoxy insist. And they would agree that there is no sharp line between the kinds of religious organization they believe to be legitimate and organizations like ethical societies. The forms such organizations may take will depend on the interests and <<other concerns>> of their members. They may be more like that of an old-fashioned church or more like that of a philosophical society. But in no case would they claim to teach doctrine authoritatively.

In their different ways, then, both demythologized orthodoxy and liberal religion wittingly or unwittingly abandon the claim in any significant sense to possess and expound revealed truth. And both have abandoned it because they accept the proposition that the claims of every traditional religion that has an orthodox form must be in conflict with the science and philosophy of any culture except the one in which it was developed, so that it is intellectually impossible for anybody who thinks in terms of the scientific culture of the twentieth century (which underlies its philosophy) to accept traditional Jewish, or Christian, or Moslem orthodoxy. Is that presupposition true?

I do not think that it is. But here a distinction must be drawn. From the time of Galileo to the present, the metaphysical assumptions, conscious or unconscious, which have formed the background of the work of most scientists have undergone radical changes. In the seventeenth century virtually all scientists presupposed that nature was a divine creation, and most of them found no difficulty in believing that God supernaturally intervened in the course of nature: indeed, such interventions were believed by Newton to be necessary to the permanence of what he called the system of the world. By the end of the nineteenth century, however, principally owing to the Darwinian revolution in biology, a majority of scientific theorists probably worked against the background assumption that there was nothing but nature, and that ideally everything that happens, if it has an explanation at all, has an explanation in terms of one or more of the natural sciences. Comparatively few scientists have gone further, and embraced the doctrine of the unity of science dear to many naturalist philosophers, that all natural sciences are reducible to a fundamental natural science—presumably physics. But we may leave that issue alone. Within modern scientific culture, and hence within modern philosophy, the principal objection to naturalism comes from the social sciences and history, the *Geisteswissenschaften*, which remain intellectually indispensable, and yet obstinately unlike the natural sciences in structure or results. The recent to-do over sociobiology is the most recent manifestation of naturalist dissatisfaction with the social sciences, which the intellectual poverty of sociobiology ensures will be futile.

What are the implications of orthodox forms of Judaism, Christianity, and Islam for modern science? I submit that they reduce to this: that science should be viewed much as Galileo professed to view it, as having to do with a system of nature created by God, within which God can intervene and has. Philosophically, the form such divine intervention may be believed to have taken is a secondary matter. Unless we demythologize it, God's communication of the Law to Moses was as much an intervention in the order of natural causes as was the sending down of fire on the prophet Elijah's altar. To think of science in this way does not impugn any of its results: what it does impugn is the naturalist doctrine that nothing ever happens in the natural realm except according to natural processes. As orthodox Jews, Christians, and Moslems all view it, the communication of the Law to Moses was genuine and supernatural. Moses was not a Jewish Solon, veneration for whose legislation was expressed by inventing the myth that God communicated it to him.

Is this incompatible with modern science? I submit not, although it is certainly incompatible with the naturalist philosophy that furnishes most natural scientists with the metaphysical presuppositions within which they work. Nor is it psychologically impossible that somebody doing serious theoretical work in natural science should embrace such a position. While it is not an argument for the forms of supernaturalism that go with religious orthodoxy that they appear more effectively to immunize their adherents against scientific quackery than does naturalism, it is worthy of remark.

The logical compatibility of orthodox supernaturalism with the results of theoretical science, and the psychological possibility for a human being in modern scientific culture of embracing it, do not, of course, imply that any form of orthodox supernaturalism ought to be embraced. Can there be any reason for taking a given form of religious orthodoxy seriously? What sort of reason could it be?

I have already, by implication, dismissed the familiar philosophical position that natural—that is, philosophical—theology is a proper *praeambulum fidei*, on the ground that the identification of any philosophically conceived God with the God of a religious faith must remain a philosophical matter. Religious teaching offers an alleged revelation, not the conclusion of a philosophical proof; and one has not accepted a revelation if one accepts what is allegedly revealed wholly on some other ground. If, however, one accepts a doctrine as revealed, one's acceptance will be independent of its supposed philosophical *praeambulum*. What we are concerned with here is this: on what kind of ground, if any, can one accept a doctrine as revealed?

In recent philosophy, questions of this kind have been discussed as having to do with the ethics of belief. Unfortunately, the favored positions both *pro* and *con* seem to me to be equally objectionable. The position *con* is that of the delightful and admirable nineteenth-century Cambridge physicist William Kingdon Clifford. It is this. It is morally wrong to grant any proposition a degree of credence that is not proportional to the weight of the evidence for it. But that is bad ethics, because what is impossible cannot be a duty. Each person's beliefs are a fabric, in which inferences with respect to one depend on the others. There is no such thing as the weight of evidence for a single belief. Whether or not evidence makes it reasonable to abandon a belief depends upon what other beliefs are held. But the Cartesian project of reconstructing the entire fabric of one's beliefs, whether on Cartesian or Cliffordian principles, is impracticable. This is true of everyday beliefs—and no reason has been given for imagining it to be otherwise with religious ones.

The favored position *pro* is that of William James. Against Clifford, he argued that, since the choice of suspending belief in an alleged religious revelation is for practical purposes, which are those that matter in religion, tantamount to rejecting it, the choice of belief or disbelief is forced. But, since the practical consequences of the choice may be momentous, given that there are no decisive arguments against it, it is anybody's right to opt for belief. The difficulty with this view, as with Clifford's, is whether it is a genuine intellectual possibility. Of course, anybody may profess belief at will, and may govern his conduct accordingly. If we set on one side self-fulfilling prophecies ("Believe that you will win, and you will"), which are not to the point here and call for special treatment, the instruction "Believe that so-and-so is the case, because the consequences of that belief will be better than those of disbelief" invites the retort "If you cannot give a better reason than that, that very fact almost forces one to disbelief." In an early paper, R. G. Collingwood remarked that "The type of all false religion is to believe what we will to believe, instead of what we have ascertained to be true; supposing that reality must be such as to satisfy our desires, and if not, go to, let us alter it."[5] To me, it seems generally to be the type of irrationality. How can anybody offer as a rational justification for believing something that thereby we may attain what Jonathan Swift described as "the sublime and refined point of felicity called the possession of being well-deceived, the serene peaceful state of being a fool among knaves"?

Instead of general reflections on the ethics of belief, philosophers would do better to consider the kinds of reason on which people otherwise reasonably intelligent have accepted an alleged revelation as genuine, and perhaps to compare them with examples of such acceptance in the Scriptures in which that revelation is canonically set out. As far as I can tell, such acceptance normally satisfies three conditions: first, the alleged revelation is perceived as communicated, not necessarily face to face, by a living member of a body of believers credibly claiming to preserve a religious tradition; second, what is communicated is offered as, at least in part, transcending anything that could be affirmed on purely philosophical or scientific grounds; and third, what is communicated purports to go some way (but only some) to making sense of human life, in such fashion as to provide human beings with a purpose in living that goes beyond those provided by ordinary practical reason.

I am afraid that you will not find the rationality or otherwise of accepting such an alleged revelation discussed in any work of epistemology with which I am familiar. That is perhaps as it should be. For, taking a class of cases of non-Jews in the first century before the present era accepting the Jewish revelation as genuine under the three conditions laid down, and supposing all members of that class to be rational, still they would not be cases of *episteme* as understood by the Greeks, or of scientific knowledge in the modern sense, whether one has the natural or the human sciences in mind. But this only serves to expose what I believe to be a yawning gap in both the philosophical and the theological literature.

To the best of my knowledge, neither Judaism, nor Christianity, nor Islam has ever offered its doctrines as examples of philosophical or scientific knowledge. In all three, religious faith is distinguished from philosophy or science—even though the man of faith is described as wiser than the man who lacks it. But equally, faith is not an unreasonable or absurd attitude (except, of course, from a point of view which unreasonably rejects its claims). It is unreasonable to embrace a religious faith if its claims to preserve a religious tradition are historically false. For example, if it could be shown historically that ancient Judaism died out with the Alexandrian empire, and that both present-day Judaism and present-day Christianity came into existence as offshoots of Islam, their Scriptures being produced in the ninth century, and cunningly constructed to claim to antedate Islam, while the references to Judaism and Christianity in the Islamic Scriptures have an even later date, being polemical interpolations, then no conviction as to the spiritual superiority of the Jewish or the Christian Scriptures could make it other than irrational to accept either Judaism or Christianity. But suppose that the claims of Judaism, Christianity, and Islam are, while not demonstrable, nevertheless, given their supernaturalist assumptions, historically defensible. (I myself believe that to be the case.) Then the question of faith will reduce to this: Does any one of the putative revelations communicate a view of the place of human life in the scheme of things in such a way as to make sense of it, and to provide human beings with a purpose in living beyond that provided by ordinary practical reason? If none does, then none is of serious religious interest. If only one does, it alone is of serious religious interest. If more than one does, it will be necessary to investigate which makes the best sense of human life.

My point is that those who accept a revealed religion do so because they believe that it makes sense of human life in a way that no other putative revealed religion does, and that no view of things that does not claim to be revealed does. Accepting such a religion, provided that it passes the rational negative tests of validity (internal coherence, historical possibility, and the like) is rational faith. What philosophy and theology have neglected to do is to investigate what, in this connection, making sense of human life is; and what it is for one view of it to make better sense than another. However, the concept of making sense to which I appeal here is clear enough for most of us to use, and to explain behavior in terms of it.

Notes

1. Étienne Gilson, *The Spirit of Medieval Philosophy*, trans. A. H. C. Downes (New York: Charles Scribner's Sons, 1940), p. 419.

2. Robert W. Funk, ed., *Translating Theology into the Modern Age* (New York: Harper and Row, 1965), pp. 168–69.

3. Ibid., p. 83.

4. Ibid., p. 169.

5. R. G. Collingwood, *Faith and Reason*, ed. Lionel Rubinoff (Chicago: Quadrangle Books, 1968), p. 232.

TWO

Can Anybody in a Post-Christian Culture Rationally Believe the Nicene Creed?

1. A Fourth-Century Creed in the Twentieth Century

The phrase "the Christian religion" stands for so many things that the question whether educated people in the western world today can rationally believe it is too vague to be worth answering. It is otherwise with the question whether they can rationally believe the Nicene creed. Many who call themselves Christians would reject it. Yet it is part of the liturgy of many Christian bodies, in particular of the largest of all, the Roman Catholic Church, the central rite of which, the mass, requires both priest and people to profess it together. A century ago, virtually all Christians would have been willing to profess it, whether or not the liturgy of their branch of the church required it, although there is one phrase in it, "one holy Catholic and Apostolic Church," which not all would have understood in the same sense.

Even so, what you commit yourself to when you profess the Nicene creed as part of a ritual like the mass is less than definite. Some (the present Anglican bishop of Durham, for example) act as though uttering the words "He [that is, Jesus] was incarnate by the Holy Spirit of the Virgin Mary" as part of the liturgy is not logically inconsistent with addressing the words "Of course, as no educated person in the twentieth century can doubt, Jesus had a natural father" to seminary students in a theology class. Yet, as far as I can tell, most educated non-Christians and most of those who say the Nicene creed as part of the liturgy of their branch of the church agree that it is logically inconsistent. They assume that "believing the Nicene creed" means believing that its various sentences are true in the same sense as they have in nonritual contexts. In what follows I shall also assume it.

As will appear later, I think that educated Christians in the western world share with non-Christians a scientific culture that is "post-Christian," in a sense to be explained. This poses a number of problems for them in professing the Nicene creed understood in its everyday sense. Of those problems that seem to me acute, I propose in this paper to consider the following three.

1. The problem of the development of Christian doctrine. The full seriousness of this problem was first made clear by Cardinal Newman, in his *Essay on Development*. There, he tried to explain to the Anglican communion he was leaving why he had come to accept the claims of the Roman communion he was entering. The Anglicans charged Rome with adding to the faith of the Apostles; but at the same time they maintained that the Nicene fathers defined part of the faith taught by the Apostles and accepted by Christians *semper, ubique, et ab omnibus*. Newman replied that, since parts of the Nicene creed would have perplexed the Apostles, the faith taught by the Apostles admits of "development" without being added to in the sense in which adding to it would be nonapostolic. But, in that case, may not the sense in which the words in which the apostolic teaching is expressed have undergone development? Why assume that the everyday sense of the words of the Nicene creed today is the same as their sense in the fourth century, or in any time but our own?

2. The problem of the variation of credibility with culture. Given the scientific-philosophical culture of the Mediterranean world in the first century, St. Paul reasonably held it to be incredible that the world has not a single divine creator (*Rom.* 1:20). However, the intellectual situation today is not what it was in the ancient world, in the Middle Ages, or even in the seventeenth and eighteenth centuries. Is the Christian faith as it was taught before the present century defensible in the ways in which it was then defended? And if it is not, is it credible now, even if it was then?

3. The problem of the historical claims of the Christian faith. According to the Nicene creed, not only was the second person of the divine Trinity incarnate in a named human individual, Jesus, or, in Aramaic, Yeshua, but that individual was sentenced to death by crucifixion by a named Roman propraetor, Pontius Pilatus, the sentence was carried out, and "on the third day, [Jesus] rose again, according to the Scriptures, [and] ascended into heaven." This part of the creed, according to orthodox Christian belief, was attested by the Apostles from the first Pentecost after Jesus' death, and what is essential in their testimony may be found in a body of writings circulated in various parts of the early church that gradually became accepted as canonical by the church as a whole. Yet this body of testimony is now widely called into

question, not only by biblical scholars outside the Christian church, but also by some within it. In view of this, is it rational to accept that body of testimony as reliable?

2. *The Problem of the Development of Christian Doctrine*

According to the Nicene creed, the Christian church is apostolic; and that is generally taken to imply that it teaches what the Apostles taught. The Apostles received a deposit of faith; they transmitted it to their successors, and it has remained unchanged. Part of it is formulated in the Nicene creed itself. If this were not so, the faith of Christians today would not be apostolic; they would accept as necessary to the Christian faith beliefs which the Apostles did not hold, and hence did not think necessary to it.

On the other hand, it is quite certain that the Nicene creed contains propositions that cannot be found in the canon of the New Testament, and which there is reason to believe would have baffled the Apostles: that Jesus is "of one substance (*homoousios*) with the Father" is an example. That Jesus is in some sense "one" with the Father was taught by the evangelist John; but the assertion that the *ousia* of Jesus and that of the Father are the same, and not merely alike, would make little sense to Christians who were unacquainted with the terminology of Greek philosophy. Can the church's claim that all its teaching is apostolic be reconciled with the historical fact that much in its later teaching cannot be found in the canonical Scriptures that are accepted as the sole authoritative source for proving what doctrines are apostolic?

The answer given to this question before the historically minded nineteenth century was that the later teachings of the church are either clarifications of what in earlier teachings had been left obscure, or deductions of what in them had been left implicit. Newman and others showed that this answer is historically false. The doctrine that the *ousia* of Jesus is that of the Father neither clarifies an obscure scriptural teaching nor is deducible from explicit scriptural teaching by recognized logical methods. Yet the church, in declaring that its teaching throughout its history neither adds to what was revealed to the Apostles nor subtracts from it, must hold that when it expressly teaches what the Apostles did not, it does not "develop" what was revealed to them in such a way as to add to it.

Although no theory of the development of doctrine has won acceptance by Christians, the holistic conception of language worked out in contemporary analytic philosophy does enable us to elucidate it in part. According to that conception, the central function of language is to enable speakers to form complex utterances, the sense of which is that certain truth conditions are satisfied. Speakers conversing in a language would completely succeed in communicating with one another, so far as this central function goes, if and only if every utterance by each of them were to be received by his hearers as his presenting himself as believing that the same truth conditions are satisfied as he himself takes it to express. However, no uttered sentence has truth conditions in isolation from others. The simplest sentence about the simplest physical things, even those used as examples by logicians, such as that snow is white, are unintelligible apart from others about colors, the weather, and the like. Hence the simplest sentence used by a scriptural writer, for example, "When the sabbath day was come, [Jesus] began to teach in the synagogue" (*Mark* 6:2) is unintelligible apart from numerous others about the institutions of rabbinic Judaism. As Donald Davidson has shown, to the extent that a hearer does not connect the truth conditions of an uttered sentence with those of numerous others with which the speaker connects them, and does not largely agree with the speaker about whether or not those truth conditions are satisfied, he will not understand what the speaker says. For the most part, contemporaries speaking or writing the same language do connect sentences in the same ways and do agree about their truth.

Communication between noncontemporaries, even when they share a common language, is another matter. For example, in the Middle Ages, educated Jews, Christians, and Muslims who uttered, in whatever language they spoke, a sentence that would be correctly translated into English as "I see a red rose" would have taken it to be false if the surface of the petals of a rose did not have a property which the presence of light enabled the air to transmit to their eyes, such that the reception of that property in their eyes was their seeing the rose's redness. Later, from Galileo to Locke and beyond, scientifically educated westerners who uttered such a sentence would have taken it to be false if the particles composing the surface of the rose's petals did not have properties of shape, size, and motion such that they reflected particles or waves of light emitted by an illuminating body, thereby causing motions of the particles composing their central nervous systems that in turn caused their minds to form a visual representation of a red rose. Nowadays, the scientifically educated have yet other views.

Does it follow that medieval Aristotelians and seventeenth-century Galileans meant something different from one another when they said that a rose they were looking at is red? No. Neither would have said what they did unless they had meant to express beliefs which, whether they knew it or not, the others believed to be false. On the other hand, neither would have retracted what they said had they become persuaded that the others' theory of color perception was true. It does not matter whether, in continuing to accept "I see a red rose" as true they changed the sense in which they used some of the words they used, or merely changed some theoretical belief they associated with uttering that sentence. What matters is that each, in saying what he does, accepts a certain theory of color perception as true, and each will continue to say what he does even if he is persuaded to change his theory of color perception.

Both philosophy and the natural sciences have made enormous advances since what Christians recognize as the revelation made by God to the Apostles. In addition, the Apostles themselves did not deny that the Greeks had a wisdom that they lacked: what they asserted was that part of that wisdom was spurious—the part that was in conflict with the revelation they had received. Hence, as the part of the wisdom of the Greeks that was not spurious was acquired by members of the Christian community, they learned new questions to ask about the deposit of faith transmitted by the church, such as the question whether the *ousia* of the only begotten Son of God the Father was identical with, or merely like, that of the Father himself. Before answering this question definitively, the church had to decide whether it is proper to speak of the *ousia* of either the Father or the Son; but, having decided that it is proper, it became part of its teaching that if philosophy were in its advance to refine the theory of *ousia*, whatever answers the church gave to questions about the *ousia* of Father or Son could be restated consistently with those refinements.

When theological questions the church recognizes as proper are framed with reference to philosophical or scientific concepts that the Apostles did not possess, the answers to them can be neither clarifications of what the Apostles left vague nor deductions of what they left implicit. They are questions which the deposit of faith enables the church—the people of God—to answer exactly, but in neither of these ways: neither by extracting something clear from a set of vague texts, each of which makes something clear that the others do not; nor by logically deriving something explicit from a set of texts, none of which by itself implies it, but which imply it as a group. They can be answered only by showing that some of the possible answers to the questions raised by the scientific or philosophical concepts the Apostles did not possess implicitly contradict something they did teach. The dogmatic teachings thus arrived at will all methodologically be of the form "It is not true that *p*, because *p*, by itself or together with propositions that are true, implies that some part of the apostolic teaching—the deposit of faith—is false." We can test this conclusion by considering dogmas proposed or accepted in some parts of the Church. I have no difficulty with accepting as possibly true the pious beliefs that the Blessed Virgin was immaculately conceived and at the end of her earthly life bodily assumed into heaven; but I do not accept them as dogmas because I do not find the reasoning conclusive by which their denial is held to imply that she is not, as the gospels unmistakably assert, the mother of Jesus, who the church teaches is God.

Just as it is reasonable to conclude that the apostolic revelation comprehends much that the Apostles did not themselves conceive, so it is reasonable to assert that what Christians of the fourth or sixteenth century affirmed as dogma in terms of scientific or philosophical concepts of their day may not only have been comprehended in the apostolic revelation, but may be restated without essential addition or subtraction in the scientific or philosophical concepts of ours. Moreover, ordinary believers can honestly profess to believe dogmas they know to be part of the church's teaching, even though they have only a sketchy understanding of how orthodox theologians would expound and establish those dogmas.

Understanding the Nicene creed sufficiently to profess it in good faith does not entail being able to pass a theological examination on it. Consider some of its principal affirmations about Jesus: that he is "begotten of his Father before all worlds, God of God, Light of Light, very God of very God; begotten not made; being of one Substance with the Father." Confronted by some theological Socrates, few worshipers who utter those words with every sign of conviction would be able to answer a series of probing theological questions on it. Yet we should not draw a counterpart of the conclusion of the Socrates of Plato's early Socratic dialogues: that his interlocutors do not know what they profess to believe. As Plato went on to show in the *Meno*, Socrates' elenctic technique depends not only on the capacity of his interlocutors to understand and answer most of his questions, but also on the adequacy of their answers, given an intellectual midwife who can ask the right questions, to solve the theoretical problems he puts before them.

Theologically uneducated believers who make the trinitarian affirmations about Jesus I have just quoted understand very well, I submit, that they mean that Jesus stands to God the Father, maker of heaven and earth, in a relation that can figuratively be described as being begotten by him, provided that it is remembered that, since this relation is between two individuals who are not independent substances or beings, one cannot speak of one as God, or true God, or Light, and of the other as not. Of course, a hostile theologian, out to show such a believer that he does not possess the theoretical knowledge he can sometimes be enticed into claiming, can often reduce him to a state of intellectual numbness about his faith. But so to employ the elenctic technique would be a malicious misuse of it, as Plato recognized by trying to show that Socrates did not so employ it.

3. A Note on the "Demythologizing" of Dogma

While they agree that the ordinary members of the body of Christ understand their faith in a nontheoretical way, some philosophers influenced by Wittgenstein's comparison of language to a kit of tools, each with different uses, contend that in professing their faith they do not think of themselves as stating facts. Thus, when they say of Jesus "He will come again, with glory, to judge the living and the dead; whose kingdom will have no end," they are expressing and embodying "a reflection on, or vision of, the meaning of life and of death," and not predicting "that certain things are going to happen."[1] The enterprise of "demythologizing" the Christian faith, and interpreting it as teaching Heideggerian authenticity, resembles the Wittgensteinian one in obvious ways. Could the content of the belief of the ordinary Christian faithful as expressed in the Nicene creed perhaps be captured by such analyses?

The answer, while nearly obvious, is not wholly so. The Last Judgment has been depicted in painting and sculpture in numerous ways, some of which have a place in the imagination of most Christians. Most Protestant groups, while obliterating such representations in their churches, continued to allow them to be printed in books regarded as edifying. Yet no moderately educated Christian would ever have claimed that any depiction of the Last Judgment represents it as it will be. They will not say what Jesus' coming again, with glory, will be like, except that it exceeds the capacity of human imagination to express it. Does it then follow that they do not believe that it is a certain thing that is going to happen? I agree with D. Z. Phillips that, in most respects that matter, the relatively uneducated people whom their fellow-Christians recognize as leading holy lives understand the doctrine of the Last Judgment better than I do; and I also agree that most of what they have to communicate about it, when it is not practical (how it can edify and not deprave), is expressed in scriptural or liturgical formulas. Yet I deny that it follows that those formulas are nothing but figurative expressions of a vision of the meaning of life. My reasons are of two different kinds.

The expression "the meaning of life" is itself figurative: it likens an individual life to a spoken or written utterance that may have or lack meaning, and if it means anything, may mean something heartening or disheartening. If Christianity were true, then it would make sense figuratively to say, with reference to it, that every individual human life has a meaning: it would amount to saying that, besides being a biological event (the event that terminates in what, in one of his last speeches, Martin Luther King called "physical death"), human life is a journey to judgment, and then to heaven or hell, and thus is not like a meaningless scribble, but like an utterance that means something edifying or unedifying. Without reference to such a specific doctrine of what human life is (I do not pretend that Christianity is the only such doctrine available to us), to affirm that human life has meaning would be almost vacuous: the equivalent of affirming that something, we know not what, is true of human life such that, if we knew it, we should be able to liken each human life to a meaningful spoken or written utterance rather than to a meaningless one. In short, we do not elucidate what is affirmed in the Nicene creed about the Last Judgment by saying that it expresses a vision of the meaning of human life and death; rather, we elucidate the figure of the meaning of life by reference to such doctrines as that of the Nicene creed.

My second difficulty is less philosophical than historical. While it is the case that most of what can usefully be said about the doctrine of the Last Judgment is practical, especially in view of the horrible evils misunderstanding of it has led to, I know of no writer whose work has been received as authoritative by any major branch of Christianity for any considerable period, who would deny that the practical teaching that can be drawn from the doctrine of the Last Judgment is drawn from it, and is not identical with it. Practical attitudes to life that can be regarded as Christian grow out of Christian beliefs about what is the case.

4. The Naturalism of Post-Christian Culture

A culture, in the sense in which I speak of "post-Christian culture," is a way of living, and in particular a way of thinking, that is transmitted from one generation of a human society to another. From the conversion of the Roman Empire to Christianity in the late fourth century, down to the late nineteenth century, the way of thinking about the world and humanity's place that was so transmitted in western Europe, and in its non-European colonies and former colonies, was largely Christian; and the teaching of the Nicene creed had a not unimportant place in transmitting it.

The fundamental idea of that way of thinking is expressed in the first verse of *Genesis*: it is that the natural universe (what is referred to in the Nicene creed as "heaven and earth"—at least so far as each is part of "all that is visible") was "made" by something else, God, whose nature the creed proceeds to describe. This idea was not a superstition of the uneducated, but part of the conception of nature taken for granted by the great scientists who created the new physics (or "natural philosophy" as Newton called it) of the seventeenth century. It was common to Galileo and to the inquisitors who condemned him, to Descartes and to Gassendi, to Newton and to Leibniz. This creationist or supernaturalist consensus was not complete: Spinoza, for one, challenged it. However, as Spinoza discovered in his correspondence with Oldenburg, his contention that what he called "the mechanical conception of nature" entails nature's self-existence, its independence of a nonnatural creator, was apt to be received not with incredulity but with incomprehension. Oldenburg's replies to Spinoza appear inept to us because Oldenburg found what Spinoza said so alien that he futilely, but I think honestly, misinterpreted it.

By the end of the nineteenth century, the culture of the educated had ceased to be creationist and supernaturalist. I do not imply that no creationist or supernaturalist groups remained within educated western society, or that none remain now. The Christian churches, like the orthodox Jewish communities, continued, and still continue, to believe and to teach what they always had. Yet the natural sciences are no longer taught, even in the most bibliolatrous institutions, as presupposing that nature was created from nothing by a supernatural being. Nature is presented, so far as the sciences of it go, as something whose existence needs no explanation; and it is accepted that the task of the natural sciences is not to explain why the natural universe is, but how it works—what the laws of its fundamental processes are and how those processes produced its present state from its past states.

Why is this change important? Cannot natural science be autonomous, and yet the natural universe ontologically depend on a supernatural creator? It cannot be denied that natural independence, as affirmed by the physical sciences, does not exclude ontological dependence; yet the change from a culture in which the natural universe is considered scientifically unintelligible without reference to its supernatural creator to one in which it is not is of the first importance. What exactly St. Paul meant by his remark that "the invisible things of him from the creation of the world are clearly seen, being understood by the things that are made" (*Rom.* 1:20) cannot now be determined; for we do not know what principles he presumed himself to share with his correspondents in Rome. If the principles he had in mind were about how nature is to be understood, such as Descartes's principle that what the fundamental laws of physics are depends on the nature of God, or Newton's principle that the stability of the "system of the world" must have a cause, and that it is not among the experimentally established mathematical principles of physics, then what he said would have radically different truth conditions from those it would have had if the principles he had in mind were metaphysical, like the principles of ontological dependence suggested to St. Thomas Aquinas by reflecting on Aristotle's philosophy of nature. And that difference would have an important implication: while if the former were true, natural scientists would be mistaken about natural science if they denied supernatural intervention in nature; if the latter were true, natural scientists could, consistently with truth so far as natural science can establish it, deny the existence of the supernatural, and hence of a supernatural creator.

Until the work of Darwin and Wallace gave scientists confidence that the variety of biological species could in principle be explained as the outcome of natural processes—a confidence the succeeding century of biological science has borne out—few of them believed that all reference to the supernatural could be excluded from the understanding of nature. What the full naturalization of the study of nature implies for Christian apologetics had been foreseen in the seventeenth century by Spinoza, and also, I think, by Pascal: namely, that the study of human beings might also be brought within the domain of the natural sciences, and the Christian religion itself be treated as a phenomenon to be explained. Already in the eighteenth century, although he excluded Christian origins from its scope, Gibbon had investigated what he called "the triumph of barbarism and superstition"—that is, of Christianity—in his *Decline and Fall of the Roman Empire* and had offered an explanation of it that did not refer to supernatural causes.

The result is familiar to us as university teachers and ought to be expressly acknowledged. It is that members of the academic community as such, whatever their Christian beliefs and commitments, do their work on naturalist principles except when the content of Christianity is under discussion—and it almost never is under discussion, even in institutions committed to religious education. As a result, belief that the natural universe was created by a supernatural God, even among those who hold it, is (in sociological jargon) "marginalized." Perhaps that is what Nietzsche meant when he decided that God had died although most academics had not noticed it.

This situation confronts Christians with two kinds of problems, an apologetic one and a pastoral one; and neither, if I am right about them, is understood as clearly as it should be. The apologetic one, which will occupy the remainder of this essay, is to defend the traditional teachings of Christianity within a scientific culture that is post-Christian in that it is naturalist: that is, while two centuries ago its scientific ways of thinking presupposed that the natural universe depends on a supernatural creator, they no longer do. The pastoral problem is that, despite the enormous sums our society spends on education, it has not transmitted the scientific culture to the bulk of its members. Within our society, when confronted with the popular frauds of the television "healers" and the demand for the *National Inquirer*, it is difficult not to deplore this; but when one learns that the Soviet Union is more afraid that visitors may bring in copies of the Bible in Russian than that they will bring in the AIDS virus, another side of the question emerges. It is deplorable that most of the public have little interest in scientific truth except when it directly makes their lives individually more comfortable—that they are credulous. On the other hand, it is not obviously deplorable that they have no faith that understanding the results of natural science would enable them to live better.

5. Apologetics and the Materialism of Contemporary Naturalism

Naturalism can take as many forms as there are conceptions of nature. Spinoza, for example, included mind as well as matter (substance as extended) in the one substance he identified with nature, and declined to reduce either to the other. In general, nature is what the natural sciences are about; and the conception of nature accepted within a culture reflects the sciences it recognizes as natural sciences. In the past fifty years in the western world, it has come to be generally accepted that psychology is properly a branch of biology; and that physics, chemistry, and biology all deal with different phenomena of the same fundamental subject matter, and to the extent that the ancient term "matter" has any scientific sense, it refers to that subject matter. Accordingly, it has also come to be accepted that, if there is nothing but nature, then there is nothing but matter in space-time. Naturalism has become materialism.

This fact has tempted some Christian apologists to defend Christianity against naturalism by refuting the contemporary form of naturalism, materialism. That was what C. S. Lewis did, in a series of exchanges, first with H. H. Price, who had called for a religion without dogma, that is, for a liberal Christianity that renounces the traditional faith embodied in the Nicene creed, by producing a philosophical refutation of naturalism, and then with G. E. M. Anscombe, in defending his refutation. When I arrived in Oxford as a graduate student in 1951, these exchanges were still audibly, if faintly, echoing. That exchange, although out of date, has much to teach us about what apologetics today should and should not be.

Lewis confidently set out to do what few philosophers would now attempt, to show that if a familiar inference based on common beliefs about belief is sound, then naturalism in its materialist form is self-refuting. This is Lewis's own summary of this argument.

> Every particular thought . . . is always and by all men discounted the moment they believe that it can be explained, without remainder, as the result of irrational causes. Whenever you know that what the other man is saying is wholly due to his complexes or to a bit of bone pressing on his brain, you cease to attach any importance to it. But if naturalism were true, then all thoughts whatever would be wholly the result of irrational causes. Therefore, all thoughts would be equally worthless. Therefore, naturalism is worthless. If it is true, then we can know no truths. It cuts its own throat.[2]

The common belief about belief on which Lewis tacitly relies is that beliefs worth considering are held because of reasons the believer accepts; and that they are appraised according as those reasons are sound or unsound. Naturalism in its contemporary form, materialism, is then dismissed on the ground that, by asserting that all beliefs are caused without remainder by physical events, it implies that they are not held because of reasons the believer accepts.

It is true, as Lewis saw, that Christianity presupposes the common belief about beliefs on which he relies. For example, St. Paul teaches that normal human beings can form enough true opinions about themselves and their situation to understand the moral law (*Rom.* 2:14–15); and that presupposes that they believe they have certain moral obligations because of sound reasons they accept. If that common belief is true, is Lewis's argument sound? I know of nobody who has studied Anscombe's objection to it who believes that it is. The flaw she pointed out is that the cause of a man's believing that he is sitting before a fire (say, that a piece of bone is pressing on his brain) is not necessarily the reason why he believes it (say, that he can see his legs stretched out toward the fire in his study grate—this reason being an illusion caused by the pressure of the piece of bone). Admittedly, when natural events cause beliefs by way of perceptual illusions, they are discounted. Yet when somebody who really does see his legs stretched out toward the fire in his study grate gives that as his reason for believing that he is sitting before a fire, the fact that his nonillusory perception has physical (i.e., irrational) causes does not entitle us to discount his reason.

Yet Anscombe herself came to perceive that her objection, although sound, is not the end of the matter. Reflecting on the episode in introducing the second volume of her *Collected Papers*, after recording that Lewis himself agreed that her objection was sound, she praised him for raising a problem the depth of which she had totally failed to recognize, and which remains unsolved: namely, "What is the connection between the grounds and the actual occurrence of [a] belief?"[3] And that is related to the implicit question of Plato's Socrates in the *Phaedo*: What is the connection between the physical causes of his limbs being in a seated posture in prison, and his conclusion that it was better for him to accept his lawful punishment than to escape? I myself know of no remotely satisfying materialist answer to either of these questions.

The most popular is that one believes something on certain grounds when the physical event that is functionally describable as the having of that belief is caused by another physical event that is functionally describable as the accepting of those grounds. This presupposes that just as the function of a physical event (say, the firing of certain neurons in a certain brain) may be described in physical terms (say, as the bringing about of the firing of certain other neurons), so it may be described in intentional or mental terms (say, as the having, by the person in whose brain neurons are thus firing, of a belief that he sees his legs stretched out toward his study fire). But there is an objection to this that has not to my knowledge been resolved: that, lacking an analytical reduction of the functional description in intentional terms to some description in physical terms, there is no reason to suppose that the two de-scriptions—the physical functional one and the intentional functional one—describe the same event. Unless the intentional description can in principle be analytically reduced to a physical one, the two descriptions would seem to be of nonidentical but correlated events.

If in reality nothing happens outside nature, and whatever happens in nature is causally explicable in terms of the natural sciences, then each real event functionally describable in intentional terms must be causally explicable in terms of the natural sciences. Although it may seem to follow that every event causally explicable in terms of the natural sciences must be identical with a physical event, it does not. All that follows is that whatever happens in reality is causally explicable in terms of *ideal* natural science: natural science as it might conceivably one day be—admitting of no progress or correction because, since all possible productive research has been done, there is no room for scientific work other than mastering and teaching what has already been discovered. Nobody believes that the natural sciences as we now have them have reached this ideal state; and it is at least questionable whether human beings, given their physical and intellectual limitations, can under any natural conditions develop natural sciences that are ideal in this sense. It follows that on the one hand, understood as the doctrine that nothing happens that is not causally explicable in terms of the natural sciences as they now are, materialism is certainly false; and that on the other, understood as the doctrine that nothing happens that is not causally explicable in terms of ideal natural science, it is something we know not what.

The familiar phenomena to which Lewis drew attention, forming beliefs and persisting in them for reasons, are not causally explicable in terms of the natural sciences in their present state—indeed, the phenomena are not even intelligible in terms of them. Naturalists profess not to be put out by this: in the past half-century, enormous advances have been made in neurophysiology and in the study of artificial intelligence, they point out, and they confidently expect that the dualism of human studies and the natural sciences will not endure much longer. That, however, is a question we can dodge. What matters for Christian apologetics is that Christianity presupposes that everyday explanations of human actions (sometimes contemptuously referred to as explanations in terms of "folk psychology") are often true. Should advances in biology and neurophysiology show that they are not, Christianity itself could not survive.

In that case, should it not be an important task of Christian apologetics to offer substitutes for Lewis's unsound argument? No. Doing so overlooks a crucial feature of the apologetic situation. Very few materialists claim that the natural sciences as they now exist furnish acceptable accounts of any of the higher mental phenomena such as beliefs. All they claim is that the progress already made gives ground for anticipating that they will, leaving it open how far the accounts they ultimately give will alter either what is commonly believed about those phenomena, or what natural scientists now believe about the subject matter of the natural sciences. In standing by folk psychology at the present stage of the natural sciences, Christians are certainly not committed to denying either that future scientific advances may revise folk psychology, or that the natural sciences of the future may not make materialism obsolete and provide acceptable causal explanations of the higher mental phenomena.

If philosophy provides any *praeambula fidei* it is in the theory of human action, and in particular in that part of it sometimes called "moral psychology." In conceiving human beings as creatures of will as well as of desire, and in refusing to think of their actions as predetermined outcomes of their desires and beliefs, Christianity presents naturalism with the task either of giving a naturalist account of the will, so understood, or of showing that it is a chimaera. The poverty of existing naturalist accounts of the human psyche, and in particular of the phenomena of special interest to Christianity—those of a will that is free (in each individual case, there are options between which it can choose), and which nevertheless predictably will not in all cases make the right choice it can make—should be better recognized than they are. These phenomena point to the unique status of human beings among known animals: they alone can recognize the difference between moral good and evil, and act on it; and yet they are compelled to judge themselves evil by virtue of the ways they in fact choose to act. Even so, these phenomena do not prove naturalism to be false: that as yet there is no useful naturalist account of these phenomena does not show that there never will be.

Despite the precision of their teaching about the nature of God and about God's dealings with humankind, the Christian churches have for the most part denied that the deposit of faith confided to them includes disputable propositions about the realm of nature. They have already come to terms with three very different philosophical and scientific conceptions of nature, the neo-Platonic, the Aristotelian, and the Copernican-Galilean-Newtonian; and if they and the world have any considerable future, it seems reasonable to suppose that they will come to terms with the philo-sophical-scientific culture now being formed, the content of which we can no more foresee than the seventeenth-century philosophers and scientists could foresee the philosophy and science of the twentieth century.

When confronted with contemporary naturalism, Christian apologists should begin by disclaiming any view about nature other than that Christian doctrine, as embodied in traditional confessions of faith such as the Nicene creed, will prove to be compatible with any authentic advance in the natural sciences. This claim is not empty: it is not logically impossible that a future naturalist psychology could give an account of human capacities that would make nonsense of what the Christian faith presupposes about them. However, Christian apologists should deprecate as intellectually vicious the present vogue for agonizing over philosophical questions generated by fictions about scientific possibilities. They will confine themselves to the traditionally agreed content of the faith (and much more was agreed than the appalling history of Christian confessional hatred and persecution would lead one to suppose), and to well-attested results of scientific investigation. Finally, they will not be in a hurry.

These principles were well understood by Cardinal Newman, and he laid them down in explaining what was the proper response to Darwin's biological discoveries.

It would ill become me, as if I were afraid of truth of any kind, to blame those who pursue secular facts, by means of the reason God has given them, to their logical conclusions; or to be angry with science, because religion is bound in duty to take cognizance of its teaching.... [T]he Catholic... does most deeply enter into the feelings of... religious and sincere minds, who are simply perplexed,—frightened or rendered desperate, as the case may be,—by the utter confusion into which late discoveries or speculations have thrown their most elementary ideas of religion.... [H]ow often has the wish risen in his heart that some one from among his own people should come forward as the champion of revealed truth against its opponents!... [B]ut [there are] several strong difficulties in the way. One of the greatest is this, that at the moment it is so difficult to say precisely what it is that is to be encountered and overthrown. I am far from denying that scientific knowledge is really growing, but it is by fits and starts; hypotheses rise and fall; it is difficult to imagine which of them will keep their ground, and what the state of knowledge in relation to them will turn out to be from year to year. In this condition of things, it has seemed to me to be very undignified for a Catholic to commit himself to the work of chasing what might turn out to be phantoms.... [4]

Newman's attitude to the natural sciences seems to me to be a paradigm of Christian faith, properly understood. He implicitly acknowledges that discoveries in the natural sciences could conceivably be incompatible with the Christian faith by leaving no room for anything supernatural, and hence that philosophical refutations of naturalism must be flawed. At the same time, he asserts the rational legitimacy of accepting the Christian faith without philosophical or scientific proof. Holding the Christian faith is believing something neither philosophically nor scientifically proved that could conceivably be scientifically (and hence philosophically) disproved. Why then believe it?

6. Why Do Christians Believe the Nicene Creed?

If some widespread belief, for example, that one's horoscope significantly affects what happens, is mostly harbored for bad reasons, and good reasons for it are not ready to hand, it would be silly to look for them. I therefore submit that, if there are good reasons for nonbelievers in a post-Christian culture to believe the Nicene creed, they should be ready to hand as the reasons why a substantial number of such persons have come to believe it. However, there is an obstacle to following this line of investigation. Conversation with such believers (of whom I am one) on what is, after all, a delicate subject, suggests that, to their embarrassment, most of them find it difficult to give any answer that seems to them more than a rationalization—and not a persuasive one. There was an intellectual process certainly, and it was complex; but what it was is hard to say.

However, in many of the intellectual processes that have culminated in many conversions, three elements can be identified.

Although all three are of philosophical interest, the only one that is strictly philosophical is not found in all conversions, but only in those of converts accustomed to think philosophically. It arises out of reflection on naturalism as a philosophy, and it is to recognize that the natural sciences as they now are cannot coherently account for human life as it is lived, and in particular for the human activity of scientific research. Perhaps the natural sciences of the future will be able to account for them, but we cannot claim to anticipate whether they will or not, as some philosophers impudently do. Once this is recognized, it must also be recognized that the explanation of part of human life as it is lived may lie outside nature.

The second element in the process by which Christianity is accepted, when it is, is ethical: it is to recognize that not only one's own life, but human life generally, whatever virtues it may exhibit, is radically tainted with evil. The gospels, in which the way for Jesus is prepared by John the Baptist preaching repentance and at the same time recognizing his own unworthiness, seem to imply that this element is to be found in all conversions.

These two elements in combination open the possibility that the remedy for human evil, if there is a remedy for it, may lie outside nature; but they establish neither that there is a remedy, nor that, if there is, it is a supernatural one. Nor, if what I have said about a possible future naturalism is true, can philosophy establish it. Our present understanding of nature is too defective for us to be able to establish either that a coherent nontheistic naturalism is possible or that it is not. We cannot take the natural science of the twentieth century along with available philosophical interpretations of it, as the medieval scholastics took the natural science of the thirteenth century and available philosophical interpretations of it, and derive from them convincing proofs of the dependence of the natural world on a supernatural God. For that a third element, a nonphilosophical one, is needed.

It is found in the religious history of the human race. Of all the religions of which we have any historical knowledge, those that have spread beyond the cultures in which they emerged fall into two groups: in the first are Hinduism and its critic and descendant, Buddhism; and in the second are Judaism and the two religions that claim to continue the Jewish revelation, Christianity and Islam. With a muddle characteristic of our age, many consider it impossible, on one hand, to acknowledge that each of these great religions has characteristic virtues and must, short of idolatry, be respected both intellectually and morally, and, on the other, to deny that more than one of them can be true. They conclude that each of the world religions is a facet of the one universal religion. Such a view is the antithesis of what it claims to be: far from respecting the great religions, it refuses to take any of them seriously; for it is impossible to take seriously either Christianity or, say, Hinduism, and also to say that they might both be true. Of the affirmations each makes, one or another will be denied by each of the others, and to dismiss any of these affirmations and denials is to dismiss the religions that make them.

Nobody would accept Christianity if he also accepted certain of the cardinal ideas of Hinduism and Buddhism, for example, the law of Karma and the doctrine of reincarnation; and those ideas seem to philosophically minded Christians philosophically objectionable. Judaism and its descendants are not objectionable in this way. Anybody who studies the Jewish Scriptures, and who concludes that they are the record of a special relation between the supernatural creator of the universe and one people on earth, through which all the others would one day be blessed, as it seems to me that anybody reasonably might, must inquire, in the light of what can be established historically, whether the Christian Scriptures record the culmination of that relation. Of course, the Christian Scriptures, or "New Testament" as they are known as a body, are the creation of the church, and not the church of them; but all present branches of the church accept the canonical texts of the New Testament as the sole repository of evidence for proving doctrine. Can it be reasonably concluded, from a historically serious study of these texts, that the Nicene creed is true?

The obvious objection to so concluding is that many biblical scholars of standing do not. I do not think that I was unusual in absorbing, as an undergraduate, the notion that biblical scholarship (of course I did not actually read any) has shown the New Testament canon is largely a second-century work of fiction, preserving some authentic elements of the original teaching of the Apostles, and much less of that of Jesus; and that the unedifying history of it from the Tübingen school in the early nineteenth century to Bultmann has shown that it is impossible to establish what the early teaching of either was. However, what it was not could be stated with some confidence: for example, Jesus did not predict his death before he entered Jerusalem for the last time; he did not teach his uncomprehending disciples that it would be sacrificial; and he did not command them to observe the rite of the Eucharist as, *inter alia* its perpetual memorial. Accepting the Nicene faith has been, for all I have talked to, in large part a matter of forming a critical attitude to much biblical scholarship.

The foundation of such an attitude is a distinction that leaps to the eye when the textual scholarship of nonreligious Greek and Latin texts is compared with that of biblical texts. As a rough rule, one can say that, to the extent that their methods are the same, biblical scholarship is sound, valuable, and modest in its claims; and that, to the extent that biblical scholarship goes its own way, it is something else. The rule is only rough; for the garden of nonreligious textual studies has its own weeds; and they are instructive for biblical studies. There is evidence that Roman historians writing just before and just after the texts of the New Testament were written used sources that have not survived: what did they contain? Differences in our earliest texts of certain classical writers might be explained by supposing that some descend from lost third- or fourth-century editions: what did those editions contain? Given a few bold but tenuously supported hypotheses, remarkable answers to such questions can be obtained and offered as fruits of scientific scholarship—the helpless past cannot complain. Peaceable scholars who know better are apt to pass over in silence work of this sort, but fortunately not all good scholars are peaceable. I recommend those who find it difficult to credit that rubbish can be passed off as the latest thing in textual scholarship to read the passage in A. E. Housman's preface to his critical edition of Lucan's *Bellum civile* which begins as follows:

> I touch with reluctance, as Gibbon might say, and dispatch with impatience an idle yet pretentious game in which Lucan's less serious critics find amusement, and which they call *Überlieferungsgeschichte*, because that is a longer and nobler name than fudge.[5]

Yet what awaits us in biblical studies is more impudent than the fudge that now and then interrupts the studies of those who work at nonreligious texts.

There is no defensible objection to attempts to determine what can be inferred from the New Testament texts about the origin of Christianity, it being expressly presupposed that nature as understood by the natural sciences of one's day is self-sufficient, and hence that whatever is narrated or reported as occurring by virtue of supernatural intervention in the natural order, whether the virgin birth of Jesus, his resurrection from the dead, or his and his Apostles' miracles of healing, is simply false. Given his naturalist assumptions, it is difficult to dispute Bultmann's conclusion that the only true history in the New Testament is the bare fact of Jesus' existence and death by crucifixion; but his scholarly caution is exceptional. For example, it has been confidently claimed that critical New Testament research establishes that Jesus was fundamentally an ethical teacher (Harnack), that he made no claim to be the Messiah (Wrede), that he was a noble but deluded fanatic who preached the imminent end of the world, and went to his death believing he could bring it about (Schweitzer), and much, much more.

Before accepting any of these results (since they contradict one another, it is impossible to accept them all), anybody who is seriously inquiring into the truth of the Nicene creed will want to know why biblical scholars should agree that nothing can happen in reality that cannot be accounted for by the natural sciences as they now are. As a day or two in a good library suffices to show, the thesis that the gospel narratives of supernatural interventions are false, although it is offered as a conclusion of textual research, is almost never a conclusion and almost always an unargued presupposition. This is sometimes concealed; for example, by working with the assumption that the authentic material from which the gospels were composed, or, more accurately, fabricated, were smaller pericopes that circulated as separate units in early Christian communities. Bultmann, for example, reduces these pericopes to sayings without context, with the result that he can deny that the authors of the gospels had any material implying a supernatural intervention to draw upon.

If the inquirer sets aside works of biblical criticism that simply presuppose that the naturalism of one's own day is true and traditional Christianity false, to what can he look? Devotional aids to the study of the Scriptures are not what he needs either. I myself neither was directed to nor found exactly what I sought; and fell back on reading the New Testament itself, with the aid of the first (1968) edition of the *Jerome Biblical Commentary* (I chose one approved by the Roman church as least likely to confound contemporary naturalist presuppositions with results of scholarship). I devoted most attention to the earliest texts, namely, the early letters of Paul; and asked myself what can be inferred from them about the beliefs and practices of the early church and whether it is consistent with the later gospel accounts of Jesus' life and teaching. Two things I found seemed to me of special importance: first, Paul's concern, in *Galatians* 1 and 2, for the unity of the church and the integrity of its doctrine, his staying for fifteen days with Peter, and his recognition of James, Peter, and John as "pillars"; and second, his description of the Eucharist, in 1 *Corinthians* 11:23–29, not only as the central rite of Christian worship, but as instituted by Jesus in terms implying that his death would be sacrificial. Both letters are reasonably believed to have been written in the 50s: less than thirty years after Jesus' death.

It seems a safe conclusion that the Apostles whom Paul recognizes as pillars were teaching soon after Jesus died that his death was sacrificial, that he was raised from the dead, and that he commanded his followers to observe the Eucharist as a memorial of his sacrifice. These teachings are the foundation of the trinitarian doctrine formulated in the Nicene creed, and they are not fabrications by unknown propagandist geniuses in the second century. The question is, are they true?

Why do converts to Christianity from pre-Christian and post-Christian cultures accept them? Part of the answer has already been suggested. When they learn what Christianity teaches, they judge it, if true, to be a remedy for their condition. In comparing it with alternatives, their verdict is, like Peter's when Jesus asked him, "Will ye also go away?" "Lord, to whom shall we go? thou hast the words of eternal life" (*John* 6:67–68). Still, a fiction may be unrivaled and still a fiction. The rest of the answer is that they judge, and reasonably judge, that, from the Pentecost after they allegedly occurred, the Apostles taught the sacrificial death and resurrection of Jesus. Unless they were insanely deluded, the Apostles were in a position to know the facts, and either reported them truthfully or lied. What they reported is incredible from a contemporary naturalist point of view. Yet from a contemporary naturalist point of view much that we all reasonably believe about ourselves is unexplained, and the misery of the condition in which serious inquirers take themselves to be would have no remedy. In this situation, faith may seem to inquirers possible, and not irrational. And then, by some means they do not understand but which the church teaches is the operation of grace, it may become actual.

Notes

From *Christian Philosophy*, edited by Thomas P. Flint. © 1990 by the University of Notre Dame Press, Notre Dame, Indiana. Used by permission of the publisher.

1. D. Z. Phillips, *Death and Immortality* (New York: St. Martin's Press, 1970), p. 67; quoted in William J. Wainwright, *Philosophy of Religion* (Belmont, Calif.: Wadsworth, 1988), p. 142.

2. "Religion without Dogma?" in C. S. Lewis, *The Great Miracle* (New York: Ballantine Books, 1983), p. 94. Originally published in *Phoenix Quarterly* 1 (1946).

3. G. E. M. Anscombe, *Collected Papers* (Minneapolis: University of Minnesota Press, 1981), vol. 2, pp. ix–x. The version of Lewis's argument which Anscombe criticized was

in chap. 3 of the first edition of his book *Miracles*, which Lewis radically revised in later editions.

4. J. H. Newman, *Apologia Pro Vita Sua* (London: Oxford University Press, 1964), pp. 272–73.

5. A. E. Housman, *M. Annaei Lucani belli civilis libri decem* (Oxford: Blackwell, 1926), p. xii; and cf. pp. xii–xviii.

THREE

⚬ ─ ⟨ ◯ ⟩ ─ ⚬

Spinoza's Theology

pinoza's theology, although original, owes much to the cultural soil that nourished it.[1] His parents were among the many "Marranos"—Portuguese Jews who in their native country had been compelled outwardly to embrace Roman Catholicism—who had emigrated to Amsterdam in the early seventeenth century. In the freedom of their new country, the immigrant Marrano community set out to recover its full religious heritage, and to shed beliefs and practices contrary to it. However, some of its members, of whom Spinoza was one, not only remained attached to non-Jewish elements in their Marrano culture, but, having embraced the revolution in the physical sciences associated with Galileo, Bacon, and Descartes, wished to pursue its implications for religion.[2] When he was twenty-three, partly because he would not renounce these non-Jewish interests, the Amsterdam synagogue expelled and cursed him. Yet even among the radical Christians who befriended him, and who repudiated the trinitarian and Christological doctrines he found absurd, only a small circle of intimates were prepared to follow him when he jettisoned the conception of God as a supernatural creator of the natural universe, and developed a "naturalized" theology, in which the natural universe, as conceived in Baconian-Cartesian natural science, derives its existence from nothing above and beyond it.

Despite its radical naturalism, Spinoza's theology is articulated much as are the supernaturalist ones he rejected. It has two major divisions, speculative and practical. Speculative theology treats of God's existence and nature, and of his relation to the natural world and the human beings in it. Practical theology treats of how human beings are to live, given God's nature and their relation to him; and it subdivides into a natural (or philosophical) part, which treats of what can be established by reason in the light of human experience, and a revealed part, which treats of what God has communicated to individual human beings.[3] While traditional speculative theology likewise had a revealed as well as a natural part, Spinoza's does not. On both historical and philosophical grounds he contended that all divine revelation to individuals is practical. It follows that little can be learned from revelation about the nature of God and his relation to the world: what is known of them that matters is philosophical. It also follows that the nature of revelation is not itself revealed: knowledge of it is derived partly from historical reports of alleged revelations, some of them spurious, and partly from philosophical considerations.

Spinoza expounded the various parts of his theology in the following writings: his speculative theology in his posthumously published *Ethics* parts 1 and 2 (the first half); his historical-philosophical theory of divine revelation and of the limits of revealed theology in the *Theological-Political Treatise*, which he published anonymously in 1670; and his practical theology in the *Theological-Political Treatise* and in *Ethics* parts 4 and 5. In what follows, I take my primary task to be to establish the sense of what he wrote, never forgetting that, consistently with his motto "*Caute*," he was reserved, especially in the *Theological-Political Treatise*, which he published during his lifetime, and in letters to correspondents who had not proved themselves friends; and that he made free use of recognized literary devices such as irony.

The chief obstacles to understanding these writings are two: one internal, and one external. The internal one is that the diction of his *Ethics* is apt to mislead readers who are not vigilant, especially if they neglect the *Theological-Political Treatise*, the Dutch version of his *Short Treatise on God, Man, and his Well-Being*, and his *Correspondence*, above all his letters to and from Oldenburg. That diction is scholastic-Cartesian; and, as he must have been aware, much of what he wrote, although not all, makes sense if his words are taken in their scholastic-Cartesian senses. However, he assigns new senses to many of the expressions he uses, sometimes explicitly, and sometimes implicitly by the structure of his reasoning or by his examples. Readers who have persuaded themselves that Spinoza is the last of the medievals or the first of the absolute idealists are apt to overlook the passages in which he does so.

The chief external obstacle to understanding Spinoza's theological writings is the notion that they are esoteric, which Leo Strauss has made fashionable.[4] According to Strauss, Spinoza's *Theological-Political Treatise*, like the writings of Plato, and of medieval Muslim and Jewish philosophers menaced by orthodox persecution, has a double meaning: the "exoteric" or surface meaning unintelligent readers like censors will take it to have, and the "esoteric" or hidden meaning intelligent readers, alert to signs such as deliberate contradictions and inapposite examples, will detect in it. The esoteric meaning may not only go far beyond the exoteric one, but may even contradict it. While I have no space to examine Strauss's case thoroughly,[5] I shall not be able wholly to avoid examining his interpretation of Spinoza's view of Jesus, "whom he regularly calls Christ," as sinister.[6]

1. Natural Theology

In natural theology, Spinoza in *Ethics* part 1 breaks with Judaeo-Christian orthodoxy by conceiving God, not as the creator of human beings and of the world they inhabit, but as an infinite being in which they exist as finite modes (E 1p15). No substance except God, he contends, can be, or be conceived; and he draws the inevitable inference that the extended and thinking things of everyday experience "are either attributes of God, or affections [that is, modes] of God's attributes" (E 1p14c2). God, he concludes, cannot create anything outside himself. He is "the immanent, not the transient, cause of all things," and not of their existence only, but also of their essence, which cannot be identical with their existence (E 1p18, 24, 25).

Notwithstanding these heresies, he implies that two of his three proofs of God's existence in *Ethics* 1p11d, as well as an additional one in its scholium, are a priori; and of these four, two not only look like the "ontological" proofs offered by Descartes and Leibniz, but one is reminiscent of those of Anselm and of Duns Scotus (E 1p11d,s). Since he also follows many orthodox theologians in deducing from God's infinity the negative "attributes" they ascribed to him, which he denied to be genuine attributes—namely, indivisibility, uniqueness, causal independence, eternity, immutability, and the indistinguishability of his existence from his essence—(E 1p13, 14c1, 17c1, 20, 20c2), many commentators have reduced Spinoza's natural theology to a stage in the supposed advance from scholasticism to Hegelian idealism. As they read him, he conceived the infinite positive attributes which he ascribed to God, such as extension, thought, and others to which human beings have no access, as attributes only in the sense that they each appear to some finite beings, human or nonhuman, to constitute God's essence, even though they do not in fact constitute it.[7] Extension, for example, is no more than a *phenomenon bene fundatum* ("well-founded phenomenon"), in the terminology Leibniz was to introduce.

While such readings will always captivate those attracted by Hegelian history of philosophy, they are incompatible not only with the great scholium to *Ethics* 1p15, but also with what Spinoza discloses in his early *Short Treatise on God, Man, and His Well-Being*[8] about the reflections on his predecessors that led him to the natural theology of the *Ethics*.

In the "Short Outline" preceding the text of the *Short Treatise*,[9] Spinoza's editor describes him as having "an idea of God" according to which: "he defines God as a being consisting of infinite Attributes, of which each is infinitely perfect in its kind. From this he then infers that existence belongs to [God's] essence, or that God necessarily exists." This reverses the order in which most medieval theologians— Muslim, Jewish, and Christian—derived the divine attributes. Both Maimonides and

Aquinas, for example, begin with the identity of God's essence with his existence (*esse*), and infer, first, that God exists necessarily and not contingently, and then that his existence cannot be limited by his essence, that is, cannot be limited to the power of any given kind of thing as opposed to that of any other. They then conclude, in Maimonides' words, that while we can know that God is infinite in the sense that "all deficiencies are negated" with respect to his essence, this knowledge is merely negative: we "cannot apprehend his quiddity"—what he is.[10]

Maimonides confined nonnegative human knowledge of God to his existence and to his works—his creation of the world and to his interventions in it, as revealed in the Scriptures.[11] Aquinas was only slightly less restrictive. He asserted that human beings can demonstrate that nonnegative terms standing for pure perfections (such as wisdom) are true of God, although the only senses they can attach to those terms when applied to God are analogical. Thus they can know that God is wise, not in the only way human experience enables them to understand positively—the imperfect and derivative one in which human beings are wise—but in a perfect way which they can only understand as not imperfect—the way in which the first cause of all wisdom is wise.[12] Yet Maimonides and Aquinas were both agreed that, since God cannot be composed of elements, he must, in the technical language of scholasticism, be "simple," and hence that the many "attributes" he can be shown to possess cannot be really distinct. In predicating different perfections of God, whether negatively or analogically, human beings do no more than ascribe to him, in different imperfect ways, a simple perfection they cannot comprehend.[13]

A caustic remark in the *Short Treatise* shows that Spinoza derided this medieval consensus at a very early stage in his thinking. "[T]he philosophers," he wrote, meaning the medieval natural theologians, "sufficiently conceded ... that they have a very slight and inconsiderable knowledge of God" when they denied that a "legitimate definition of God can be given," giving as their ground that such a definition "must represent the thing absolutely and affirmatively, and ... [that] one cannot know God affirmatively, but only negatively" (ST I.7). And he went on to attribute their complacency in ignorance to their Aristotelian mistake that legitimate definitions of substances—that is, of beings neither predicated of nor present in another—or of accidents, of which there are nine fundamental categories,[14] *"must be by genus and difference."* Descartes had corrected this mistake by showing that the essences of created substances are only two, each constituted by a single principal attribute that is the subject matter of a fundamental science, and that Aristotelian accidents of a substance—beings that exist only as "present in" it—are each no more than modifications, or "modes," of the attribute constituting its essence. Thus a noncomplex body, or corporeal substance, is constituted by the attribute of extension (i.e., spatial three-dimensionality); and its modes at any given time are its shape, size, and state of motion or rest relative to other bodies. Aristotelian accidents of a complex body that are not reducible to modes of extension—for example, its hue as seen—are not present in it at all, but are propensities of the modes of the bodies composing it to cause certain modes of thinking in embodied thinkers.

From the beginning, as his *Short Treatise* shows, Spinoza saw Descartes's scheme as the foundation of a new theology as well as of a new physics. A definition in Cartesian science is not by *genus* and *differentia*; and that of a substance simply states what its Cartesian principal attribute is. Such attributes "require no genus, or anything else through which they are better understood or explained; for since they, as attributes of a being existing through itself, exist through themselves, they are also known through themselves" (ST I.7). Definitions of modes, by contrast, specify in what modifications of the principal attribute of their substances they consist, and exist wholly "through" those attributes (ST I.7). Like most of his scientifically minded contemporaries, Spinoza believed that Descartes had shown that the physical universe is an unbounded extended plenum, in which bounded or finite things exist as modifications by virtue of internal motions the quantity of which is conserved. Empty space is a nonthing; for an attribute must be an attribute of something, and the extension of an empty space would be an attribute of nothing. Since a vessel emptied of everything extended must collapse, one that seems to be empty, for example, a glass jar emptied by an air pump, can have been emptied only of whatever stuff (air) an air pump pumps, not of the finer stuff it cannot pump. And since no extended body can move from the place it occupies unless some other extended body or bodies replace it, all motion in the infinite plenum must be vortical, like the motion goldfish swimming in a bowl produce in the water in it. The infinite plenum, however, is not absolutely infinite; for it has no modes that are not modes of extension. It cannot, for example, think. But in its kind—*res extensa*—it is infinite.

Rightly apprehensive that his physics would prompt heretical theological speculation, Descartes himself protested that the extended corporeal plenum is *not* infinite in any legitimate sense, but merely "indefinite":

> [I]n the case of God alone, not only do we fail to recognize any limits in any respect, but our understanding positively tells us that there are none. [But]...
> in the case of other things, our understanding does not in the same way tell us that they lack limits in some respect; we merely acknowledge in a negative way that the limits they have cannot be discovered by us.[15]

This, however, obfuscates a distinction that Spinoza saw, and is there for anybody to see: that between infinity in a kind and absolute infinity, or infinity in every kind. In discussing the corporeal universe in its kind, that is, as an extended substance, Descartes wrote:

> [T]his world, that is, the whole universe of corporeal substance, has no limits to its extension. For no matter where we imagine the boundaries to be, there are also some indefinitely extended spaces beyond them, which we not only imagine *but also perceive to be imaginable in a true fashion, that is, real.*[16]

This implies, not only that "we merely acknowledge...that the limits [this world has] cannot be discovered by us," but that there are no such real limits, because beyond any finite extended thing there are real extended spaces.

What of the scholastic objection[17] that, since what is extended is divisible, it must be made up of finite parts, and so cannot be an infinite *substance*? Spinoza had found its refutation as early as when he wrote the *Short Treatise*, and repeated it in Letter 12 and *Ethics* 1p15s. Neither the parts human beings distinguish in extended space, nor the whole considered as composed of those parts are "true or actual beings, but only beings of reason" (ST I.2). The extended universe is in fact indivisible, although for some practical purposes we must think of it as divided into parts; but the parts into which we mentally divide it are not true and actual beings but mere *entia rationis*, like the hours into which we divide the day. Not only is this infinite extended plenum not created, as Descartes had mistakenly believed, but two predicates are true of it which traditional theology held to be true only of God: namely, "exists in itself" and "is conceived through itself." In other words, like all infinites, it is a substance.

By saying that the infinite extended plenum "exists in itself" Spinoza meant that it is its own immanent cause, that is, it depends on itself for its existence. Immanent causation is the self-dependence of an independent existent, and the other-dependence, or dependence on an independent existent, of any dependent existent or mode. Although the only laws of immanent causation discovered by human beings about the extended plenum are laws of conservation—that both its infinite quantity and the proportion of motion to rest in it are always the same—it can be inferred from the nature of substance in general that there must be others by which it immanently causes the changing states of motion and rest that occur in it. That inference is confirmed by the discovery of laws of transient causation according to which one state of motion and rest is succeeded by another. When E. W. von Tschirnhaus suggested in a letter that of itself the infinite extended substance must be an inert mass, Spinoza flatly denied it, and declared that the nature of the actual infinite extended substance—that is, the laws by which it immanently causes whatever it does—must determine not only whatever motion and rest occur in it, but also what unchanging laws of transient causation govern the continual changes in the motion and rest of finite bodies in it.[18]

Having affirmed what Descartes had denied, that extension is an attribute expressing an essence that is infinite in the strict sense, and that the medieval objections to the infinity of the extended universe are unsound, Spinoza naturally proceeded to inquire whether thought (*cogitatio*), the second of the really distinct attributes that constitute Cartesian created substances, also expresses an infinite essence.

Jewish and Christian theologians, while speaking with the vulgar in referring to God's intellect and in ascribing infinite knowledge to it, at the same time endorsed a principle which Maimonides had said "should be established in everybody's mind," namely,

> that our knowledge or our power does not differ from [God's] knowledge or
> His power in the latter being greater and stronger, the former less and weaker,

or in other similar respects, inasmuch as the strong and the weak are necessarily alike with respect to their species, and one definition comprehends both of them. ... [E]verything that can be ascribed to God, may He be exalted, differs in every respect from our attributes, so that no definition can comprehend the one thing and the other.[19]

According to that principle, thought, so far as it expresses either the essence of any individual human mind (as Descartes believed) or that of a substance of which individual human minds are modes (as Spinoza believed), neither can be an attribute of God nor can express an infinite essence. Here too, Spinoza boldly rejected both the principle and its implications. Just as he had maintained that a finite extended thing must be a mode of an infinite extended substance through the attribute of which, namely extension, it is conceived, so he urged that a finite set of ideas, which is what a human mind at bottom is, must be a mode of an infinite substance through the attribute of which, namely thought, it is likewise conceived (E 2p1 and E 2p2d). Nothing in any human idea, however inadequate, forbids that it be part of the complex infinite adequate idea that is an infinite mode of such an infinite thinking substance.

Yet even if Spinoza were right—even if all finite bodies and their states were modes of an infinite corporeal substance, and all finite minds and their thoughts were modes of an infinite thinking substance—Descartes's doctrine that essences expressed by really distinct attributes must be of really distinct substances would not be impugned. And if it were true, Spinoza's infinite extended substance and an infinite thinking substance would each be a really distinct substance of one attribute. No infinite thinker who was infinitely extended could be more than a *union* of two distinct substances, as Descartes believed a human being is. Nor could any such substantial union be a substance, because it would need an external cause.

Spinoza would have nothing to do with this line of thought. "[T]he more reality or being a thing has," he declared, "not only do the more attributes belong to it," but each of these attributes "must be conceived through itself"—that is, must express an infinite essence by itself, and not merely in conjunction with the others (E 1p9–10). This doctrine raises two questions that go to the heart of Spinoza's metaphysics and continue to be disputed by commentators on it. First, how can really distinct attributes, which express really distinct essences, each infinite in its kind, constitute the essence of one and the same substance? And second, even if an infinite substance consisting of really distinct attributes *can* exist, is there any good reason to believe that one *does*?

In *Ethics* 2p7—"The order and connection of ideas is the same as the order and connection of things"—Spinoza furnishes a clue to how he conceives the unity of a substance that is both extended and thinking. It suggests that the unity of any substance consisting of really distinct attributes is the *necessary* identity, under each of those attributes, of the order and connection of its modes. But what are order and connection? Presumably, the order of a thing's modes as constituted by really distinct attributes is the same if and only if, considered in their causal order—both immanent and transient—those constituted by any one attribute correspond one to one with those constituted by any other. Sameness of connection is more obscure. It cannot be determination by the same causal laws, because the causal laws determining the order of the modes under any one attribute must be conceived through that attribute. I conjecture that Spinoza thought that there must be transattribute laws of nature determining, for a substance's modes as constituted by any one attribute, how they are constituted by any other. Given what those laws of nature are, and how the totality of the substance's modes are constituted under any one attribute, it would follow, for any mode as constituted under one, how it is correspondingly constituted under any other. If that is so, and I know of no coherent alternative that does not contradict his text, Spinoza conceived God as a substance consisting of every one of the infinite attributes that constitute an infinite essence, the constitutive laws of whose nature determine, for any mode constituted by any of its attributes, both that it will also be constituted by every other, and how it will be so constituted.

Why believe that God, so conceived, exists? This question reduces to "Does each of the various attributes that express an infinite essence express the essence of a unique being consisting of infinite attributes, or are those attributes distributed among more than one being?" If the former, Spinoza's God exists; if the latter, he does not. The fundamental argument Spinoza offers for the former runs: "[s]ince being able to exist is power, it follows that the more reality belongs to the nature of a thing, the more powers it has, of itself, to exist. Therefore, an absolutely infinite Being, or God, has, of himself, an absolutely infinite power of existing. For that reason, he exists absolutely" (E 1p11s; cf. ST I.2). This amounts to a principle of plenitude: that the possible substance that has most reality must exist. Unfortunately, Spinoza's argument for it is unsound; for, as Leibniz was to show, possible independent existents are possible worlds rather than possible substances. Spinoza himself recognized that how much reality a substance has is determined by how many attributes it has. If so, as long as all the attributes there are are somehow distributed over substances in a possible world, how much reality it has cannot be increased or decreased by distributing them differently: it must remain the same, whether they all constitute a single substance, or each a different one. Hence an argument on Spinoza's lines can at best show that every attribute expressing an infinite essence must be instantiated in some set of substances, not that they must all be instantiated in a single one.

Although Spinoza presumably never perceived that his form of the principle of plenitude is flawed, in his *Short Treatise* he supplemented it by arguing a posteriori that the attributes Extension and Thought must both belong to the same substance, "because of the unity which we see everywhere in Nature; if there were different beings in Nature, the one could not possibly unite with the other" (ST I.2). Since the only attributes "we," that is, human beings, cognize are Extension and Thought, the only attributes we can in any sense "see" united everywhere in Nature are Extension and Thought. But, since we cannot see Thought, how can we see that? Presumably by experiencing in ourselves that the primary object of human thought is the corporeal universe, as mediated through the changing states of particular human bodies. While it does not strictly follow that all the primary finite modes of thinking in the infinite thinking substance have modes of the corporeal universe for objects, if the ones we immediately cognize do, and if there is no reason to believe them unique, then it is at least a reasonable conjecture that the infinite thinking being of which our minds are complex finite modes has for its primary object the infinite extended thing of which our bodies are complex finite modes, and that it truly represents that primary object because the causal order of the modes of that thinking thing and that of the modes of that extended thing are one and the same.

A further conjecture seems natural, although Spinoza explicitly stated it only in a letter. Given that the absolutely infinite divine substance consists of infinite attributes besides Extension and Thought, and that, as thinking, it cognizes all its modes under all of them, his correspondent Tschirnhaus inquired why human beings, who are modes of the divine substance, cognize only one attribute besides Thought, namely Extension (Ep 63). Spinoza answered that since, as thinking, God must adequately cognize every one of his attributes, and since each complex idea in him that adequately represents him under a given attribute must be infinite, God as thinking must consist of an infinity of minds, each primarily representing him as infinite in one of his kinds (Ep 66). Human minds are finite modes only of one of the infinite minds in the infinite idea that is an eternal mode of God as thinking, namely, that mind whose primary object is God as extended. God as thinking cognizes all his infinite attributes; but just as each infinite attribute is really distinct from every other, so is the idea of each in the infinite idea of God really distinct from the idea of every other. Accordingly, each finite mind is a mode of the idea that is God's self-cognition of one of his infinite attributes, and of himself as cognizing it. Each human being is both a human body, a finite mode of God constituted by the attribute Extension, and a human mind, the finite mode of God as thinking that is primarily constituted by an idea of that body *and of nothing else*; and for each further attribute of God, A_i, that same finite mode will also be constituted by A_i and by a mind that is primarily constituted solely by the idea of that mode as constituted by A_i. Hence God, so far as he constitutes the idea of that finite mode, will be a series of ideas, each primarily constituted by an idea of it under a different attribute other than Thought. Not only is the finite mode that as extended and thinking is a human being much more than a human being, but, as thinking, it is much more than a human mind.

In writing the *Theological-Political Treatise*, Spinoza thought it prudent to explain to his readers what he meant both by the word God and by the traditional theological terms he applied to God. By God he meant the absolutely infinite substance, which he identified with Nature, considered as an infinite all-embracing immanent cause, and not simply as the corporeal universe. He wrote:

[S]ince nothing can be or be conceived without God, it is certain that all those things which are in nature involve and express the concept of God, in proportion to their essence and perfection. Hence the more we cognize natural things, the greater and more perfect is the cognition of God we acquire, or (since cognition of an effect through its cause is nothing but cognizing some property of that cause) the more we cognize natural things, the more perfectly do we cognize the essence of God, which is the cause of all things. So all our cognition, that is our greatest good, not only depends on the cognition of God but consists entirely in it. (TTP iv.11)[20]

It follows that to happen according to the laws of Nature and to happen according to the knowledge and will of God are one and the same. Spinoza makes this point with an example from geometry, but he would certainly have accepted one from physics.

[W]hen we attend only to the fact that the nature of a triangle is contained in the divine nature from eternity, as an eternal truth, then we say that God has the idea of the triangle, or understands the nature of the triangle. But when we attend afterwards to the fact that the nature of the triangle is contained in the divine nature in this way, solely from the necessity of the divine nature, ... then that very thing which we called God's intellect we call God's will or decree. (TTP iv.24)

In a later chapter he sums up his doctrine of the identity of Nature, the absolutely infinite substance, with God:

[S]ince nothing is necessarily true except by the divine decree alone, it follows quite clearly from this that the universal laws of Nature are nothing but decrees of God, which follow from the necessity and perfection of the divine nature. Therefore, if anything were to happen in Nature contrary to her universal laws, it would also necessarily be contrary to the divine decree, intellect and nature. ... We could also show the same thing from the fact that *the power of nature is the divine power and virtue itself.* Moreover, the divine power is the very essence of God. (TTP vi.8–9; emphasis added)

Spinoza's theology, in short, naturalizes God.

This naturalization transforms the sense of two terms which Spinoza continued to apply to God: the predicates "eternal" and "perfect." Following Boethius, both medieval and Cartesian theologians had conceived eternity as timeless existence. Spinoza redefined it as "existence itself, insofar as it is conceived to follow necessarily from the definition alone of the eternal thing" (E 1d8). The existence of an absolutely infinite being, as Spinoza describes it, follows necessarily from its definition because it is defined as immanently causing its own existence;[21] and a thing immanently causes its own existence if and only if it is such that it is a law of nature that it is conserved, that is, can neither be created nor destroyed. Eternity so understood does not exclude the passage of time in the everyday sense;[22] for motion and rest is an eternal mode of infinite extended substance, and motion is relative change of position in time.[23]

Again, both medieval and Cartesian theologians conceived "perfection" a priori, as a standard by which Nature and everything in it can be judged imperfect. Spinoza, without redefining it, treats it as equivalent to "infinite." Hence, since the extended corporeal universe is infinite in its kind, it is perfect in its kind too, not because it satisfies some a priori standard of perfection, but because, as far as extension is concerned, it is itself the only rational standard of perfection. God, as absolutely infinite being, is likewise absolutely perfect, not as satisfying some a priori human standard, but as providing the only ultimate standard by which human beings can judge anything as imperfect. As Spinoza put it, "[T]he perfection of things is to be judged solely from their nature and power; things are not more or less perfect because they delight or offend men's senses, or because they agree with human nature or are repugnant to it" (E 1ap).

In declaring that the absolutely infinite being whose existence he claimed to demonstrate is the true God whom orthodox Jews and Christians ignorantly worship, was Spinoza concealing his atheism from himself by a play upon words? Maimonides would have thought so:

> I shall not say that he who affirms that God, may He be exalted, has positive attributes either falls short of apprehending Him or ... has an apprehension of him that is different from what He really is, but I shall say that he has abolished his belief in the existence of the deity without being aware of it.[24]

When confronted with a letter in which Lambertus van Velthuysen reprobated the author of the *Theological-Political Treatise* (not knowing who he was) for "teaching pure Atheism with hidden and disguised arguments" (Ep 42), Spinoza indignantly asked, "Does that man ... cast aside all religion who declares that God must be recognized as the highest good, and that he must be loved as such with a free spirit?" (Ep 43).[25] But, as Maimonides would properly have answered, anybody who identifies God with Nature confounds the highest good with a being who is nothing like the God of Abraham, Isaac, and Jacob. He did not make the heavens and the earth, he did not create our ancestors and place them on earth, and he is not, through the calling of the Jews, engaged in blessing all the nations of the earth. Spinoza's God cannot rationally be worshiped as the God of orthodox Judaism and Christianity can: human beings are not made in his image, and their relations with him are not those of like with like in any sense at all. And yet human beings would have to Spinoza's God, if he existed, something not wholly unlike the relations they would have with the God of Judaism and Christianity, if he existed. They are causally totally dependent on him for their existence. Nobody who is not so insane as to hate his own existence can, as Spinoza pointed out, hate Spinoza's God (E 5p18). Our attitude to him will, however, be one of "intellectual love" in a sense to be defined, which is identical with an attitude Spinoza called "*acquiescentia.*" If God is conceived as traditionally minded Jews and Christians conceive him, Spinoza denies his existence, and can legitimately be accused of atheism. Not of idolatry; for he does not offer to his "God" the sort of worship that pagan polytheists offered to theirs. Spinoza's God, however, is more like the Jewish and Christian one than like those of paganism; and the intellectual love Spinoza thinks due to his God, while unlike monotheistic worship, has some analogy to it. Spinoza can legitimately claim that his absolutely infinite being is sufficiently like the Jewish and Christian God, and the attitude it would be rational to take to such a being sufficiently like worship, for it to be proper to describe it as "God."

2. Revelation, Imagination, and Universal Religious Faith

Those who identify God with Nature, if they have a theology at all, usually confine it to natural theology, and dismiss divine revelation as a superstition. In the *Theological-Political Treatise*, Spinoza does neither. Defining revelation (or, from its recipient's point of view, prophecy), as "certain (*certa*) cognition of something revealed by God to men" (TTP i.1), he accepts the Jewish and Christian Scriptures as records of a long tradition of divine revelation, and, economically investigating that tradition, develops a general theory of revelation and deduces from it the tenets of a universal religious faith.

Spinoza recognized that his definition of revelation is satisfied by natural cognition, or cognition of the second and third kinds as defined in *Ethics* 2p40s2; for such cognition is both certain and immanently caused by God. However, he also recognized that, while what God certainly reveals through science is in no way inferior to what he certainly reveals in other ways, Europeans generally (the *vulgus* among whom the *Theological-Political Treatise* was published) take revealed cognition to exclude the scientific, and recognize as revelation only the specimens of it recorded in the Jewish and Christian Scriptures. He himself was no bigot: while accepting the Jewish-Christian revelation as authentic, he took care to point out that the Jewish Scriptures attest that "the other nations had their own prophets also, who prophesied to them and to the Jews" (TTP iii.35).

Spinoza's philological principles for studying the Jewish and Christian Scriptures were not original. Among philologists in the Netherlands, especially since J. J. Scaliger's appointment to a chair at Leiden in 1594, they were regularly followed in studying nonscriptural texts.[26] As Richard H. Popkin shows in chapter 9 of the present volume,[27] they had been stated and employed by a succession of biblical scholars, both Jewish and Christian, most of whom were perfectly orthodox, like the medieval rabbi Abraham ibn Ezra,[28] whose commentary on the Pentateuch was printed alongside the Hebrew text of the Venetian Bomberg edition of the Jewish Scriptures. (A few others were not, like Spinoza's friend and correspondent Lodewijk Meyer.) However, classical philologists tended to leave biblical studies to theologians,[29] with the result, as Popkin also shows, that nobody before Spinoza explored what would follow from combining good philology with his naturalized theology.

This is how Spinoza states and defends his philological principles for studying Scripture:

> [J]ust as the method of interpreting nature consists above all in putting together a history of nature, from which, as from certain data, we infer the definitions of natural things, so to interpret Scripture it is necessary to prepare a straight-

forward history of Scripture and to infer the mind of the authors of Scripture from it, by legitimate reasonings, as from certain data and principles. For if somebody has admitted as principles or data for interpreting Scripture and discussing the things contained in it only those drawn from Scripture itself *and its history*, he will always proceed without any danger of error. (TTP vii.8; emphasis added)

Spinoza makes two general claims about what can be established by following these principles. First, it can often be shown whether a sacred text has in fact been transmitted from antiquity or has been interpolated or added to out of "the blind and reckless desire to interpret Scripture and to think up new doctrines in religion" (TTP vii.3). Second, it can often be demonstrated that a report of an alleged revelation is a mere fabrication—whether by the alleged prophet himself, or by somebody in a position to ascertain whether or not he claimed to have had this or that revealed to him. By contrast, invalidating the reasons offered for interpolation or addition can approach a proof of authenticity.

Both the Jewish Scriptures and the nonepistolary part of the Christian ones largely consist of historical narratives: some of divine revelations to individuals, of the actions they prompted, and of reactions to them; others simply of revelations and of the situations in which they were vouchsafed. Of those narratives, some purport to have been written by those who received the revelations they record, but most do not. Spinoza argues that the Pentateuch, *Judges, Ruth, I* and *II Samuel,* and *I* and *II Kings,* "were all written by one and the same Historian, who wanted to write about the past history of the Jews from their first origin up to the first destruction of the City" (TTP viii.42). Who that historian was, he does not claim to be able to prove, but he suspects that it was Ezra (TTP viii.48), and thereafter refers to him, whoever he was, by that name (TTP ix.2). Ezra, however, left his work incomplete. In parts, it is incoherent, although later editors have removed some of its gaps and incoherencies by additions and interpolations of more doubtful authority (TTP ix passim).

Since it can be inferred from the Jewish Scriptures themselves that "before the time of the Maccabees there was no canon of the Sacred Books, but the ones we now have were selected from many others by the Pharisees of the second temple, . . . and those books were accepted only because of their decision"—which neither was divinely inspired nor was claimed to be—Spinoza declares that "those who want to demonstrate the authority of Holy Scripture are bound to show the authority of each separate book," and the authenticity of any given passage in it (TTP x.43). Yet he doubts neither that Ezra had honestly used authentic materials, nor that his work can usually be distinguished from that of later editors. Hence he does not impugn the authority of most of the Scriptures as edited, even though little in them had been written by the prophets whose thoughts or deeds they report. Even less does he impugn the authority of the Pentateuch because of such trifles as that Moses could not have written the whole of it: for example, the preface to *Deuteronomy,* which implies that it was written after Jews had crossed the Jordan, which they did not do until after Moses' death (TTP viii.6).

Despite the weight he attaches to philological evidence, Spinoza could not have arrived at his more important conclusions about revelation from it alone. He acknowledges that two philosophical principles are needed as well.

The first is a corollary of his naturalism: namely, that, although the specific causes of nonscientific revelations are usually beyond human knowledge, they fall wholly within the natural causal order, and are not supernatural interventions in it. According to *Ethics* 1p29, "in nature there is nothing contingent, but all things have been determined from the necessity of the divine nature to exist and produce an effect in a certain way." In his discussion of miracles in the *Theological-Political Treatise*, Spinoza points out what this implies for revelation: namely, "that nothing happens in nature that does not follow from her laws, that her laws extend to all things that are conceived by the Divine intellect itself, and finally, that nature maintains a fixed and immutable order," and hence that "the term 'miracle' cannot be understood except in relation to men's opinions, and means nothing but a work (*opus*) whose natural cause we cannot explain by the example of some other [to which we are] accustomed, or at least which cannot be so explained by the one who writes or relates the miracle" (TTP vi.13). Far from helping us to understand God's true nature, miracles distract us from it; for "those who run back to the will of God when they are ignorant of something are just silly; it is a ridiculous way of professing ignorance" (TTP vi.23).

The second philosophical principle on which Spinoza's revealed theology rests has to do with cognition. According to *Ethics* 2pp32–43, to cognize is to have an idea. Cognition is imaginative (of the first kind) if it consists partly of inadequate ideas; it is properly intellectual (of the second or third kinds) if it consists wholly of adequate ones. Adequate ideas are either "of things that are common to all, and are equally in the part and in the whole" (E 2p38), or of what is common and proper both to the human body and to an external thing customarily affecting it, and is in the whole of each and in every part (E 2p39). Cognition by adequate ideas is either (i) discursive—by "reason (*ratio*) or cognition of the second kind"—in which an effect is cognized by deriving its idea from the idea of its cause, or (ii) intuitive—"*scientia intuitiva* or cognition of the third kind"—in which the essence of a thing is cognized by forming an idea that presents it as immanently caused by God, the absolutely infinite substance (E 2p40s2). Spinoza also believes that, in *Ethics* parts 3 and 4, he has shown how, by analyzing the affects of the human mind functionally, to develop a theory of them that is intuitive in this sense.[30]

As he himself observes (TTP i.2), natural intellectual cognition of either kind satisfies his formal definition of revelation or prophecy, that is, "certain cognition of some thing, revealed by God to man"; for "the things we cognize by the natural light depend solely on the cognition of God and his eternal decrees" (TTP i.2). But, as he also observes, most people do not speak strictly. Partly because they spurn their natural gifts, and partly because they thirst for things that are rare and foreign to their nature, they call no cognition revelation or prophecy unless it "extends beyond the limits of [natural cognition] and...the laws of human nature, considered in themselves, cannot be its cause" (TTP i.3).

After examining, in the light of his naturalism and his theory of cognition, the parts of the Jewish Scriptures that he considers Ezra to have edited, Spinoza concludes that

> all those things God revealed to the prophets were revealed to them either in words, or in visible forms (*figurae*), or in both words and visible forms. The words and visible forms were either true, and outside the imagination of the prophet who heard or saw them, or else imaginary, [occurring] because evidently the imagination of the prophet was so disposed, even while he was awake, that he clearly seemed to himself to hear words or to see something. (TTP i.9)

He also infers, from the report in *Numbers* 12:6–7, that God made the following declaration to Aaron and Miriam in Moses' presence and by an actual voice: "If there be a prophet among you [i.e., the Jews], I the Lord will make myself known unto him in a vision, and will speak unto him in a dream. My servant Moses is not so, who is faithful in all mine house. With him will I speak mouth to mouth" (TTP i.21). And finally, he endorses the Jewish belief that Moses was unique among the Jewish prophets: all the others received their revelations through imaginary words and visible forms which only they cognized, but Moses received his through real sounds, which bystanders could hear (TTP i.10–13,19–22).

Here, if anywhere, a doubt intrudes whether Spinoza believed what he wrote; although if he did not, he betrays it neither by exaggeration nor by any other turn of style. If Moses received his revelations from God by a real voice, that voice would have been a miracle, according to his own definition: "a work [of God] whose natural cause we cannot explain by the example of another customary thing, or at least which cannot be so explained by the one who writes or relates the miracle" (TTP vi.13). This conception of a miracle implies, of any reported miracle, either that it really occurred and has a natural cause, or that it lacks a natural cause and did not really occur. If Spinoza had believed that the former is true of the scriptural reports of the real voice through which God revealed to Moses what he did, would not he have speculated about what the natural cause of that voice was?

His treatment of the miracle which the Roman Holy Office adduced as evidence against Galileo's Copernicanism suggests that he would have. That miracle is reported in *Joshua* 10:12–14:

> Then spake Joshua to the Lord in the day when the Lord delivered up the Amorites before the children of Israel, and he said in the sight of Israel, Sun, stand thou still upon Gibeon; and thou, Moon, in the valley of Ajalon. And the sun stood still, and the moon stayed, until the people had avenged themselves upon their enemies. Is not this written in the book of Jasher? So the sun stood still in the midst of heaven, and hasted not to go down about a whole day. And there was no day like that before it or after it, that the Lord hearkened unto the voice of a man.

Spinoza acknowledges that, when Joshua said, "Sun, stand thou still," he believed that God would arrest the sun's rotation about the earth long enough for his victory to be decisive, and later, that God had so arrested it; and that Joshua's belief was so far false, because, according to the new physics, the earth is a planet rotating about the sun, and the appearance of sunrise and sunset is not produced by the sun's motion (TTP ii.26). But he denies it to follow either that there was no miracle, or that, since Joshua's cognition of it was false, and hence not certain, it was not prophetic.

> Are we [he asked] bound to believe that Joshua, a soldier, was skilled in astronomy? and that the miracle could not be revealed to him, or that the light of the sun could not remain longer than usual above the horizon unless Joshua understood the cause of this? . . . I prefer to say openly that Joshua did not know the cause of the greater duration of that light. . . . [He] did not allow for the fact that a refraction greater than usual could arise from the great amount of ice which was then in that part of the air (see *Joshua* 10:11), or from something else like that, which we do not inquire into now. (TTP ii.27)

However absurd his scientific speculation appears today, when much more is known about refraction, it was not excluded by the state of physics when he wrote.

Would not Spinoza have offered a similar speculation about the natural causes of the voice by which Moses received his revelations if he had believed it to be real? A parallel should be considered. Just as the reality of Moses' voices is crucial to orthodox Judaism, so that of Jesus' bodily resurrection is crucial to orthodox Christianity. How does Spinoza treat the reports of resurrections of the dead in *II Kings* 4:31–37 (the Shunammite's son), and in all four gospels (Jesus)?

In the former case, by offering a natural explanation of it, he has no difficulty in accepting that the revival of the Shunammite's son really occurred (TTP vi.47). In the latter, by his striking silence, when expounding the true nature of Jesus' teaching, about his reported resurrection, he plainly implies that Jesus' body did not return to life—an implication which he expressly confirms in a letter to Oldenburg (Ep 75). Presumably part of the reason why he accepts the former and not the latter is that he does not think the restoration to life of the Shunammite's son to be a genuine resurrection: he was merely revived by the warmth of the prophet's body, and so was only apparently dead. By contrast, on the evidence of the gospels, he accepts that Jesus really died on the cross, but maintained to Oldenburg that the reported appearances of his resurrected body, contrary to the Apostles' sincere belief, were imaginary—"not unlike the appearance by which God appeared to Abraham, when he saw three men whom he invited to dine with him" (Ep 75). Oldenburg expostulated that "in the gospels, Christ's resurrection seems to be reported (*tradi*) equally literally with [his passion and death]" (Ep 79), presumably having in mind the story of doubting Thomas (*John* 20:24–28); but unfortunately no answer to his letter, dated only a year before Spinoza's death, has been preserved.

Spinoza asserts, as his general conclusion about scriptural reports of miracles, that

> . . . everything that is truly narrated in Scripture to have happened necessarily happened, as all things do, according to the laws of nature. And *if anything*

can be found which can be conclusively demonstrated to be contrary to the laws of nature, or not to have been able to follow from them, it should simply be believed that it has been added to the Sacred Texts by sacrilegious men. (TTP vi.51; emphasis added)

This, however, is far from Hume's doctrine in his essay "Of Miracles" that all reports of phenomena are suspect that are not of kinds customarily observed. By defining a miracle as "a work whose natural cause we cannot explain by the example of another customary thing" (TTP vi.13), Spinoza implies both that phenomena that are not of kinds customarily observed really do occur, and that they are naturally caused. He makes that implication explicit by declaring that, "if we find in the Sacred Texts certain things whose causes we do not know how to give an account of, and which seem to have happened beyond, indeed contrary to, the order of nature, that ought not to cause us to hesitate to believe unreservedly that what has really and truly happened has happened naturally" (TTP vi.45). It is, also, confirmed by his examples. Daylight is not customarily prolonged, even when there is a great amount of ice in the air, as reported in *Joshua* 10; nor are those whose observable vital functions have ceased after suffering severe pains in the head customarily restored to life after somebody has lain on their apparently dead bodies, as reported in *II Kings* 4. A consistent Humean would be obliged to reject both reports as fabrications. A consistent Spinozist, however, is obliged only to reject philologically authenticated reports (as Spinoza took these to be) if they are excluded by Cartesian physics; and Cartesian physics, as Newton was later to complain, is licentious in the speculative hypotheses it sanctions.[31] With respect to these reports, if it does not exclude those Spinoza accepted, I do not see how it excludes those he did not.

That Moses' voices and Jesus' resurrection were real are each believed, by those who believe them, on the ground of scriptural reports which Spinoza accepts as based on reliably transmitted oral or written records of original observations. If either in the *Theological-Political Treatise* or in his correspondence Spinoza gives a defensible reason for accepting the former but not the latter I have not found it. The evidence for the latter, while far from conclusive, is stronger. Although some Jewish commentators have accused Spinoza of tendentiously preferring to attack Judaism rather than Christianity,[32] in the *Theological-Political Treatise* he chose to accept the miracle crucial to orthodox Judaism while conspicuously refraining from accepting the one crucial to orthodox Christianity. Apart from this, his theoretical treatment of both is even-handed, although some of his remarks about Judaism are not.[33]

He endorses as authentic the bulk of the revelations reported in the Jewish Scriptures from *Genesis* to *II Kings*. He then argues that, when studied according to correct philological and philosophical principles, those Scriptures show that the Jewish prophets, even Moses, received their revelations wholly through cognition of the first kind, namely imagination: Moses receiving it through a real voice, and the rest through purely imaginary words and visible forms. That the medium of revelation is imagination supplies a principle for interpreting the scriptural record. The case of Moses shows that the greatest of the prophets was not the one who knew the most. As a man of his time, he was ignorant of much that became commonplace to rabbinical students: for example, "he taught that ... [Yahweh] chose, for himself alone, the Hebrew nation and a certain region of the world (see *Deuteronomy* 4:19, 32:8–9), but that he left other nations and regions to the care of the other gods substituted by him" (TTP ii.38). The same holds for the lesser Jewish prophets. What was revealed to them was "accommodated" to the speculative beliefs about God and his relation to the world they already had, and so did not derive from revelation (TTP ii.41). Since many have been deluded that they were receiving revelations but were not, how does God make a prophet certain that a cognition vouchsafed him is a revelation? Spinoza's answer is that every prophet who receives a new revelation both "has a heart inclined only to the right and the good," and imagines what is revealed "very vividly" and with "signs" accommodated to his imagination—they differ from prophet to prophet—that render him totally certain of it (TTP ii.10–12). This answer unfortunately fails to tell those who are deluded into thinking that they are prophets how to find that out.

Cognition is either speculative (of what is the case) or practical (of what to do). Hence, if no revealed cognition is theoretical, it must all be practical. Practical cognition, in turn, is either general or particular. The general practical cognition revealed to Moses is the Jewish Law which he promulgated only to the Jewish people, and which therefore only they were bound to observe. It includes, besides general rules of individual conduct (summed up in the Decalogue), ceremonial rules for divine worship, among them rules for instituting a hereditary priesthood and offering various forms of sacrifice, and judicial rules for adjudicating disputes, trying charges of criminality, and punishing those found guilty. Later prophets added other provisions, as when the prophet Samuel anointed first Saul and later David as king. Particular revelations were accorded to political leaders (judges and then kings) as well as to private individuals (those usually referred to as "prophets") about what should be done, by given individuals (not necessarily the prophet) or by the state, in individual situations.

Spinoza expressed the greatest admiration for "how far this [Moses'] way of constituting the state (*imperium*)"—that is, the way it was constituted before the kings—"could moderate people's hearts (*animos*) and contain both the rulers and the ruled so that the latter did not become rebels and the former did not become Tyrants" (TTP xvii.62).[34] He conceded only one defect in it: that the sacred ministry was reserved to the tribe of Levi, although, before the brief apostasy in which everybody except the Levites worshiped the golden calf, it was to have consisted of the firstborn in each family (TTP xvii.96–97). The new arrangement caused dissension between people and sacred ministry which repeatedly tempted the political leaders to introduce forbidden forms of worship, which in turn caused the prophets to denounce them. While suggesting that the character of the people made it inevitable that their sacred ministry would either apostatize or cause dissension, Spinoza somberly described the situation in prophetic terms: "At that time, the security [of the Jewish people] was not the concern of God, but vengeance" (TTP xvii.97).[35] Had it not been for this causally intelligible defect, "in the state (*rempublicam*) of the Hebrews ... the government (*imperium*) would have been everlasting" (TTP xvii.112). Even as it was, it repeatedly overcame great dangers, but sometimes only because of "God's external aid" through individual prophets (TTP iii.17).

Spinoza offers his conclusion that the nearly flawless constitution of the Hebrew state was the work of prophets and not of political theorists as a matter of historical fact, which, like facts of any kind, theorists ignore at their peril. He recognized that the kind of cognition most needed for competence in practical affairs is the first—imagination; it is not the second and third—reason and *scientia intuitiva*—although the latter are needed for explaining that competence ex post facto. Here it must not be forgotten that Spinoza uses the words "imagination" and "reason" in connection with prophecy in senses he carefully defines in the second scholium of *Ethics* 2p40. Executive power accomplishes its particular purposes only by correctly perceiving the individual situations in which it is exercised. Such situations are "sized up" imaginatively, and possession of correct theories does not ensure that they will be sized up well. Spinoza saw clearly that those whose powers of imaginative perception are extraordinary and whose rational attainments moderate often do better in constitution-making and legislation, in establishing creeds and forms of worship, and even in formulating moral codes, than those whose rational attainments are extraordinary and whose powers of imaginative perception moderate. And when somebody of strong imaginative power founds an enduring constitution, although the power by which he does it is natural, he and his followers, believing that nobody could have done it without supernatural help, may well ascribe his doing it to such help.

Because Spinoza finds Christian teaching to be directed to the whole world and Jewish only to the Jewish people, and explains this partly by the mode in which Jesus received the revelation he did, some commentators have imputed to him a prejudice against Judaism. But he is usually evenhanded. Just as he dismissed the speculative doctrines of orthodox Judaism as not part of what was revealed to the Jewish prophets, so he dismisses those of orthodox Christianity, which he professes not to grasp (*capere*) (TTP i.24), as not part of what was revealed to Jesus or to the Apostles. The revelation to Jesus, he wrote, "as the apostles preached it, doubtless by relating the simple story of Christ, does not fall under reason, yet everyone can easily appreciate by the natural light that, like the whole of Christ's teaching, it consists chiefly of moral lessons" (TTP xi.15). And he finds it to differ from the Jewish revelation only in this: "before the coming of Christ the Prophets were accustomed to preach religion as the law of their own Fatherland (*Patriae*) and by the force of the covenant entered into in the time of Moses; but after the coming of Christ the Apostles preached *the same religion* to everyone as a universal law, solely by the force of the passion of Christ" (TTP xii.24; emphasis added). The Christianity of Jesus and the early Church was therefore a reduced rather than an augmented Judaism: for example, it lacked laws for a state, for a sacerdotal system, or for religious rites.[36] Substantially, it taught what Spinoza called "the tenets of the universal faith, or the fundamental principles of the whole of Scripture," which are seven: (1) that there is a supreme being, supremely just and merciful; (2) that the supreme being is unique; (3) that the supreme being is omnipresent; (4) that the supreme being has the supreme right and dominion (*dominium*) over all things; (5) that the supreme being is worshiped and obeyed only by justice and charity, or love of one's neighbor; (6) that only those who obey the supreme being by living in the way prescribed in (5) are saved (*salvos*); and (7) that the supreme being pardons all who repent. This was the substance of Moses' religious teaching of the Jewish people: the primary function of the Christian revelation was to teach it to all people (TTP xiv.24–28).[37]

These fundamental principles not only leave it open whether God is identical with Nature or is its supernatural creator, but they also describe God as just, merciful, and forgiving. It therefore falls short of the theology Spinoza expounds in the *Theological-Political Treatise* in failing to make plain either that God is identical with Nature (TTP vi.7–22), or that it is only because of "a defect in [the multitude's] thinking" that God "is described as a lawgiver or prince, and called just, merciful &c" (TTP iv.37). In itself, this should not trouble readers. If, as Spinoza has maintained, prophets characteristically receive their revelations through their imaginations, and interpret them according to their antecedent beliefs, Jesus, who had been taught the speculative beliefs of the early rabbinic Judaism, would have interpreted whatever was revealed to him compatibly with those beliefs.

This explanation, however, is excluded by a series of passages in Chapter i of the *Theological-Political Treatise*. First of all, Spinoza confesses that he believes nobody but Jesus to have arrived at "so great a perfection above others" that it enabled him "to perceive by the mind alone certain things that are not contained in the first foundations of our cognition, nor can be deduced from them" (TTP i.22). He then proceeds to acknowledge that, according to the reports in the Christian Scriptures, God did not reveal things to Jesus by appearing to him, or through angels: "if Moses spoke with God face to face, . . . Christ communicated with God mind to mind" (TTP i.24). To Jesus alone

> God immediately revealed—without words or visions, God's appointed conditions (*placita*), which lead men to salvation. So God revealed himself to the Apostles through Christ's mind, as formerly he had revealed himself to Moses by means of a heavenly voice. And therefore Christ's voice, like the one Moses heard, can be called the voice of God. And in this sense we can also say that God's Wisdom, that is, a Wisdom surpassing human wisdom, assumed a human nature in Christ. (TTP i.23)

Hence Jesus, and he alone, received God's revelations without the aid of imagination, that is, without the aid of words or of images.[38]

Finally, in *Theological-Political Treatise* iv.29–32, Spinoza asserts that, unlike Moses and the Jewish prophets, who "did not perceive God's decrees adequately, as eternal truths," Jesus "perceived things truly and adequately"; and that therefore "it would be as contrary to reason to maintain that God accommodated his revelations to the opinions of Christ as to maintain that God previously accommodated his revelations to the opinions of the angels [through whom he revealed them], that is [to the opinions] of a created voice and of visions"[39] (TTP iv.29–31). And he adds,

> ...from the fact that God revealed himself immediately to Christ, or to his mind, and not, as he did to the Prophets, through words and images, we can understand nothing but that Christ perceived or understood truly the things revealed; for a thing is understood when it is perceived with a pure mind, without words and images. And so Christ perceived the things revealed truly and adequately. (TTP iv.32)

As a result, Jesus was able to teach human beings how to live, not merely by pro- mulgating a law to be obeyed, but by revealing the eternal causal truths by virtue of which that law is not simply a command to be obeyed, but a dictate of reason, which only prescribes what is for their advantage (*utile*). Spinoza did not deny that, when speaking to those who did not understand the kingdom of heaven, Jesus may have taught what was revealed to him as law; but he inferred from Paul's epistles that, when speaking to those who did understand, Jesus taught it as eternal truth, and not as law. By thus writing it in their hearts, he paradoxically both confirmed and stabilized it as law, and freed them from a servile relation to it (TTP iv.33–34).

That these passages are difficult does not excuse the license with which Strauss has interpreted them. According to Strauss,

> Spinoza asserts first that no one except Jesus (whom he regularly calls Christ) has reached the superhuman excellence sufficient for receiving, without the aid of the imagination, revelations of supra-rational content; or that he alone—in contradistinction to the Old Testament prophets in particular—truly and ade- quately understood what was revealed to him.[40]

As we have seen, Spinoza did assert that nobody but Jesus arrived at so great a perfection above others ("*ad tantam perfectionem supra alios pervenisse*") that God revealed to him things he did not reveal even to Moses. But that implies, not that his perfection was "superhuman," but that it excelled that of *other* human beings like himself. Again, Spinoza did assert that Jesus perceived what was revealed to him "adequately, as eternal truths," and not "as precepts and things instituted," as Moses perceived what was revealed to him (TTP iv.29). But far from implying that the content of what was revealed to Jesus was "supra-rational," adequate perception is necessarily rational. Fi- nally, Spinoza did assert that what was revealed to the Jewish prophets was accom- modated to their opinions, and that they interpreted it in the light of their opinions. But that does not imply that there was any defect in how they understood what it was revealed to them that they should do. Since nothing speculative was revealed to them, their speculative mistakes were not revelations inadequately understood.

Strauss's misunderstanding of what Spinoza writes in these passages is of a piece with his radical misunderstanding that, in implicitly asserting in some passages that "revelation or prophecy as certain knowledge of truths which surpass the capacity of human reason is possible," and explicitly denying in others "the possibility of any supra-rational knowledge," Spinoza "contradicts himself... regarding what may be called the central subject of his book."[41] The "certain knowledge" he ascribes to the Jewish prophets is (extrinsically) true cognition of the first kind—imagination—which the prophet is unable to doubt. As cognition, it is subrational rather than superrational, and the cause of the prophet's certainty is natural. It surpasses the capacity of the higher forms of cognition (reason and *scientia intuitiva*) because, while they can supply the general dictates of reason (roughly, the moral law, and the general principles of politics), they cannot supply certain cognition of how to act to advantage in particular situations. There is no contradiction whatever in asserting that, although the provisions of the Jewish law divinely revealed to Moses through a voice included the moral dictates of reason that apply to all human beings, it was not revealed to Moses *that* it did include them. Nor is there any contradiction in asserting that, although reason and *scientia intuitiva* are higher forms of cognition than imaginative insight into particular situations, one variety of which is prophecy, there are many practical problems that can only be solved by recourse to the latter.

Yet a problem of consistency remains after the fogs of Straussian misreading have been dispersed. Spinoza depicts Jesus not as a philosopher, but as a prophet in the colloquial sense: as receiving sure cognition from God, not as philosophers do, "from the first foundations of our cognition" (TTP i.22), that is, from the principles laid down in *Ethics* part 1, but in a way that, although natural, nobody yet understands. He is a greater prophet even than Moses; but he *is* a prophet, not a philosopher. Yet if Jesus understood what he taught "truly and adequately," must his cognition of it not have been of the second or third kind, and hence philosophical? And in that case, how could he have been a prophet?

Closer scrutiny of what Spinoza wrote in the crucial passages of the first and fourth chapters of the *Theological-Political Treatise* shows that this difficulty too springs from misreading. What was revealed to Jesus? Presumably, the tenets of the universal faith, various applications of those tenets, and many of the theorems in *Ethics* part 4 about the effects of various dispositions to act, both virtuous and vicious, together with solutions, according to those theorems, of many practical problems that confronted him during his ministry. Let us assume that Jesus understood what was revealed to him "truly and adequately." What would that involve? An adequate idea is one that has all the intrinsic properties of a true idea, as distinct from the extrinsic property of agreement with its object (E 2d4); and this is to be understood in the light of the axiom that "Cognition of an effect depends on, and involves, cognition of its cause" (E 1a4). Because everything is an effect, including God or Nature, which as cause of itself is also effect of itself, adequate cognition of anything whatever is cognition of its cause. Thus adequate cognition that it is advantageous to accept and observe the tenets of the universal faith, or to observe certain rules of conduct, or to adopt a particular course of action, is cognition of such practices and actions as causing advantage. Yet although such causal cognition is attainable by anybody capable of studying the *Theological-Political Treatise* thoroughly, Spinoza did not think it can be deduced from the first foundations of our cognition, and in the *Ethics* he showed why it cannot. In advancing to the theories of the affects and of servile and free action in *Ethics* parts 3 and 4, from the fundamental metaphysics and theory of mind in *Ethics* parts 1 and 2, he makes it plain that six postulates in *Ethics* part 2 (stated after 2p13) and two in *Ethics* part 3 are indispensable, none of which is deduced from "the first foundations of our cognition" as laid down earlier. They are derived according to the theorem that "if something is common to, and peculiar to, the human Body and certain external bodies by which the human Body is usually affected, and is equally in the part and in the whole of each of them, its idea will also be adequate in the Mind" (E 2p39). The practical cognition imparted in *Ethics* parts 3 and 4 is all attainable by what Spinoza called "cognition of the second kind"—by certain "common notions," and by adequate ideas of what is common and peculiar to the human body and to certain bodies that affect it. Such practical cognition is not in itself philosophical: that is, it is not the *scientia intuitiva* attainable only when its principles as set out in *Ethics* parts 1 and 2 have been mastered. What can be adequately cognized ("perceived") by the mind alone is not the same as what can be deduced from the first foundations of our cognition. The mind alone adequately cognizes certain things from common experience which it cannot deduce from the first foundations of our cognition—even though those foundations determine when common experience yields adequate cognition and when it does not. Adequate cognition remains adequate even though the principles determining its adequacy have not even been thought of.

Jesus' adequate cognition, as Spinoza conceived it, was not accompanied by cognition of the principles determining its adequacy. His perfection exceeded that of his fellow men because he "perceive[d] by the mind alone things that are not contained in the first foundations of our cognition, and cannot be deduced from them," even though he did not perceive by the mind alone the metaphysical and epistemological principles according to which his perceptions or cognitions were adequate. Jesus' mind, Spinoza declared, "would necessarily have to be more outstanding and far more excellent than the human mind is" (TTP i.22–23); but that does not imply that his mind was raised to that level of excellency by external causes of a kind that do not operate on other human minds, or that it was superhuman by nature, much less divine. No mind, according to Spinoza, is anything but a complex idea; and to act on a mind is to cause the ideas that compose it to be other than they would have been but for that action. Hence God could externally cause Jesus to perceive something by the mind alone only if he *directly*—without imaginative mediation—caused certain ideas to be among those composing his mind that otherwise would not have been among them. It is not contrary to Spinoza's theory of mind, as far as I can tell, that natural causes might directly introduce into the ideas composing Jesus' mind either the partly inadequate ideas expressed in the tenets of the universal faith, or the adequate ideas set out in *Ethics* parts 3 and 4 of the advantage or disadvantage actions of this or that kind tend to cause; and no matter what those natural causes might be, they would be God or Nature acting.

Spinoza's position, in short, is that God introduced into Jesus' mind both the tenets of the universal faith and the dictates of reason stated in *Ethics* parts 3 and 4. Jesus' cognition of the latter was adequate, even though he had no notion either of the metaphysical propositions from which a philosopher would derive those theorems, or of their proofs. The difference between Jesus' moral and religious teaching and Spinoza's is that between the conception of God expressed in the first four tenets of the universal faith and that expressed in *Ethics* part 1 and the latter half of part 5; and that difference explains why to Spinoza Jesus is a prophet in the colloquial sense, not a philosopher. Since he lacks cognition of the principles by which his prophetic cognition can be shown to be adequate, he cannot demonstrate its adequacy, as a philosopher must, from "the first foundations of our cognition."

Spinoza's theory of divine revelation is therefore consistent both with itself and with his natural theology. Yet to most who follow his philological treatment of Scripture, his explanatory theory is much more persuasive than his religious conclusions. Given his naturalized theology, not only his explanation of the phenomena of Jewish and Christian prophecy, but his extraction of the tenets of his universal faith as the rational core of both Judaism and Christianity, are alike defensible. True, his universal faith was stillborn as a religion, and was not, as a matter of history, the essence of either Judaism or Christianity. But Spinoza's deficiencies as a religious teacher do not show that his theology was defective.

One of the attractions of Spinoza's theory of prophecy is that it explains why this is so. Even the ablest theorists have shown themselves poor at designing institutions, whether religious or political, that work at all, much less that go on working. Spinoza's universal religion, like Hobbes's state Christianity, is designed to subserve political rather than religious needs. Adopting it would certainly curb the persecuting clergy whom Spinoza detested; but it does not satisfy the religious needs that the faiths proclaimed by Moses and Jesus did. In his theory of prophecy Spinoza not only recognized that the two religious faiths embraced by most of his contemporaries were instituted not by philosophers but by prophets, but began to explain why. To complete his explanation, the histories of both faiths must be investigated more thoroughly than he investigated them. Just because he does not try to make the Jewish prophets respectable from the point of view of his naturalist philosophy, his depiction of them is nearer to the truth than his depiction of Jesus and the Apostles.

If Spinoza's naturalist theology is true, then the claims of Judaism and Christianity to revealed truth are false. However, his theory of Judaism as founded on imaginative cognition would remain plausible in itself, and extensible to Christianity. The source of their power as faiths would have to be sought in a theory explaining how certain kinds of error about ultimate questions can become foundations of shared ways of living. There is no obvious reason why the *Theological-Political Treatise* could not be revised along these Spinozist lines. And even if Spinoza's naturalist theology is not true, at least he saw, what few theologians and fewer philosophers see, that religions are sustained by prophecy, not by philosophy or theology.

3. Practical Theology

Spinoza's revealed practical theology is that of "the universal faith" which he believed to be the true core both of Judaism and Christianity. It is, like all revealed theology, practical. However, its practical directions are expressed by imagining God as the perfect model for human conduct; and, so far, its expression is false. Spinoza's definitive practical theology is the natural one found in *Ethics* parts 4 and 5. Its practical content is summed up in the "dictates of reason" for human life there expounded. It is therefore identical with his ethics as ordinarily understood, which Don Garrett studies in chapter 6 of this volume.[42] What it signifies theologically is found by examining the dictates of reason from the point of view of the relation of human beings to God.

Everything human beings do or undergo—all their actions and passions—are done or undergone according to the laws of immanent causation that constitute God's or Nature's essence. Since God's essence is perfect, it is absurd to wish that anything that happens should happen otherwise. From God's point of view, human violations of the dictates of reason are as necessary to his perfection as human observances of them. As Spinoza explained to his correspondent Willem van Blijenbergh,

> ... if *good in relation to God* implies that the just man does some good to God, and the thief some evil, I answer that neither the just man nor the thief can cause either delight or disgust (*taedium*) in God. If it is then asked whether each of those actions, so far as it is something real and caused by God, is equally perfect, I say that if we attend to the actions alone, and in the way proposed, then it can turn out that each is equally perfect. (Ep 23)

Since God, as even traditional theology had taught, is wholly active, and so without passions, "strictly speaking, [he] loves no one, and hates no one" (E 5p17c). Hence to God, considered as he is in himself, and not as he constitutes this or that individual finite mind, nothing any human being does or undergoes is good or bad, just or unjust. It is irrational even to ask whether anything whatever might be better than it is, because nothing can happen except as it does in God—the absolutely infinite substance that is the only being that can exist.

It follows that, although human beings can and should inquire what is the best way for human beings to act, and what is the best attitude for them to take to God or Nature, and to Nature's course, they should not delude themselves that what is best for them is more than that. Since the nature of everything is a *conatus* to persevere in being what it is, what is good for a thing is what promotes its perseverance in being—what is advantageous (*utile*) for it; and what is bad for it is what hinders its perseverance in being. However, a human being does not persevere in being simply because his or her vital functions, such as breathing, continue. The highest good to which any human being can aspire is to be as free as a human being can be: that is, to be able to take advantage of every opportunity to increase his or her power to act that circumstances can make possible. The greatest opportunity anybody can have is to live in a free society as one among many who are fully capable of taking advantage of its freedom; but to take advantage of that opportunity, each must develop the cooperative virtues of good faith and benevolence. Spinoza contemptuously dismissed the objection that the virtues necessary for making the most of the greatest opportunity are not unqualified advantages, because they unfit human beings for saving their lives in circumstances in which they can only be saved by servility, treachery, or cowardice (E 4p72d). If you cannot survive without servile complicity in crime, the lesser evil, that is, what is advantageous (*utile*), is to refuse and die, as Seneca did (E 4p20s); for nobody capable of saving his life by such complicity can thrive in the only circumstances in which a rational human being can: those in which one can live without violating the dictates of reason.

While he forcibly asserts that reason imposes on the rational a set of dictates very like those of traditional Judaism and Christianity, Spinoza as forcibly denies that it permits them to reprobate those who violate those dictates as both Jewish and Christian preachers have done. He writes of them:

> They seem to conceive man in nature as a government (*imperium*) within a government. For they believe that man disturbs, rather than follows, the order of nature, that he has absolute power over his actions, and that he is determined only by himself. And they attribute the cause of human impotence, not to the common power of nature, but to I know not what vice of human nature, which they therefore bewail, or laugh at, or (as usually happens) curse. And the more he knows how eloquently and bitingly to rail at the impotence of the human Mind, the more he is held to be Godly. (E 3pr)

Such denunciations are in fact more blasphemous than godly. The dictates of reason require every human being to produce as much good as he can, and to reduce evil as much as he can; but how much of either he can do depends not on him, but on how things necessarily are. To the extent he can do neither, he should neither decry the state of the world as evil, nor heap contumely on those wrong actions he cannot prevent. "He who rightly knows (*novit*) that all things follow necessarily from the necessity of the divine nature . . . will certainly find nothing worthy of Hate, Derision, or Contempt, *nor anyone whom he will pity (miserebitur)*" (E 4p50s; emphasis added). He will try to have only affects that prompt him to benevolent action, which pity, or "sadness, accompanied by the idea of an evil that has happened to somebody we imagine to be like ourselves" (E 3da18), will not. To one already committed to active benevolence, sadness at what he cannot do can only distract him from what he can, and at the same time impair his love of God. Spinoza, however, scrupulously added that "one who is moved to help others *neither* by reason *nor* by pity is rightly called inhuman" (E 4p50s; emphasis added).

The love Spinoza's God attracts from those who rightly know him is described by Spinoza as "intellectual." That love is an action, not a passion: the action of a rational finite being whose essence is a *conatus* to persevere in being, and who adequately cognizes that, since God is the substance of which he is a finite mode, his own existence would be unthinkable unless God were exactly as he is. Unlike the love of God preached by Moses and Jesus, gratitude for benefits received, whether in answer to prayer or as a reward for worship, has no part in it. Nor is it a due return for God's love to us. It is our participation in "the very Love of God by which God loves himself" (E 5p36); and nobody who so loves God can "strive that God should love him in return" (E 5p19). To love God intellectually is to be intellectually at peace (*quies*) with how things are: ourselves, and the absolutely infinite substance of which we are finite modes. The highest blessedness (*beatitudo*) is true acquiescence of spirit (*vera animi acquiescentia*) (E 5p42s).

Spinoza argues that nobody can hate God, because to the extent that we consider God as immanent cause of all that exists we are active, and so not sad—hate being the passive affect of sadness, accompanied by the idea of an external cause (E 5p18). His premise, however, seems to me false. Considering God as the immanent cause of all that exists is an action so far as one strives to exist oneself, for it contributes to directing that active striving rationally; but it is not an action if external causes so overwhelm one's *conatus* to persevere in existence that one wishes never to have existed at all. Spinoza might, indeed, save his proof if he could show that extreme pain could not overwhelm one's *conatus* to persevere in existence without obliterating our power to consider God as immanent cause of all that exists. But he did not show it, and I do not believe he could have. Of course, even if he could not, it would not follow that it can be rational to hate God: that some finite mode in the absolutely infinite being wishes it had never been does not show that it is irrational for the infinite being itself to will to exist.

Notoriously, Spinoza has embarrassed many of his admirers by claiming to demonstrate that "the human Mind cannot be absolutely destroyed with the Body, but something of it remains which is eternal" (E 5p23). Most recent commentators have rejected his proof as either fallacious or sheerly unintelligible. It is, however, a natural development of his conception of the human mind as a subset of the ideas that are modes of the eternal mode he refers to as the infinite idea of God, when taken together with his doctrine that a human individual's adequate idea of itself, if that individual has one, is a functional idea of its existence as caused at a certain stage in the course of nature. Given that all adequate ideas are eternal elements in the infinite idea of God, it appears to follow that if an adequate idea of itself is part of an individual human mind, that part of it not only will remain eternally after the individual body that is the primary object of that mind has been destroyed, but has eternally pre-existed the coming into existence of that body.[43]

Theologically, the question raised by Spinoza's doctrine that part of the human mind remains after the dissolution of the body that is its primary object, is what bearing it has on how human beings should live. I think the answer is that the eternal continuance of part of one's own mind in the mind of God cannot but be something a mind that wills to persevere in existence must will. However, it does not have the place in the lives of Spinozists that the hope of resurrection has in the lives of many

Jews and Christians. What exists eternally is part of what exists during life, and is neither better nor worse than it is then. If we (that is, God, so far as he constitutes our minds) adequately cognize our lives as worth living, then we (that is, he, so far as he is us) shall so cognize them forever. Our deaths will not be followed by divine judgment, and our continuation after death will be neither glorification in heaven nor damnation in hell. But neither will our deaths be wholly the end of us.

Notes

From *The Cambridge Companion to Spinoza*, edited by Don Garrett. ©Cambridge University Press 1996. Reprinted with the permission of Cambridge University Press.

1. The following abbreviations are used in this paper: (A) Titles of Spinoza's Writings: E: *Ethics, Demonstrated in Geometric Order;* Ep: *Letters;* ST: *Short Treatise on God, Man, and His Well-Being;* TTP: *Theological-Political Treatise;* (B) Subdivisions of E: a: Axiom; ap: Appendix; c: Corollary; d: (not following a reference to a proposition) Definition; d: (following a reference to a proposition) Demonstration; da: Definitions of the Affects; le: Lemma; p: Proposition; pr: Preface; s: Scholium. References to "the present volume" refer to *The Cambridge Companion to Spinoza*, ed. Don Garrett (Cambridge: Cambridge University Press, 1996). Ed.

2. Yirmiyahu Yovel, *Spinoza and Other Heretics*, vol. 1, *The Marrano of Reason* (Princeton: Princeton University Press, 1989), is the best comprehensive treatment of Spinoza as a dissident Marrano. It draws on a large and growing body of studies of the Amsterdam Jewish community and his relations with it. His relations with Protestant groups were authoritatively examined by K. O. Meinsma in 1896, in a book now most accessible in Henri Méchoulan and Pierre-Francois Moreau's French edition of it, with appendices, titled *Spinoza et son cercle* (Paris: J. Vrin, 1983), and they continue to be closely investigated by many scholars. The influence of Franciscus van den Enden, an ex-Jesuit with whom Spinoza studied as a young man, remained largely unexplored until the recent investigations of Wim Klever, who has announced his discovery of a number of van den Enden's writings, which he plans to present in a forthcoming book, *Van den Enden, Biographical Documents and Works*.

3. Spinoza's Latin name for God, "*Deus*," is masculine; and his name for an infinite being he held to be identical with God, "*Natura*," is feminine. He sometimes refers to this individual as "*Deus sive Natura*"—"God or Nature." In the genders of the pronouns I use in place of these names, I follow Spinoza for the first two: "he" for "God" and "she" for "Nature." For "God or Nature" I use "it."

4. Leo Strauss, *Persecution and the Art of Writing* (Chicago: University of Chicago Press, 1988), chap. 5. (This book was originally published in 1952.)

5. Only a thorough examination could convince. Errol E. Harris in *Is There an Esoteric Doctrine in the "Tractatus Theologico-Politicus"?* (Leiden: Vanwege het Spinozahuis, E. J. Brill, 1978) has done much of what is needed by showing that what Strauss considers the eight chief signs by which Spinoza indicates the esoteric sense of the *Theological-Political Treatise* are nothing of the sort.

6. Strauss, *Persecution and the Art of Writing*, p. 171.

7. The "subjective" interpretation of what Spinoza meant by "*attributum*" is sometimes supported by translating "*tanquam*" in Spinoza's definition of an attribute, namely, "*id, quod*

intellectus de substantia percipit, tanquam ejusdem essentiam constituens" (E 1d4), as "as if" rather than as "as." The decisive examination of the question of the objectivity of Spinoza's attributes is Martial Gueroult, *Spinoza: I Dieu* (Paris: Aubier-Montaigne, 1968), Appendix 3, "*La controverse sur l'attribut*," pp. 428–61.

8. Mignini (in Filippo Mignini, ed. and trans., Spinoza, *Korte verhandeling van God, de mensch en deszelvs welstand/Breve trattato su Dio, l'uomo e il suo bene* (L'Aquila: L. U. Japadre Editore, 1986) has persuasively argued that Spinoza wrote the first half of this work in Latin in the middle of 1660, and amplified it as objections were made or occurred to him. According to Mignini, he permitted a friend to translate it, with additional notes, into Dutch, after which he revised the translation and added to the text. By early 1662, having decided to restate his conclusions *more geometrico* (in the geometrical method), he began to rework it into what became the *Ethics*. Edwin Curley judiciously surveys the theories that have been offered of the composition of the *Short Treatise* in his *The Collected Works of Spinoza* (Princeton: Princeton University Press, 1985), I:50–53.

9. The author of this outline has usually been thought to be the Amsterdam philosopher Willem Deurhoff. Some, however, attribute it to Monnikhoff. Cf. G. C. Gebhardt, ed., *Spinoza Opera* (Heidelberg: Carl Winter, 1925), I:436, and Curley, *The Collected Works of Spinoza*, I:53, n. 1.

10. Moses Maimonides, *The Guide of the Perplexed*, trans. Shlomo Pines (Chicago: University of Chicago Press, 1963), I, 57–58 (Pines, pp. 132–37); Aquinas, *Summa theologiae* I, 12, 11–12.

11. Maimonides, *The Guide of the Perplexed*, II, 13–31 (Pines, pp. 280–359); III, 25–26, 51 (Pines, pp. 502–10, 618–28).

12. Aquinas, *Summa theologiae* I, 13, 1–3.

13. Maimonides, *The Guide of the Perplexed*, II, Introduction, 1, 9b–10b (Pines, pp. 235–41, 249–52); Aquinas, *Summa theologiae* I, 13, 4 ad 3.

14. Aristotle, *Categories*, 1ᵃ16–2ᵇ7; cf. *Metaphysics* VII, 1028ᵃ8–1028ᵇ8.

15. René Descartes, *Principia Philosophiae* I, 27 (C. Adam and P. Tannery, eds., *Oeuvres de Descartes* [Paris: J. Vrin, 1964–75], VIIIA:15).

16. Ibid., II, 21 (*Oeuvres*, VIIIA:52); emphasis added.

17. Cf. Maimonides, *The Guide of the Perplexed*, II, 1, esp. 9b–10b (Pines, pp. 249–52); cf. Aquinas, *Summa theologiae* I, 3, 1 (*secundo*).

18. Part of this correspondence was conducted through an intermediary, G. H. Schuller. The relevant passages in Spinoza's letters are Letter 64, where he referred Tschirnhaus to E 1p25c,s and to E 2p13le7s, and Letter 83. My disagreements both with Abraham Wolf's translation of Gebhart, *Spinoza Opera*, IV:334/24–25 of Letter 83, and with his commentary on the passage cited (A. Wolf, trans. and ed., *The Correspondence of Spinoza* (London: Frank Cass, 1966), pp. 61–62, 365) are explained in Alan Donagan, *Spinoza* (London: Harvester/Wheatsheaf, 1988, and Chicago: University of Chicago Press, 1989), pp. 100, 120.

19. Maimonides, *The Guide of the Perplexed*, I, 35, 42a (Pines, p. 80).

20. Here as elsewhere, my translation closely follows E. M. Curley's draft of a translation that will appear in the second volume of his *The Collected Works of Spinoza* (forthcoming from the Princeton University Press). I thank Professor Curley for his kindness in providing me with a copy of his draft, and for permitting me to use it. I have also consulted Samuel Shirley's excellent translation in Baruch Spinoza, *Tractatus Theologico-Politicus* (Leiden: E. J. Brill, 1989). While I do not record minor divergences from

Curley's renderings (mostly intended to be more literal if less elegant), readers should take note that I always render Spinoza's *"cognoscere"* and *"cognitio"* as "cognize" and "cognition," and not as "know" and "knowledge." My chief reason is that Spinoza held that human beings often cognize falsely.

21. That "necessarily" in Spinoza's definition means "by (immanently) causal necessity" and not "by logical necessity" is plain from the structure of *Ethics* part 1. See Donagan, *Spinoza*, pp. 60–64, 73–75.

22. He does deny it in a technical sense. See Donagan, *Spinoza*, pp. 109–13.

23. This has been denied by some, on the ground of some passages in which Spinoza uses the word *"tempus"* in a technical sense. See Jonathan Bennett, *A Study of Spinoza's "Ethics"* (Cambridge: Cambridge University Press, 1984), pp. 202–3.

24. Maimonides, *The Guide of the Perplexed* I, 60, 76b (Pines, p. 145).

25. I have falsely asserted that Spinoza's contemporaries accused him "not of disbelieving what he professed to believe, but of concealing the heretical implications of what he professed" (*Spinoza*, p. 15). In "Van Velthuysen, Batelier and Bredenburg on Spinoza's Interpretation of the Scriptures," a paper presented in April 1991 to a conference at Cortona organized by the Scuola Normale Superiore di Pisa, Dr. Wiep van Bunge has shown that van Velthuysen did what I denied any of Spinoza's contemporaries did. The distinction I drew is philosophically suspect as well as historically false, because the distinction between difference in meaning and difference of belief is (as Quine has shown) indeterminate.

26. For the development of philology in the Netherlands see U. von Wilamowitz-Moellendorff, *History of Classical Scholarship*, trans. Alan Harris (Baltimore: Johns Hopkins University Press, 1982), pp. 50–53, 65–76.

27. Richard H. Popkin, "Spinoza and Bible Scholarship," in *The Cambridge Companion to Spinoza*, pp. 383–407. Ed.

28. Born *c.* 1090 in Tudela, Spain; died 1164. Cited by Spinoza as "Aben Ezra."

29. "No other text [than that of the New Testament] posed the problem of the Textus Receptus . . . in so stark a form; and no other text was necessary to salvation. The character of the Vulgate established by Erasmus, Beza, and Stephanus was so obviously haphazard that thoughtful critics, in countries where it was allowable to do so, had the strongest motives for questioning its authenticity" (E. J. Kenney, *The Classical Text* [Berkeley: University of California Press, 1974], p. 99). Even though, as Kenney adds in a footnote on the same page, "there are almost no doctrinal issues of any significance which turn on the criticism of the text, as was remarked by Bentley"—but thirty years after Spinoza's death.

30. Spinoza's theory of the three kinds of cognition is discussed in Margaret Wilson, "Spinoza's Theory of Knowledge," *The Cambridge Companion to Spinoza*, pp. 89–141. My own treatment, which is largely derived from Alexandre Matheron, *Individu et communauté chez Spinoza* (Paris: Editions de Minuit, 1969) and "Spinoza and Euclidean Arithmetic: The Example of the Fourth Proportional," in Marjorie Grene and Deborah Nails, eds., *Spinoza and the Sciences*, Boston Studies in the Philosophy of Science (Dordrecht: Reidel, 1986), pp. 125–50, may be found in Donagan, *Spinoza*, pp. 135–40.

31. For a scientific example of Spinoza's licentiousness in hypothesis, see his controversy with Boyle (with Oldenburg as intermediary) about the reconstitution of nitre (Ep 6,11,13). For why Newton found it necessary to formulate a principle limiting what hypotheses scientists should consider, see A. Rupert Hall and Marie Boas Hall, "Philosophy

and Natural Philosophy: Boyle and Spinoza" in *Mélanges Alexandre Koyré II: L'aventure de l'esprit* (Paris: Hermann, 1964), pp. 241–56.

32. E.g., Hermann Cohen in the nineteenth century, and (less vehemently) Leo Strauss in this. See Leo Strauss, *Spinoza's Critique of Religion*, trans. E. M. Sinclair (New York: Schocken Books, 1965), pp. 19–20; and *Persecution and the Art of Writing*, pp. 190–91.

33. I say what I think necessary about his offensive incidental remarks about Judaism in Donagan, *Spinoza*, pp. 26–27.

34. Here I have included a translation of this passage by Edwin Curley that is superior to the one used by Donagan and published in *The Cambridge Companion to Spinoza*. This translation was kindly supplied to me by Don Garrett. Ed.

35. As he acknowledged, he took his words from Tacitus: "*[Nec] enim umquam atrocioribus populi Romani cladibus magisve iustis indiciis adprobatum est non esse curae deis securitatem nostram, sed ultionem*" (*Historiae*, I, 3).

36. "As for the ceremonies of the Christians, viz. Baptism, the Lord's Supper, feasts, liturgies (*orationes externas*), and whatever others there may be in addition which are and always have been common to all Christianity, if Christ or the Apostles ever instituted these (which so far I do not find to be sufficiently established), they were instituted only as external signs of the universal Church, but not as things which contribute to blessedness or have any Holiness in them" (TTP v.32). As philology, this is fantastic with respect to the Eucharist (the Lord's Supper).

37. The most illuminating treatment of Spinoza's project for a universal faith, and of its relation to Christianity, is Alexandre Matheron, *Le Christ et le salut des ignorants chez Spinoza* (Paris: Aubier-Montaigne, 1971).

38. "Except for Christ, nobody received revelations from God unless by the help of imagination, that is, by the help of words or of images" (TTP i.25).

39. Spinoza's point seems to be that just as God, in causing a voice or an image that conveys a revelation, does not accommodate the revelation to the (nonexistent) opinions of that voice, so, in causing an idea in Jesus' mind, he does not accommodate himself to the other ideas in that mind. Angels, it must be remembered, are not real, but figments of the imaginations of the prophets who ascribe to them the voices they hear or the visual appearances they see.

40. Strauss, *Persecution and the Art of Writing*, p. 171.

41. Ibid., p. 169. The passages Strauss cites for the former of the two allegedly contradictory propositions are: TTP i.1–4,6–7,22–23,25 and xv.22,26–27,44 (with vi.65, vii.8–10,78, xi.14–15, xii.21–22, xiii.6–8,20, xvi.53–56,61,64 for comparison); and those cited for the latter are TTP v.49, xiii.17, xiv.38, and xv.21,23,42 (with iv.20 and vii.72 for comparison).

42. Spinoza's Ethical Theory, in *The Cambridge Companion to Spinoza*, pp. 267–314. Ed.

43. I have examined elsewhere how Spinoza derives *Ethics* 5p23, and defended its validity, given his axioms, in Donagan, *Spinoza*, pp. 191–200. Strictly, it is not part of his theology.

FOUR

St. Thomas Aquinas on the
Analysis of Human Action

*A*t least two distinct purposes may be discerned in Aquinas's various writings on
human action. One is to complete and correct Aristotle's treatment of it in
the *Nichomachean Ethics* and elsewhere, to which he of course pays close and
respectful attention. A second springs from his primary commitment to theology.
Reflecting on what is said in the Scriptures and the writings of the Fathers about
such topics as the fall of Adam, sin, conversion, and the operation of grace, theologians
produced a body of doctrine about various aspects of human acts. It is unsystematic,
but it has been tested in the pastoral and missionary work of the Church, especially
in the discipline of confession and penance; and to Aquinas's mind, it settles certain
questions authoritatively: as when it declares that voluntary human acts are commanded by their agents freely, and not by necessity. In addition it introduces certain
concepts into the theory of action, for example, those of enjoyment and consent, in
ways that have virtually no counterpart in the philosophical tradition. Aquinas undertakes to incorporate these contributions of theology, where sound, into a revised
Aristotelian theory.

Aristotelian theories of action are causal, and causal in a distinctive way. To do
something, to perform an act, is to cause something. And causing something is always
to be investigated in terms of a pair of fundamental concepts, *dynamis* and *energeia*,
which appear in Aquinas's Latin as *potentia* (potency) and *actus* (act). The power or
capacity of an object to cause something—whether a change of state, or a persistence

in a state—largely determines what that object is. Brute animals are distinguished by their possession of powers of sensation and bodily movement: an animal's behavior, as Aristotle understood it, is a matter of its activation of the tendencies to bodily motion characteristic of its species, as a result of its exercise of its characteristic powers of sensation. Human beings are differentiated from brute animals by their further possession of intellectual powers, making it possible for them to cause changes or persistences in the state of things in rationally pursuing ends they have rationally set themselves. So to cause a change or persistence is to perform a human act. And an Aristotelian theory of human acts is a theory of what exercises of what distinctively human powers are involved in performing such acts.

Unless two distinctions that pervade Aquinas's work on action are kept in mind, not only his, but any Aristotelian theory is apt to be unintelligible. The first, drawn in *Summa theologiae* I–II, 1, 1, is that between those doings of human beings that are human properly speaking and those that are not. A human act, properly speaking, is an act over which the human agent is master (*dominus*), that is, an act in which he exercises the distinctively human capacities of reason and will (*facultas voluntatis et rationis*) (I–II, 1, 1c.). Accordingly, acts in which those capacities are not exercised, like absent-minded twitches of hand or foot, or strokings of the beard, although acts of a human being (*actus hominis*) are not human acts (*actus humani*) (I–II, 1, 1 *ad* 3). The second is Aquinas's equally sharp distinction between the complete human acts in which the human capacities of will and intellect are exercised, and the exercises of those powers which go to make up complete human acts. A complete human act is a unity in which, by virtue of certain intellectual acts, some possible act is commanded, and by virtue of certain acts of will, the commanded act (*actus imperatus*) is performed.[1] Neither an intellectual act, such as thinking that it would be good to have a higher salary, nor an act of will, such as willing to do what needs to be done to get more money, are by themselves considered complete human acts by Aquinas. Yet both may be components in a given person's complete act of working overtime.

It is a sheer mistake to suppose that Aristotelian theories in which a complete human act is analyzed, inter alia, into a number of component exercises of the powers of will and intellect can be undermined, as Gilbert Ryle undermined various introspectionist psychological theories, by demanding the introspectionist credentials of the various postulated acts of those powers, and then, for good measure, questioning the relevance for a theory of action of whatever the results of an introspectionist inquiry may be.[2] Aristotle's and Aquinas's investigations of human action are strictly conceptual and analytic.[3] They begin with the distinction between human action and merely animal behavior that was presupposed in the dealings between man and man in the culture of either, and they seek to establish what exercises of what human powers must be involved in human action if that distinction can validly be drawn. The question "What evidence have we that that distinction is a valid one?" must indeed be investigated; but its investigation forms no part of the treatise on the nature of human acts (*de conditione humanorum actuum*), Aquinas's final and most elaborate treatment of human action, which occupies *Summa theologiae*, I–II, 6–17.

According to Aristotle, an act is voluntary (*hekousion*) if its moving principle is in the agent himself, he being aware of the circumstances of his act and of the objects with which it is concerned (*Eth. Nic.* 1110^{b}32–33; 1111^{a}22–23). Hence brute animals, acting from bodily appetites such as hunger, act voluntarily (1111^{b}8). Human action is distinguished from that of brutes as exemplifying not only voluntariness, but also choice (*prohairesis*). Choice involves not only will (*boulesis*) for an end, but also deliberation (*bouleusis*) about how to attain it (1139^{a}31–32). Both call for intellect; for deliberation is an intellectual operation, and will presupposes an intellectual grasp of what is willed. However, since he held that human beings by nature will to live a good life, and that their characters reveal what they take a good life to be, Aristotle was reluctant to acknowledge that a man acting out of character or on impulse genuinely chooses at all, because the deliberation that gives rise to such actions is not about an ethically good end (1139^{a}31–34). Yet he did concede that "the incontinent man and the bad man, if he is clever, will reach as a result of his calculation what he sets before himself (*protithetai*)" (1142^{b}18). Drawing attention to this passage, Professor Anscombe justly observed that "Aristotle ought ... to have seen that he was here employing a key concept in the theory of action, but he did not do so."[4]

Aquinas appreciated Anscombe's point, although it did not accord with the conventions in which he wrote for him to state it. And so, while he retained the structure of Aristotle's analysis of chosen acts (his key elements, will (*voluntas*), deliberation (*consilium*), and choice (*electio*) correspond to Aristotle's *boulesis*, *bouleusis*, and *prohairesis*), he saw that, if human acts as such involve choice, then choice cannot be subject to the Aristotelian restrictions, according to which acts that are out of character cannot be chosen. Aristotle's restricted concept of choice follows from his restricted concept of will. Aquinas therefore proposed a new and less restricted concept of willing an end, which in turn made it possible for him to introduce, as the fundamental explanatory concept in the theory of action, the derivative concept of intention.

In Aquinas's theory, the class of voluntary human acts is identical with the class of human acts involving choice. The members of both classes are exercises of the same power, the power of will (*voluntas, potentia voluntatis*), in defining which Aquinas simply appropriates Aristotle's definition of the power of choice: " 'Will,' " he writes, "means rational appetite" (I–II, 6, 2 *ad* 1; cf. *Eth. Nic.* 1139^{b}4). As rational, will is moved to activity by the activity of the related power of intellect; as appetitive, its activities are for the attainment of ends. Just as every power, according to its nature, is directed to a certain kind of object as proper to it, as the power of vision is directed to the visible, the power of will, as rational appetite, is directed to the rationally appetible, that is, to the character of good (*ratio boni*), which is intellectually grasped as being common to all things (*bonum in communi*) (I–II, 8, 1 and 2; 10, 1 and 2). And just as a particular act in which the power of vision is exercised can be directed to an object only inasmuch as it is visible, so a particular act in which the power of will is exercised can be directed to an object only inasmuch as it is taken to be good (*sub ratione boni*) (I–II, 8, 1c.).

Exercises of an appetitive power, which by its nature has to do with the attainment of an end, necessarily involve two kinds of subordinate acts: acts directed to the end to be attained (*in finem*), and acts directed to the means by which the end is to be attained (*in ea quae sunt ad finem*). Systematic inquiry will begin with the former.

The power of will, according to Aquinas, is exercised in no fewer than three kinds of acts directed toward ends. One, however, is fundamental; and with unfortunate ambiguity, Aquinas calls it by the same name as the power of will itself, namely, "*voluntas.*" Fortunately, when using this ambiguous word would mislead, he usually has recourse to the less ambiguous phrases "*actus voluntatis*" (act of will), sometimes preceded by the epithet "*simplex*" (simple), and "*motus voluntatis*" (motion of the will) (e.g., I–II, 8, 2 and 3; 10, 2 and 3). A simple act of will is a "motion" of an agent inasmuch as he is intellectual (an interior motion, therefore, and not an exterior bodily one) toward the attainment of a particular thing taken to be good as an end.

It is of the first importance to follow Aquinas's example (in I–II, 8, 2c.) and to distinguish between what he says about the power of will and what he says of the acts in which that power is exercised. Only of the power of will is the object said to be the character of good (*ratio boni*) (I–II, 8, 2c.). And the sense of saying that is clear: namely, that nothing can be an object of an act of that power except as having that character. Acts of will, accordingly, have as their objects particular ends *sub ratione boni*. By contrast, the traditional interpretation is obscure, according to which Aquinas holds that the first act of will in a complete human act has good *in communi* for its object.[5] What would it be to will something incompatible with good *in communi*? But, whether or not such a doctrine makes sense, there is sufficient reason to conclude that Aquinas does not hold it. First, while there are several passages in which *ratio boni* or *bonum in communi* is expressly asserted to be the object of the power of will, there is no unambiguous one in which it is asserted to be the object of any act in which that power is exercised. Second, and decisively, Aquinas insists that the simple acts of the power of will have only ends as their objects, while at the same time arguing that the power of will has as objects means as well as ends "because the character of good (*ratio boni*), which is the object of the power of will, is found not only in the end, but also in those things which are for the end" (I–II, 8, 2c.). Hence, to foist on him the doctrine that there is a simple act of will having the character of good as its object, with the implication that there are simple acts of will extending to means as well as to ends, would gratuitously make him contradict himself.

Any intellectual act in which something is affirmed to be an attainable good can give rise to a simple act of will directed to attaining it. The intellectual act in question may be in error. Aquinas insists that an end willed need not be good as a matter of fact (*in rei veritate*), finding for this Aristotelian credentials of a sort in *Physics* II, 195ᵃ26 (I–II, 8, 1c.). From this, taken together with the theological doctrine that the only good attainable by man that is complete and lacks nothing, namely, the beatific vision, cannot be intellectually grasped by natural means, he further concludes that in this life the will is not moved to any end necessarily (I–II, 10, 2). Of course, no end by itself can move the will at all, because the power of will includes the power to refuse to think of any given object. But even if he does think of it, no end any human being can think of by his natural powers can move his will necessarily, because, since no such end is completely good, it is open to him to incline instead to some good he recognizes that end to lack (I–II, 10, 2c.).

Besides what he called simple acts of will, Aquinas recognizes two other kinds of acts of will directed toward ends: enjoyment (*fruitio*) and intention (*intentio*). By the former, he enriches the Aristotelian theory from theological sources, above all from the writings of St. Augustine, whence are drawn the proof texts in all four articles of the question *de fruitione* (I–II, 11). By the latter, he further develops his revision of Aristotle.

The Aristotelian characterization of the will as rational appetite captures what is essential to its function in explaining what we do and why we do it. But that characterization says as little as possible about what willing an end is like. And it says both less than can be said about why human beings persist in ends despite accumulating evidence of their unsatisfactoriness, and less than theologians have taught about the rewards of persisting in ends that are satisfactory. St. Augustine had distinguished enjoyment from passive pleasure by maintaining that it is through the will that we enjoy.[6] And he had defined enjoying as "cleaving with love to something for its own sake" (*amore inhaerere alicui rei propter seipsum*).[7] Since anything simply willed as an end is willed for its own sake, although it may be willed for the sake of some further end as well, it is natural to ask whether every simple act of will is accompanied by an act of enjoyment. Aquinas's answer is implicit. "Anyone," he declares, "has love or delight from what he ultimately looks for (*de ultimo exspectato*), which is [his] end" (I–II, 11, 1c.). This implies that every simple act of will must have an act of enjoyment as its counterpart.

Why did Aquinas not simply add "involving cleaving with love" to his account of a simple act of will as an interior motion to something as an end *sub ratione boni*? Two reasons can be found in his text. First, while either one simply wills something as an end or one does not, one enjoys an end more the better it seems, and only the beatific vision completely (I–II, 11, 3c.); moreover, one enjoys an end perfectly only when it is possessed, and imperfectly when it is merely intended (I–II, 11, 4c.). Enjoyment, in short, has degrees, but simple willing has not. Second, with the actual possession of the beatific vision, "the delighted will comes to rest" (I–II, 11, 3c.); but that is when enjoyment is at its height.

Although Aquinas for good reasons distinguished acts of enjoyment from simple acts of will, what he writes about each shows conclusively that he holds every simple act of will to be immediately and intimately connected with an act of enjoyment. It is almost perverse to describe the enjoyment which, in some degree, pervades every human act, and which is found even in the acts of brute animals (cf. I–II, 11, 2c.), as something that occurs only at the conclusion of a successful human act. Yet it is common. Aquinas's placing of the question *de fruitione* immediately after the three questions concerning simple acts of will is enough to give the alarm.[8]

The fundamental theme of an Aristotelian theory of action is that willing an end generates action by way of the agent's deliberation about means (literally, "those things that are for the end"). Following Nemesius, Aquinas held that means are possible acts by which the end can be attained (I–II, 14, 4c.). Unless an appropriate act of deliberation ensues, simple acts of will remain barren. But once an appropriate act of deliberation has disclosed means by which an end willed can be attained, the simple act of willing that end generates a further act directed toward it: namely, an act of willing it through the means. Aquinas offers a simple but effective illustration. When we simply (*absolute*) will to be healthy, our act is a simple act of will (*voluntas*), and no more; but when we will to be healthy as an end to which some possible act is ordered, we perform a further act, an intention (I–II, 12, 1 *ad* 4; cf. 4c.). The deliberation by which an intention is generated can be more or less complete. Aquinas remarks that "there can be an intention of an end even though the means have not yet been determined" (I–II, 12, 4, *ad* 3). As soon as it is judged that there is a possible act by which an end can be attained, the end may be willed through that possible act. Intentions, in short, may be more or less determinate.

It is evident from Aquinas's exposition that intending does not differ from simple willing in the same way as enjoying does. Enjoying differs from simple willing, not in the object toward which it is directed, but in the intrinsic nature of the act that is directed toward that object. Intending, by contrast, is an act of exactly the same intrinsic nature as simple willing. They differ extrinsically, in the objects to which they are directed—simple willing being directed toward an end absolutely, and intending toward it through some means.

From the point of view of investigations of intention today, Aquinas deals primarily with the concept of the *intention with which* an agent acts.[9] In his moral writings, he used his results in exploring the distinction between acting intentionally (*secundum intentionem*) and not intentionally (*praeter intentionem*). The English usage according to which "What do you intend?" means "What have you decided to do?" falls outside of Aquinas's concept of intention, and is treated by him under the concept of choice.

For reasons which will become plain, Aquinas's treatment of choice largely recapitulates his treatment of intention. He adopted not only Aristotle's view that willing an end gives rise to choice (*electio*) by way of deliberation (*consilium*), but also his conception of acts of deliberation as consisting of analytical questioning (*quaerere et resolvere*) terminating in a judgment (*iudicium*), in which the end willed as the effect of the contemplated action is resolved into its simple causes—the means by which it may be attained (I–II, 14, 1 and 5; cf. *Eth. Nic.* 1112^{b}12–31).

A further complication can no longer be put aside. Deliberation is itself often a complete human act; for example, doing a sum in my head as part of the act of balancing my monthly accounts. Hence many human acts must be complex, in the sense of having other complete human acts as components. Familiar examples given today are repetitious acts, such as driving home a nail by repeated blows with a hammer.[10] But what may be called organized acts, consisting in a number of different complete human acts, the performance of which in a certain temporal order (some or all may be simultaneous) is designed to bring about a certain result, are more common and more important. Making a cake and tying a complicated knot are homely examples.

The fact that the act of deliberation which, according to any Aristotelian theory, is a component of any complete human act, may itself be a complete human act, raises the specter that deliberation is a process that must go on *in infinitum*. This would necessarily be the case if *every* act of deliberation were a complete human act. However, Aquinas argues that some are not. It is true that any question may be made an occasion for a complete human act of deliberation. But, since human action does occur, there must be simple human acts in which the act of deliberation is not itself a complete human act. This will be so when the agent's end is resolved into means unproblematically, because the resolution is a matter either of the agent's scientific knowledge (*disciplina*) or technical skill (*ars*), or has to do with a trifle (*res parva*) in which nothing that might come to mind would seem possibly to be in error (I–II, 14, 4 and 6). Thus in making a cake according to a recipe I know by heart, my technical skill enables me to judge how much of a given ingredient it is good to add as soon as the question comes up, without any process of calculation.

Aquinas points out that the judgment or verdict in which a "practical syllogism" of deliberation terminates (I–II, 13, 1 ad 2) is not apodictic.[11] An agent resolving the attainment of an end into its simple causes will produce a premise to the effect that it will be attained on a certain condition: say, "If M is adopted, E will be attained." Quite obviously, from such a premise, taken together with the judgment, "E is good to attain," which led to E's attainment being willed, it does not follow that "M is the suitable means to adopt." For the conditional premise does not exclude others: for example, "If N is adopted instead of M, E will be attained" (I–II, 13, 6 ad 2).

As soon as his deliberation has resulted in a judgment that it would be well to adopt some determinate means for the sake of the end willed, it is open to the agent to exercise his will and choose that means—or not to, either abandoning the end willed, or choosing to deliberate further. If he chooses the means indicated by his deliberation, however, is his choice not identical with his intention? True, there is a difference between the concepts of choice and intention to which attention has already been drawn: choice is of some determinate possible act, but intention may be of a possible act specified with any degree of determinateness. Yet the act to which two concepts apply may be the same act, even though the concepts by which it is referred to differ. When the means, that is, the possible act through which an end is intended, is determinately specified, are intending and choosing the same act?

Aquinas leaves no doubt that they are. In the body of I–II, 12, 4 he lays it down that "to tend towards an end and to tend towards that which is for the end is one and the same motion of the will in subject (*subiecto*)"; and he goes on to say that that same motion of the will, which is one in subject, differs according as we think about it (*ratione*) either primarily in terms of the means (choice), or primarily in terms of the end (intention) (I–II, 12, 4 *ad* 3). The reason why Aquinas's treatment of choice largely recapitulates his treatment of intention is now plain: when its object is determinate, an intention is the same act as the corresponding choice.

Just as the Aristotelian treatment of acts of will directed toward ends seemed defective to Aquinas in omitting to recognize that an agent does not merely tend to his ends, but cleaves to them with love, so he found a parallel defect in its treatment of acts of will directed toward means. Having in deliberation arrived at a judgment as to what means to his end are good, the agent does not simply tend to those means, but approves and loves them (*disponit et amat*) (I–II, 15, 3). This Aquinas calls "*consensus*" (consent), identifying it with what the translators of St. John of Damascus referred to as "*sententia.*" However, unlike enjoyment, which is full only when the end of all human action has been attained, consent is logically prior to choice, and may precede it in time. For consent, unlike choice, is accorded to suitable means to one's ends as soon as they are judged to be such. In most simple human acts, only one means to his end ever comes into the agent's mind, and he consents to it and chooses it together; but as Aquinas remarks, it may happen (*potest contingere*) that deliberation discloses several suitable means, one of which is judged most suitable, and in such cases, the agent approves and loves all the means judged suitable, while going on to choose the one judged most suitable (I–II, 15, 3 *ad* 3). Yet it would be a mistake to divide all acts of deliberation into two stages, deciding what means are suitable, and then deciding which is most suitable, giving rise to acts of consent and of choice respectively: what Aquinas has set out is a single act of deliberation, the verdict of which may be complex (that, of several suitable means, one is most suitable), which gives rise to an act of consent directed to all the suitable means, and an act of choice directed to one only.

Aquinas has now developed his revision of Aristotle's theory of action sufficiently to elucidate his own conception of a complete human act as a unity, among the components of which are a commanded act (*actus imperatus*) and an act of command (*imperium*) (I–II, 17, 4c.). Commanded acts are commanded by the will, but only as a subordinate power (I–II, 1, 1 *ad* 2): ultimately they are commanded by the intellect (I–II, 17, 1c.). This follows from his definition of commanding as "ordering (*ordinare*) somebody to something that is to be done, with a certain intimative motion (*intimativa motione*)" (I–II, 17, 2c.); for he explains that intimation is primarily expressed by indicative sentences containing gerundives, of the form "*Hoc est tibi faciendum*" (this is to be done by you), and only secondarily by imperatives (I–II, 17, 1c.). In a complete human act, a commanded act will be that component which the agent judges is to be made to happen, and which *does* happen as a result of an act of will which he performs in view of that judgment. Taking the theory as so far developed, it is natural to identify the act of command (*imperium*) with the judgment that terminates deliberation; and to identify the mediating act of will, as a result of which the commanded act happens, with the act of choice. Aquinas, as we shall see, adds a further act of will (namely, *usus*), and provides it with an appropriate generating intellectual act; but that, I shall argue, is muddled.

Yet it is essential to Aquinas's theory, as nobody seriously disputes, that in no complete human act can the component commanded act be identical with any of the acts of intellect and will that give rise to it. For every one of those latter acts— judging an end good, willing to attain it, enjoying it, deliberating about what would be the suitable means of attaining it, consenting to such means as there are, choosing the most suitable, and, if Aquinas is right, an additional act of intellect leading to an additional act of will which he calls *"usus"*—is an immediate exercise of the power of intellect or of will, which excludes any exercise of any subordinate power (I–II, 1, 1 *ad* 2; 6, 4c.). Each of them is *elicited*, not commanded.

What acts, then, *are* commanded? The most obvious complete human acts are bodily, for example, raising one's arm.[12] When an act is a bodily act, the commanded act will be a motion of one's bodily members (*corporis membra*), for example, one's arm's going up. The occurrence of such a commanded act is always an exercise of what Aquinas calls the agent's executive power (*potentia executiva*) with regard to his body, an exercise that is immediately caused by some act of will (I–II, 16, 2c.; 17, 9c.). Each human being finds out by experience the range of his executive power with regard to his body (I–II, 17, 9 *ad* 2 and 3). But although certain motions of the bodily members are the most familiar examples of commanded acts, Aquinas expressly declares that both acts of intellect and acts of will can also be commanded, and even, up to a point, acts of sensitive appetite (I–II, 17, 5–7).

Why he does so appears most clearly from what he says about commanded acts of intellect. It follows from the nature of elicited acts, as we have seen, that no elicited act of intellect can be commanded: one cannot command dissent from what immediately strikes one as true. But not all acts of intellect are elicited. To begin with, their execution or performance (*exercitium*), as distinct from their content if performed, never is: it is because they have a shrewd notion that, if they ask themselves whether black is white, the judgment that it is not will immediately be elicited, that human beings sometimes judge that <<not>> asking it will serve their ends better than asking it. In short, whether an act of intellect is performed or not can be commanded. Furthermore, when human beings ask themselves whether a certain answer to a question is true or false, it often happens that no judgment is immediately elicited. Should their intellectual powers fail them in this way, it is open to them to deliberate whether their ends will be served better by assenting to a given answer, or by dissenting from it. And so, in the absence of an elicited act of assent or dissent, assent and dissent themselves may be commanded (I–II, 17, 6).

The article (I–II, 17, 5) in which Aquinas treats of commanded acts of will is perilously succinct. It will be misunderstood if it is forgotten that, when a certain possible act is commanded in an act of intellect and then chosen in an act of will, what is commanded is the possible act that is chosen, and not the act of choosing or willing it. The crucial premise in Aquinas's demonstration that acts of will are commanded is that a man "can judge that it is good that [he] will a certain thing" (*potest iudicare quod bonum sit aliquid velle*) (I–II, 17, 5c.). He has not forgotten that what is judged in deliberation is that a certain means is most suitable: his point is that sometimes the means judged most suitable for attaining an end may itself be an act of will. And so the act of choice that ensues, if one does, will be an act of willing that act of will. Unfortunately, in the article itself, Aquinas gives no examples at all. But they are not far to seek. Not all acts of will are, like the act of choice in complete bodily human acts, directed upon a possible movement to be made here and now. One may resolve to act in a certain way in the future, either at a certain time and place, or in certain circumstances whenever and wherever they occur. And, since making such resolutions is one of the means by which moral virtues are acquired, it is one kind of act of will that can be commanded.

The carrying out or execution of a commanded act, as Aquinas describes it, is a matter of the operation of certain human "interior principles" (*principia interiora*), namely, the powers of the soul (*potentiae animae*) such as intellect, will, and sensible appetite, their trained dispositions (*habitus*), and the organs or bodily members, each conceived as the seat of powers such as to see, to feel, to move in such and such a way, and the like (I–II, 16, 1c.). These principles are also referred to as executive powers (I–II, 17, 3c.). They are set in operation by acts of will (I–II, 16, 1). Aquinas therefore holds that, in a complete human act, the actual execution of the commanded act is related to a certain elicited act of will—necessarily the last one—as effect to cause. And the causal relation will not be that of an agent to his complete human acts, or to those of their component acts that are elicited, but that of any event that is an effect to any event that is its cause.

It remains to determine what is the last act of will in a complete human act: the act of will which causes the operation of the executive powers that constitutes the commanded act. There is an obvious reason for identifying it with the act of choice, and so for identifying the intellectual act of command with the act of judgment that terminates deliberation: namely, that Aquinas himself lays it down that "inasmuch as [the power of will] is in the person willing as having a certain proportion or order to that which is willed" (*secundum quod est quodammodo in volente per quamdam proportionem vel ordinem ad volitum*), the last act of will with respect to the means is choice (I–II, 16, 4c.).

Aquinas's argument for interpolating a further act of will between choice and the commanded act is confused on its face. It begins with the premise that, besides the relation which the power of will can have to the willed inasmuch as it is in the person willing as having a certain proportion or order to the willed, there is a second relation which it can have inasmuch as the willed is in the person willing as an end which he really possesses (*ut habeat ipsum finem realiter*) (I–II, 16, 4c.). The means, as well as the end, is then declared to be included in this second relation. And finally, it is argued that, since choice is the last act of will in the first relation,

> *Usus* belongs to the second relation of the will to the thing willed by which it tends to its bringing about (*ad consequendum rem volitam*). From which it is manifest that *usus* follows choice, provided that the word "*usus*" is adopted inasmuch as the will uses the executive power, by moving it (*secundum quod voluntas utitur executiva potentia, movendo ipsam*). (I–II, 16, 4c.)

This seems to be one of those sheer blunders into which even the greatest philosophers fall. For if the second relation of the will to the willed in fact obtains—namely, the relation it has when the willed is something really possessed—then the executive power by which the willed has been brought about must already have been exercised. Hence if *usus* is an act which belongs to the second relation of the will to the willed, it cannot be directed to the operation of an executive power which *ex hypothesi* has already operated. "Using" the executive powers can only be an act belonging to the *first* relation of the will to the willed. And Aquinas himself concedes that the last act of will in that first relation is choice. *Usus*, understood as the "using" of the executive powers, should therefore be identified with choice. And *imperium*, as the act of judgment which gives rise to *usus*, need not be identified with an elicited intellectual act alleged to follow choice (cf. I–II, 17, 3 *ad* 1): it should simply be identified with the judgment with which deliberation terminates.

Shorn of excrescences that contradict his own principles, Aquinas's analysis of the structure of a simple complete human act can be set out in the schematic table below (see figure 1).

Aquinas's analysis of human action is rightly held by his admirers to be a major contribution to philosophy. In taking Aristotle's theory as his point of departure, he anticipated most action theory today; and his revision of Aristotle's concept of *boulesis*, and the introduction of the explanatory concept of intention and the revision of Aristotle's theory of choice which followed from it, appear now to be common property of unknown origin. His treatment of enjoyment and consent, although derived from theology, seems to me phenomenologically sound. Internally, the only serious defect in his theory is his interpolation of two superfluous elicited acts, *imperium* and *usus*, between choice and the execution of the commanded act.

To his immediate successors, the most controversial point in Aquinas's theory of action was the priority it affirms of intellect over will. Freedom of will, according to it, is wholly a matter of the nonnecessity of any judgment a man can arrive at by his natural powers as to the goodness of an end or the suitability of a means. Even when will seems to fly in the face of intellect, there is always a (foolish, perhaps vicious) judgment which directs it. Duns Scotus was to develop the doctrine that the source of the will's freedom is internal to it, and not external, as Aquinas holds.[13] To the run of twentieth century philosophers, the feature of Aquinas's theory that is most objectionable is his retention of Aristotle's conception of causation as the exercise of a power or capacity, which allows him to think of human beings themselves, and not only of events occurring within them, as genuine causes of their actions—"agent causes." Some of the most important recent work in action theory has attempted to work out a revised Aristotelian position very like Aquinas's, but in which the post-Humean conception of causation as a nomological relation between events is substituted throughout for the Aristotelian one.[14] On the other hand, there are philosophers today who contend that the concept of action implicit in our practice is unintelligible without something like the Aristotelian conception of agent causation.[15]

A Simple Complete Human Act
(e.g., Socrates's raising of his arm)
consists of

I. Acts of intellect   II. Acts of will

A. *with regard to the end*

Elicited acts {

1. Judging that an attainable end is good (e.g., Socrates's judging that it would be good to attract Plato's attention and that he can).

2. Willing to attain that end (e.g., Socrates's willing to attract Plato's attentions).
3. Enjoying that end.
4. Intending that end throught suitable means (cf. 7).

B. *with regard to the means*

5. Deliberating how to attain that end, that is:
(a) asking what within one's power would most suitably cause the attainment of the end willed, and
(b) judging that a certain act (= the commanded act) in one's power would be most suitable (e.g., Socrates's judging that the most suitable means would be his arm's going up). [Aquinas should have identified this judgment with *imperium*, or command.]

6. Consenting to all the means judged suitable.
7. Choosing the means judged most suitable (e.g., Socrates's choosing that his arm go up). [This is identical with intending, given that one's intention is fully determinate.]

III. Act of the executive power caused
by the last elicited act of will

Executed act   8. The commanded act takes place, the relevant executive powers having been set in operation by the act of choice (e.g., Socrates's arm's going up).

Figure 1.   Aquinas's Analysis of a Human Act, Corrected according to the Present Interpretation.

Little has been said of the vulgar objections, or rather slogans, by which the philosophical work of Aquinas and other scholastics is now and then ignorantly dismissed. The commonest, probably, is that Aquinas's theory of action is a "faculty-psychology" in which human beings are resolved into a collection of faculties or powers, each of which is then treated as a quasi-agent. Although, for convenience, Aquinas often speaks of what a power like the intellect does or can do, I have detected no statement indispensable to his theory of action that cannot readily, if sometimes cumbrously, be reformulated as a statement about what human beings, as possessing that power, do or can do. He himself annihilates the objection that acts of will cannot be commanded because "the will cannot understand a command" (*voluntatis non est intelligere imperium*) (I–II, 17, 5 obj. 2) by pointing out that "a *man* enjoins an act of will on *himself* inasmuch as *he* understands and wills" (*homo imperat sibi ipsi actum voluntatis, inquantum est intelligens et volens*) (I–II, 17, 5 ad 2).

As for the scarcely less common objection that the elicited acts which according to Aquinas are components of even the simplest complete human acts are too numerous to be credible, and correspond to nothing in our experience of our own acts, the reply—made also by action theorists today—must be that the components of simple complete human acts are ascertained, not by introspecting what happens when we perform them, but by examining various cases in which an act is begun but not completed. We recognize cases in which we or others will to attain an end, and then do not bother to consider means at all; cases in which we or others think about suitable means but fail to settle on any as most suitable; cases in which we or others settle upon some means as most suitable, and then do not choose to adopt it; and finally (as when we or others suffer some unanticipated impairment of our executive powers) cases in which we choose to bring about some act which we think possible, and find that it is beyond our power. It is by reflection on such cases, and not by introspection, that Aquinas constructs his theory (e.g., I–II, 12, 2 ad 4; 12, ad 3; 15, 3 ad 3; 16, 4 ad 3; 17, 5 ad 2).

Notes

From *The Cambridge History of Later Medieval Philosophy*, edited by Norman Kretzmann, Anthony Kenny, and Jan Pinborg. © Cambridge University Press 1982. Reprinted with the permission of Cambridge University Press.

1. "...imperium et actus imperatus sunt unus actus hominis, sicut quoddam totum est unum, sed est secundum partes multa" (*ST* I–II, 17, 4c.). "...nihil prohibet, in his quae sunt multa partibus et unum toto, unum est prius alio; sicut anima quodammodo est prius corpore" (*ibid. ad* 3).

2. Cf. Gilbert Ryle, *The Concept of Mind* (London: Hutchinson and Co., 1949), chap. 3, "The Will."

3. Cf. Anthony Kenny, *Will, Freedom and Power* (Oxford: Blackwell, 1975), pp. 13–15.

4. G. E. M. Anscombe, "Thought and Action in Aristotle," in *New Essays on Plato and Aristotle*, ed. Renford Bambrough (London: Routledge and Kegan Paul, 1965), p. 147.

5. By the "traditional" interpretation, I mean the interpretation that was to be found in most manuals of Thomist philosophy until very recently. The source of many of these treatments appears to be the article "Acte" in *Dictionnaire de théologie catholique*, by A. Gardeil, whose interpretation of Aquinas's analysis of a complete human act is summed up in the following schematic table, which, save for simplifications of items (10) and (11), is translated from one presented in that article, col. 343. Compare the scheme presented by Thomas Gilby in *Summa theologiae* (London and New York: Blackfriars, in conjunction with Eyre and Spottiswoode and McGraw-Hill, 1963–76), vol. 17, p. 211.

I. Acts which concern the end
(*Ordo intentionis*, I–II, 8)

Acts of Intellect (I–II, 9, 1 ad 3)	Acts of Will (I–II, 9 ibid.)
1. One sees the good (9, 1)	2. One loves it (*Appetitus inefficax boni propositi*—8, 2)
3. One judges rationally that it ought to be sought for (*Judicium synderesis proponens objectum ut conveniens et assequibile*—19, 4)	4. One wills to attain it (*Actus quo voluntas tendit in objectum ut assequibile et conveniens*—9, 7)

II. Acts which concern the means
1. *Ordo secundae intentionis vel electionis*

5. One seeks after the means of attaining it (*Consilium*, I–II, 14)	6. One gives one's consent to the means found (*Consensus*, I–II, 16)
7. One judges what is the means best suited to attaining the end (*Judicium practicum*, I–II, 14, 6; 13, 3)	8. One chooses it (*Electio*, I–II, 13) (One decides)

2. *Ordo Executionis*

9. One efficaciously decides to employ the means (*Imperium*, I–II, 17)	10. The will puts into action the powers whose operation is needed (*Usus activus*, I–II, 16) (Utilization)

11. Execution (*Usus passivus*, I–II, 16, 1) The powers whose operation is needed operate
12. Enjoyment of the intellect and the will in the possession of the end (*Fruitio*, I–II, 11)

6. St. Augustine, *De trinitate*, X, 10 (*Patrologia Latina* 42, 981); quoted in *ST* I–II, 11, 3 obj. 3.

7. St. Augustine, *De doctrina christiana*, I, 4 (*Patrologia Latina* 34, 30); quoted in *ST* I–II, 11, 1c.

8. "Why the genetic order of volition, intention, and enjoyment is not followed does not appear," Gilby notes (*Summa theologiae*, Blackfriars ed., vol. 17, p. 49). It did not occur to him that Aquinas's genetic order may not have been that of his interpreters.

9. On the scope of such investigations, see G. E. M. Anscombe, *Intention* (Oxford: Blackwell, 1957), p. 1.

10. Cf. Alvin I. Goldman, *A Theory of Human Action* (Englewood Cliffs, New Jersey: Prentice-Hall, 1970), pp. 35–37.

11. Anscombe, "Thought and Action in Aristotle," pp. 152–53.

12. Ludwig Wittgenstein, *Philosophical Investigations*, trans. G. E. M. Anscombe, 3d ed. (New York: Macmillan, 1953), I § 621, has made this example the standard one.

13. See Bernardine M. Bonansea, "Duns Scotus's Voluntarism," in J. K. Ryan and B. M. Bonansea, eds., *John Duns Scotus: 1265–1965* (Washington, D.C.: Catholic University of America Press, 1965), esp. pp. 97–113.

14. For example, Donald Davidson, *Essays on Actions and Events* (Oxford: Clarendon Press, 1980), in "Agency," "How is Weakness of Will Possible?" and "Freedom to Act."

15. For example, Roderick M. Chisholm, *Person and Object: A Metaphysical Study* (London: G. Allen and Unwin, 1976), esp. pp. 69–88.

FIVE

Human Ends and Human Actions:
An Exploration in St. Thomas's Treatment

1. The Two Teleologies

There are at least two different ways in which human beings explain one another's actions. One, the most common, is by treating the action to be explained as behavior with a purpose, and a purpose as an end to be brought about. When we know what somebody proposed to bring about when he acted in a certain fashion, and why he believed that so acting was, in his situation, the way to bring that end about, we can claim so far to understand his action. Philosophy furnishes us with a word for such explanations: the word "teleological." Human action is characteristically directed to *tele*, or ends; and a *telos* is an event of a certain kind to be made to happen, or (less accurately, I believe) a state of affairs of a certain kind to be brought about. Sometimes this event is fairly simple, such as at last getting in your first serve in a tennis game, after an ignominious string of failures; sometimes it is highly complex, such as living a happy life.

A second way of explaining human actions, although less common, is nevertheless familiar. You have match point in a tennis game against an opponent to whom you mostly lose, and he makes a nearly impossible return which only you are in a position to see. With much inward grief, you have to call "In!" You are not a moral masochist. Giving calls against yourself in such situations is not one of your purposes in life. And yet we understand your doing it, even if, in your shoes, we should not have.

How do we understand it? Perhaps to begin with, in terms of fairness and sportsmanship. But what lies behind the rules of fairness and sportsmanship? Is it not simply that your opponent is somebody to whom you owe the truth, miserable wretch though he is for bringing that return off? You acted for his sake, not to realize any purpose of your own.

The phrase "for his sake" is inescapably teleological. It signifies that on account of which your action was done. You did what you did, not for any outcome it might have produced, but out of concern for your opponent. You were certainly not concerned to concede him the point. If his return had been in and neither he nor you had seen it, you would not have repined at all. Yet, for his sake, you regarded cheating as out. Your opponent was the end of your action in a way quite different from that in which any purpose you had might have been.

Even so, is not the fundamental sense of "*telos*" the first: that of an event to be made to happen? Not for St. Thomas, as we shall see. But that is not immediately evident in his language, as it was to be in the language of his great successor, the blessed John Duns Scotus. Scotus distinguished *finis*, an end (that is, *telos*) from what he called "*finitum*," literally an "ended," namely, that which stands to an end as that which is brought about stands to what brings it about.

> [A] *finitum* depends for its being upon a *finis* as [essentially] prior [Scotus declared] just to the extent that the *finis* as loved moves an efficient [cause] to confer being on it.

And so, he proceeds,

> a corollary follows, which should not be passed over in silence, namely, that a certain opinion about the *finis* is a *falsa imaginatio*. [That opinion is] that the final cause of a being is the last operation [in causing it], or the object brought about through that operation.[1]

His line of thought, I take it, is this. Sometimes, as in official or productive activity, the end of an action is either the last operation performed (such as the granting of an official permission), or is something produced by that operation (such as a finished product turned off an assembly line); but in neither case do the actions that lead up to the end depend on it as essentially prior to them, for it is prior to them only as something thought by the agent or designer. By contrast, when the end of an action is essentially prior to it, it cannot be either an operation that forms part of it or something produced by it. It can only be a pre-existent thing that is loved by the agent, and for the sake of which he acts. And an ultimate end must be essentially prior to any action of which it is the end.

It is evident that the two kinds of *telos* disclosed by these examples are connected with two different conceptions of morality. Events to be brought about are *tele* of the kind that are recognized in consequentialist conceptions of it, and persons are *tele* of the kind that are recognized in conceptions of it as a limit to be observed in trying to realize our purposes.

Anybody who, like myself, is interested in these two kinds of *telos* will be refreshed by St. Thomas's treatment of the ends of human action in both his moral philosophy and his moral theology. For, unlike most of our contemporaries, he did not embrace one of the two kinds of *telos* and ignore the other. Nobody has reaffirmed more emphatically than he the Aristotelian doctrine that "all men agree in seeking an ultimate end, which is happiness (*beatitudo*)."[2] Nor has anybody confessed more passionately than he the Mosaic and Christian faith that "the end of human life and society is God."[3] And God is not, as some process theologians would have us believe, an event to be brought about.

Unfortunately, I have not enough learning to investigate St. Thomas's teleology of human action thoroughly and systematically. At best, I can lead you on a free ramble through some things he wrote about it in the two of his works with which I am least unfamiliar: the two *Summae*. Even here, when the mountain air makes breathing hard for me, I shall retreat to the valleys of more recent philosophy. However, as you will see, that is not because I think any philosopher to have done better than St. Thomas on the questions I shall consider. My hope is that I may irritate somebody better equipped into providing us with something more systematic.

2. *The Two Teleologies in St. Thomas*

St. Thomas's commitment to both of the kinds of teleology I have distinguished is evident in what he had to say about the difference between the relation of intellectual creatures to what he referred to as "the ultimate end of the whole of things" and that of nonintellectual ones. "Only the intellectual creature reaches the very ultimate end of the whole of things through his own operation, which is the knowing and loving of God: whereas other creatures cannot attain the ultimate end except by a participation in its likeness" (*Summa contra gentiles* III, iii, 1). Here, while the ultimate end of the whole of things is unmistakably God, presumably the operation by which intellectual creatures reach that end is also an end for them. God is indeed the being for whose sake they act, but the operation by which he is attained is an event they aim at bringing about.

Although the cheerful remark I have quoted from the *Summa contra gentiles* seems clear enough, it must be acknowledged that some philosophers have found it difficult to conceive how any existing being can be an end. For example, Sir David Ross, the great British Aristotle scholar of the first half of our century, wrote, in another connection, that "an end is an object of desire, and an object of desire is something that does not yet exist."[4] If Ross were right, attaining an end could not be anything except bringing it into existence. And so it would be nonsensical to describe God, who exists now and always, as an end to be attained by rational creatures in one way, and by nonrational creatures in another.

Before we dismiss Ross's objection as fatuous, which I think it is, we should acknowledge that St. Thomas himself, when he wrote about the end of human life, as distinct from the end of the whole of things, usually referred to it as something not yet existing which we hope may be brought into existence. For example, in *Summa contra gentiles* III, 25, 7, he wrote:

> . . . a thing has the greatest desire for its ultimate end. Now, the human intellect has a greater desire, and love, and pleasure, in knowing divine matters than it has in the perfect knowledge of the lowest things, even though it can grasp but little concerning divine things. So, the ultimate end of man is to understand God, in some fashion.

Here the ultimate end of human beings in this life is presented as an object of desire that does not yet exist. And a little later in the same chapter St. Thomas went on to identify it with *felicitas*, the commonest equivalent in the *Summa contra gentiles* of Aristotle's *eudaimonia*. Apparently, whatever his opinion may have been about the ultimate end of the whole of things, he agreed with Ross that the ultimate end of human beings in this life is to attain a state they have not yet attained.

How are such pairs of passages as these to be reconciled? One way would be this. The ultimate end of everything in each order of being—inanimate things, plants, brute animals, rational animals, and separate substances—is to attain a state it is not in; and since those states are definable only by reference to God, God is the ultimate end of the whole of things in the sense that he and he alone is that by reference to which the ultimate ends of all things are defined. What is wrong with this will be evident to you. It is that there must be some reason why the ultimate ends of all things can be defined only by reference to God; and that reason must yield a deeper sense in which God is the ultimate end of the whole of things than that their specific ends can all be so defined. What is that deeper sense?

St. Thomas's first answer to this question in *Summa contra gentiles* was metaphysical. An end is a final cause. From this it follows that

> the end holds first place over other types of cause, and to it all other causes owe the fact that they are causes in act: for the agent only acts for the sake of the end. . . . Therefore the ultimate end is the first cause of all. (III, 17, 9)

And the first cause of all is, of course, God: the first cause, and the first agent. Now, St. Thomas continues,

> . . . an end that is produced by the action of an agent cannot be the first agent; it is, rather an effect of an agent. Therefore, God cannot be the end of things in this way, as something produced (*constitutum*), but only as something pre-existing (*praeexistens*) to be obtained. (III, 18, 3)

The ultimate end of human action, or of action of any other kind, cannot be something that does not yet exist, if that end is, as all good Aristotelians believe, the ultimate final cause. Hence we must distinguish between the end of an action, which exists before it, and what St. Thomas calls the "obtaining" of that end. *Obtaining the end is not the end.* Nor does "obtaining," as St. Thomas uses it here, stand for any kind of exclusive ownership or dominion.

Of course, this line of thought does not find favor with many metaphysicians today. And on this point I imagine that most of us here, including many who would call themselves Thomists, stand with the majority of our contemporaries. If we accept, as I do, St. Thomas's doctrine that God is something like the final cause of things as that is conceived in Aristotle's metaphysics (of course that is not all he is), it is not for Aristotle's reason that the universe has a final *natural* cause. For what reason then? I believe that St. Thomas gets at it in an observation about the ends of productive actions generally.

> [T]he ultimate end of any maker, as a maker, is himself; it is for our own sakes that we use things made by us, and if sometimes a man makes a thing for some other purpose, this has reference to his own good, either as useful, or delectable, or right. (*honestum*)

Now, what holds for all makers holds for God.

> God is the productive cause of all things.... Therefore, he himself is the end of all things. (III, 17, 8)

This argument implies that creatures as well as God may be ends. Later in the third part of *Summa contra gentiles* St. Thomas went on to draw that conclusion when he came to address himself to the foundations of morality. Rational creatures excel all others not only in the dignity of their end, but also in the perfection of their nature.

> In perfection of nature, only the rational creature has dominion over its acts, freely moving itself to doing them (*ad operandum*). Other creatures are moved to the activities (*opera*)proper to them rather than move [themselves to them]. (III, 111, 1)

Among creatures, only the intellectual ones (St. Thomas uses the words "rational" and "intellectual" interchangeably in this connection) are principal agents, as distinct from instruments.

> What is moved only by another has the nature (*ratio*) of an instrument: but what is moved *per se* has the nature of a principal agent. Now, an instrument is wanted, not for its own sake (*propter seipsum*), but so that a principal agent may use it. Hence all the careful work that is devoted to instruments must be referred to the principal agent as end; but what is done for the principal agent, either by himself or by another, is for his sake (*propter ipsum*), inasmuch as he is a principal agent. Therefore intellectual creatures are treated by God as things cared about (*procuratae*) for their own sakes.... (III, 112, 1)

To this, St. Thomas added a parallel argument: namely, that intellectual creatures are ends—things cared about for their own sakes—not only as principal agents, but also as attaining what they do through their own efforts.

> [W]henever things are ordered to any end, if any among them cannot attain the end through their own efforts (*per seipsa*), they must be subordinated to those that attain it and are ordered to it for their own sakes.... Now... God is the ultimate end of the whole of things. An intellectual nature alone attains to God in himself, that is, by knowing him and loving him.... Therefore the intellectual nature is the only one in the universe that is wanted (*quaesita*) for its own sake, and all others for its sake (III, 112, 3).

Moreover, creatures of intellectual nature are wanted for their own sakes as individuals. "A rational creature," St. Thomas declared, "stands to divine providence as governed and provided for for his own sake, not only for the sake of his species, as other corruptible creatures are" (III, 113, 2).

That rational beings as such are ends, creator and creature alike, is the foundation of the moral law. "Law is nothing but a certain reason and rule of operation (*ratio et regula operandi*)" (III, 114, 3). In governing themselves according to that reason and rule, human beings "participate in a certain likeness of divine providence" (III, 114, 2). But "the end of every law, and above all of divine law, is to make men good," and what makes a human being good is "possessing a good will" (III, 116, 3). A person of good will wills, first of all, "to cling to God ... through love," and next, to love his neighbors (III, 116, 1 and 117, 1). That he do so, St. Thomas pointed out, is the sense of what St. Matthew's gospel recognizes as the two fundamental commandments on which the whole Mosaic Torah hangs (III, 116, 6 and 117, 7).

In explaining the reason of these commandments—that is, why they are laws—St. Thomas makes it clear that the first holds because God is an end: "the will is good because it wills a good object, and especially the greatest good, which is the end" (III, 116, 3). However, he does not make it as clear that the same is true of the second. Indeed, the reason he gave for it is easily mistaken for an anticipation of Hume's.

> [T]here ought (*oportet*) to be a union in affection among those for whom there is a common end [he wrote]. Now men share in common the one ultimate end which is happiness.... So, men ought to be united with each other by a mutual love. (III, 117, 1)

And he continued,

> [I]t is natural to all men to love each other. A sign of this is that by a certain natural instinct, a man comes to the help of any man in need, even one he does not know.... Therefore, mutual love is prescribed for men by the divine law. (III, 117, 6)

Unlike Hume, however, St. Thomas saw in natural instinct not a substitute for a requirement of practical reason, but a sign that such a requirement underlies it.[5] And his assertion that happiness (*beatitudo*) is the ultimate end shared by all men must be understood in the light of his doctrine that happiness itself presupposes a pre-existent end.

The structure of morality as St. Thomas presents it in *Summa contra gentiles* accordingly seems to be this. God, the first cause and first agent, is the ultimate pre-existing end of the whole of things, before all produced ends (*fines constituti*). Rational creatures also, by the providence of God, act for their own sakes. But what their own sakes require is that they obtain the ultimate end of the whole of things by loving and understanding it. A necessary condition of their doing that is that their wills be good: that is, that they will according to law. Law is reason and rule. And reason and rule require, first of all, that they love God, and second, that they love their neighbors—all other rational beings. The Mosaic Torah lays down in detail what these fundamental commandments imply.

However, *Summa contra gentiles*, written between 1258 and 1264, is one of St. Thomas's earlier works. In the later *Summa theologiae*, written between 1266 and 1273, morality is treated much more elaborately, and at first sight, differently. The morality of *Summa contra gentiles* is unmistakably a deontology based on a distinctive teleology of pre-existent ends; that in *Summa theologiae* is for the most part a theory of virtues and vices based on a theory of right reason. Yet, despite the obvious differences of subject, differences of doctrine turn out to be largely in emphasis.[6]

A brief survey must suffice. That the treatise *De lege* in *Summa theologiae* (I–II, 90–97) expands the treatment of moral law in the earlier *Summa*, but without contradicting it, is, as far as I know, not seriously questioned. What is called in *Summa contra gentiles* "divine law," that is, the reason and rule of operation in which human beings participate in a certain likeness of divine providence, is now called "natural law (*lex naturalis*)" (*ST* I–II, 91, 2). And, as in *Summa contra gentiles*, all the moral precepts of the Mosaic Torah are declared to be contained in the natural law, and to be summed up in the two *prima et communia praecepta* "Love God" and "Love your neighbor" (*ST* I–II, 99, 1 ad 2; 100, 3). The additions to Mosaic moral teaching made by Christianity are declared to be few, and chiefly to be a matter of forbidding internal acts not forbidden in all cases by Moses (*ST* I–II, 107, 4).

That both God and human beings are recognized to be pre-existent ends in *Summa theologiae* is equally evident. As far as morality is concerned, it is explicitly laid down that all morality arises from love of the pre-existent ends, God and human beings. St. Thomas commented on St. Paul's at first sight surprising assertion that "If there is any other commandment it is comprised in this saying: 'Thou shalt love thy neighbor as thyself,' " that

> [T]he whole of the law is summed up in this single commandment... as the
> end to which, in a certain sense, all the commandments are directed. For when
> one loves one's neighbor for God's sake, then this love includes the love of God
> also. (*ST* I–II, 99, 1 ad 2)

I shall therefore assume that, early and late, St. Thomas thought of morality as a matter of law (law itself being understood as a matter of reason), and of law as resting on a teleology of pre-existent ends.

3. Human Tragedy and Philosophical Comedy

It is now time to return to a topic briefly introduced and then laid aside: St. Thomas's unwavering Aristotelian teaching that "the ultimate end of man, and of every intellectual substance, is called *felicitas* or *beatitudo*; for this is what every intellectual substance desires as [its] ultimate end, and for its own sake alone" (*Summa contra gentiles* III, 25, 14). Can St. Thomas reconcile this with the Christian doctrine that the ultimate end of human action is not something brought about by it, but something that pre-exists it?

The chief difficulty in doing so is that, according to Aristotle, happiness or blessedness—*eudaimonia* or *to makarion* in Greek, *felicitas* or *beatitudo* in Latin—is something rational beings naturally seek. As we shall see, there turn out to be difficulties in this concept that compel a distinction within it. Still, what do human beings naturally seek? Aristotle's answer to this question is well known, but worth repeating:

> ... human good turns out to be activity of soul in accordance with virtue, and if there are more than one virtue, in accordance with the best and most complete. But we must add "in a complete life." For one swallow does not make a summer, nor does one day; and so too one day, or a short time, does not make a man blessed and happy. (*Eth. Nic.* I, 1098^{a}16–19)

On any unsentimental view of the conditions of human life, two grim consequences follow. The first is that, since they will not receive the nurture and training of a free citizen of an Hellenic *polis*—and that is what is necessary for engaging in activity in accordance with virtue—many human beings will never have the capacity to attain the human good. The second is that, since not even capacity and virtue together ensure good fortune in this world, the virtuous and able will sometimes fail to attain it.

Human life, as Aristotle conceived it, is inescapably tragic. Some individual lives are happy; but nobody, however great or noble, can count on it.

> [A] multitude of great events ... if they turn out ill ... crush and maim blessedness (*tomakarion*); for they both bring pain with them and hinder many activities. ... [T]he man who is truly good and wise, we think, bears all the chances of life becomingly and always makes the best of circumstances. ... And if this is the case, the happy man (*ho eudaimon*) can never become miserable (*athlios*)—though he will not reach blessedness (*makarios*), if he meet with fortunes like those of Priam. (*Eth. Nic.* I, 1100^{b}25–1101^{a}8)

No doubt it is better to have been Hector or Priam than to have been a lifelong slave; but to say that a tragic hero like Hector attained the end of human life would be absurd.

Aristotle's investigation has led him to distinguish two varieties of ultimate human good: a happiness attainable by anybody whose nurture and training has endowed him with the capacity for virtuous action—a happiness he calls *eudaimonia*; and a happiness for which luck is needed as well, which he calls *to makarion*. Neither is palatable to a Christian or post-Christian mind, for whom no human being should be conceived as excluded from the human good. Yet is there any alternative? Light is thrown on St. Thomas's medieval rejection of Aristotle's tragic view by the vain struggles of two representative modern philosophers, Immanuel Kant and Henry Sidgwick, to find such an alternative.

Both Kant and Sidgwick found the tragic view of life unacceptable because of what they believed to be demands of practical reason. Both maintained that practical reason imposes on those who have it two distinct principles, which would generate inconsistent precepts unless certain further postulates were true. Since rational creatures cannot practically reject those principles, neither can they practically refuse to postulate what is necessary for their reconciliation.

Since Sidgwick's reasoning is more elementary, I begin with it. Of the two principles which he believed practical reason to impose, the first is universalistic: namely, the utilitarian greatest happiness principle, that among the courses of action open to him, a truly rational agent would choose one that would produce the greatest amount of happiness on the whole.[7] If he had thought that practical reason imposed no principle but this, Sidgwick would not have questioned the finality of the verdict of experience that life is tragic. After all, most human beings, for no apparent fault of theirs, do not lead lives that are happy on the whole; and, owing to their inescapable ignorance of many effects of the different courses of action open to them, even those who sincerely try to act on the greatest happiness principle often do not succeed. But Sidgwick was convinced that practical reason also imposes a second principle: namely, the egoist one that a truly rational agent would always choose, among the courses open to him, one from which he would get for himself the greatest surplus of pleasure over pain.[8] It would profit nothing to examine either Sidgwick's reasons for this principle, or how he answered objections to it. Both, in my opinion, have worn at least as well as his reasons for the greatest happiness principle. What matters here is that Sidgwick believed that this "dualism of practical reason," as Schneewind has called it, gives us ground to reject the finality of tragedy in life.[9] Why did he believe that?

Sidgwick allowed that philosophy can tolerate the world's being so ordered that what practical reason demands that we try to attain is in fact unattainable. But he dismissed as ridiculous any suggestion that practical reason might demand the logically impossible in any situation to which its precepts apply. In themselves, his two principles of practical reason do not collide. It may be that, in any situation to which they apply, a course of action that will yield the greatest amount of happiness on the whole may be identical with one from which the agent would get for himself the greatest surplus of pleasure over pain. Unfortunately, experience leaves no doubt that this is not always so. Yet if any human being should ever be confronted with a situation in which he could not get for himself the greatest surplus of pleasure over pain by an action that would yield the greatest amount of happiness on the whole, then, on Sidgwick's principles, practical reason would demand of him both that he do something that would yield the greatest amount of happiness on the whole, and that he not do it. And in that case, there would be "a fundamental contradiction in one chief department of our thought"—namely, ethics.[10]

Sidgwick therefore held that our practical reason feels a "vital need" to "prov[e] or postulat[e]" a "connexion of Virtue and self-interest, if it is to be made consistent with itself."[11] But is this vital need a philosophical necessity? Proving it seems out of the question. Are we then entitled to postulate it? Only if we are entitled to postulate that there cannot be contradictions in fundamental departments of our thought; and Sidgwick acknowledged that whether we are or not is "profoundly difficult and controverted."[12] However, there are those who hold that "the edifice of physical science is really constructed of conclusions logically inferred from self-evident premises"— Sidgwick himself was so inclined—and if they are right, if "in our supposed knowledge of the world of nature propositions are commonly taken to be universally true, which yet seem to rest on no other grounds than that we have a strong disposition to accept them, and that they are indispensable to the systematic coherence of our beliefs," then, Sidgwick declared, "it will be more difficult to reject a similarly supported assumption in ethics, without opening the door to universal scepticism."[13]

Such a conclusion is less convincing than astonishing. If intuitively held principles generate a contradiction, then the beliefs to which they give rise cannot be systematically coherent, and one or more of them must be false. The natural inference from Sidgwick's argument is not that his principles must be supernaturally reconciled, but that something must be wrong with one or both of them. St. Thomas, it is hardly necessary to say, would have dismissed both.

Kant's variation on the same theme is more persuasive, because he made no mention of intuitively self-evident principles. Instead, he began by distinguishing two senses in which a good can be the "highest." A good may be *supreme*, that is, there may be no other to which it is subordinate; or it may be *perfect* (*consummatum*), that is, it may be a whole that is no part of a larger whole. A good will, that is, a will that wills for the sake of duty, is the supreme good: it is subordinate to no other, and is the sole necessary condition of anything's being unqualifiedly good. But it is not the perfect or complete good. For that

> happiness is also required, and indeed not merely in the partial eyes of a person who makes himself his end, but even in the judgment of an impartial reason, which in general regards persons in the world as ends-in-themselves. For to be in need of happiness and also worthy of it and yet not partake of it could not be in accordance with the complete volition of an omnipotent rational being, if we assume such for the sake of the argument.[14]

Now, "even though they belong to a highest good which they jointly make possible," virtue (good will) and happiness are distinct, and the maxims *Pursue virtue* and *Pursue happiness* are "wholly heterogeneous and far from being at one in respect to their supreme practical principle."[15] Nevertheless,

Since ... the furthering of the highest good, which contains [the] connection [of virtue with happiness] in its concept, is an a priori necessary object of our will and is inseparably related to the moral law, the impossibility of the former must prove the falsity of the latter also.[16]

Yet practical reason cannot entertain the possibility that the moral law is false. It must therefore postulate whatever is necessary to avoid entertaining it. And two postulates are necessary: the immortality of the soul (so that a virtuous person's failure to attain happiness in this life will not be final), and the existence of God (so that the afterlife will not repeat the failure of the present one).

This is not the place for an adequate appraisal of Kant's argument: for that I recommend Allen W. Wood's sympathetic study, *Kant's Moral Religion.*[17] However, I beg to draw your attention to a feature of it that bears on what St. Thomas would have thought of it. The theoretical possibility Kant rejects as practically absurd is that a virtuous man be required by practical reason to seek the highest good—the union of virtue and happiness—in a world in which he cannot attain it. But is any human being virtuous in the sense in question? Certainly there are those who have lived virtuous lives by ordinary human standards, and even those who have acted with heroic virtue in circumstances in which almost nobody would have; but were their wills unwaveringly good in all circumstances? If not, does the question of Kant's *absurdum practicum* arise at all?

In his later writings on religion, as Wood points out, Kant acknowledged that

in spite of the differing conditions in which we find man, a propensity to evil, to lie, to kill his fellows, or to enslave and exploit them, to adopt any course of action which leads to the satisfaction of personal wishes, is always characteristic of him. And hence Kant conclude[d] that each of us has grounds for saying, in the words of Romans 3:9: "They are all under sin,—there is none righteous, no, not one."[18]

Well, if none are virtuous, nothing in practice would follow from the world's being so ordered that, if any were virtuous, they would not be assured that they could attain happiness, and hence nothing absurd in practice would.

It does not follow, of course, that it is not our duty to strive for a more equitable distribution of happiness in the world, or that the misery many of the best of humankind have endured should not sicken us. But there is no practical absurdity in asserting, on one hand, that it is an absolute duty to act with good will, and to try to ensure happiness to all who do; and on the other, that among human beings, flawed individuals in flawed societies, the best will often fare worst. The best have never drawn the conclusion that, unless it is legitimate to postulate a supernatural world to redress the iniquities of the natural one, the duty to act with good will would be a chimera. Rather, they have agreed with Edgar, in Shakespeare's *King Lear*, that

> Men must endure
> Their going hence, ev'n as their coming hither:
> Ripeness is all.

4. St. Thomas on the Limits of Aristotelian Eudaimonia

The happiness rational beings seek on principle, according to both Kant and Sidgwick, is natural. And Kant's account of natural happiness is in the main Aristotelian. (Sidgwick's was more hedonistic than is now fashionable.) I do not think we know how St. Thomas would have answered the question, "Given that human beings are rational inhabitants of a natural universe, seeking happiness as Aristotle understood it, and that there are no nonethical grounds for asserting the existence of anything supernatural, would there be any reason to suppose that the virtuous cannot be finally unhappy?" Since he believed himself to have demonstrated nonethically that a natural universe cannot exist without a supernatural creator, he denied that the question could arise except on a false view of things; and he was not interested in answering such questions.

Even so, I think that St. Thomas would have acknowledged that false philosophical positions can be internally coherent. Hence I also think that he would have admitted that the question I have asked arises. So, although he neither answered it nor affirmed anything from which an answer can be directly deduced, it is not senseless to ask what a Thomistic answer to it would be. In the language of today, I conjecture that it would be something like this. "In deciding whether, on the false suppositions given, it is practically reasonable to accept that the virtuous can be finally unhappy, two things must be remembered about the human situation as, without revelation, it would be reasonable to believe it to be. The first is that the virtuous are far from completely virtuous. The second is that most of the evils that afflict human beings are caused by other human beings, and that there is no evil in the wills of others that has not a counterpart in our own. Given these facts, no human being can say, 'The undeserved evil that is done to me is done by beings with whom I have no kinship, and is utterly unlike anything I myself have willed.' This neither excuses it nor makes that person in any way responsible for it. But it does show that a world of beings like ourselves is one in which it is to be expected that the virtuous will often be finally and irremediably unhappy. Yet it does not follow that it is unreasonable to strive to be virtuous. On the suppositions given, the finality of tragedy in human life must be accepted."

Of course, St. Thomas did not begin either where Aristotle did in the ancient world, or Kant and Sidgwick in the modern. While accepting, as common wisdom, that no human being in the present dispensation is wholly virtuous, they would all have dismissed as mythical his assumption, which he admitted cannot be philosophically demonstrated, that the innocent beings originally created were much more than free and guiltless of wrongdoing—much more than what Pelagius took human beings now to be. Contrary to both pre-Christian and post-Christian opinion, St. Thomas held that human beings in a state of innocence had,

> as Augustine says . . . *a tranquil avoidance of sin, and while that lasted, there could be no sort of evil at all.* . . . [F]rom the very rightness of that original state . . . as long as

the soul remained subject to God, the inferior things in man would be put under the superior, and the superior would not be hindered by the inferior. (*ST* I, 94, 4c.)

In this state, human beings know God "with a higher sort of knowledge than we do now; so [their] knowledge was somehow halfway between (*media . . . inter*) knowledge in our present state and knowledge in the home country (*patria*), where God is seen through [his] essence" (*ST* I, 94, 1c.). And this knowledge was not natural, that is, not by experience or connaturality: "the first man had knowledge of everything through ideas (*species*) infused by God" (*ST* I, 94, 3 *ad* 1).

Why remind you of medieval notions that those among you who want St. Thomas to be taken seriously today may well prefer to forget? Mainly because Christianity as traditionally understood is committed to treating the myth of the Garden of Eden, which St. Thomas accepted literally, as expressing an anthropological truth. If traditional Christianity remains an intellectual option, then it remains an intellectual option that the state of human beings as we know it neither was original nor will be final. To inquire into the ultimate end of human life as though that is not an option flatly dismisses Christianity. I am unwilling to dismiss it, and I assume that you are too. But in that case, we must hold, with St. Thomas, that just as it would be a mistake to infer, with respect to the happiness they can attain, that human beings originally were what they now are, so it would be a mistake to infer that they always will be what they now are. St. Thomas took it to be a revealed truth that in their original state human beings once knew God by a halfway infused knowledge they can no longer have. And he also held that, in their *patria*, the world to come, they will know God directly.

What this direct knowledge will be they cannot know now. But in the *Summa contra gentiles*, assuming the correctness of Aristotle's theory that human thought about anything is by way of something in the human mind that serves as an intelligible species of it, St. Thomas ventured to draw the following conclusions about it.

> [T]he divine essence may be related to the created intellect as an intelligible species by which it understands. . . . Yet, [the divine essence] cannot be the form of [a created intellect] in its natural being, for the result of this would be that, once joined to [that created intellect], it would make up one nature. This could not be, since the divine intellect is in itself perfect in its own nature. But an intelligible species, united with an intellect, does not make up a nature; rather, it perfects it for [an act of] understanding. . . . This immediate vision of God is promised us in Scripture: "We see now through a glass darkly; but then face to face" (*ICor.* 13: 12). It is wrong to understand this in a corporeal way, picturing in our imagination a bodily face of the Divinity. . . . [W]e shall see God face to face, in the sense that we shall see him without a medium, as is true when we see a man face to face. (*SCG* III, 51, 4–5)

If we presuppose that a direct vision of God is attainable by divine grace, and that it will totally satisfy those who are granted it, then our inquiry into what is the happiness that all men seek is transformed.

There are two cases to consider. The first, and philosophically the less interesting, is that of those who believe the Christian revelation. Even Aristotle, in a passage to which St. Thomas drew attention, noted that because *eudaimonia* is a *telos* that is "telic" in every way, even those who are active in accordance with complete virtue, and are sufficiently equipped with external goods throughout a complete life, can only be said to be *makarioi* as men are; for, since the future is always obscure to them, their *eudaimonia* is not "telic" in every way.[19] By contrast, nobody who believes the Christian revelation can seriously imagine that those who see God face to face can have anything more to want: their end as intellectual beings would be completely attained (*ST* I–II, 3, 8c.).

The more interesting case is that of those who do not believe the Christian revelation. St. Thomas's view of their state reminded me of the analysis of desire generally offered by Bertrand Russell in his *Analysis of Mind*, one of the several volumes in which, according to C. D. Broad, he "laboured ... to make a coherent philosophy out of the thin crudities of behaviourism."[20] According to Russell, what is essential to desire is an initial state of a person (called "discomfort") that gives rise to restless activity which continues until a new state is reached in which restless activity ceases. What is desired is not what the person believes he seeks, but what in fact puts an end to his discomfort.[21] Now, according to St. Thomas, although the only thing that will put an end to the restless striving of human beings is the vision of God, most of them do not know it. Moreover, except by revelation, nobody can know it, not even those in a state of innocence.

> [F]or the direction of one's own and others' lives, besides knowledge of things that can be learned naturally, one needs to know things beyond natural knowledge, because human life is directed to a certain supernatural end; and so for the direction of our life it is necessary to know matters of faith. (*ST* I, 94, 3c.)

We can have natural knowledge that the only thing that will pacify us is some sort of activity in accordance with virtue, completely realized in complete life (cf. *ST* I–II, 3, 2c.). But we can learn about that sort of activity only by faith, and can share in it only by grace.

> [T]he final happiness (*beatitudo*) prepared for the saints surpasses both the intellect and the will of man. *Eye hath not seen, nor ear heard, neither hath it entered into the heart of man, what things God hath prepared for them that love him.* (*ST* I–II, 5, 5c.)

In this way, Aristotle's theory of the end of human life, while preserved, is transformed.[22]

5. Divine Comedy

St. Thomas's transformation of Aristotle's theory of happiness also transforms the problem of whether human life is ultimately tragic. Not, however, by finding anything ethically impossible in its being tragic.

The cardinal point in St. Thomas's theory is that the ultimate end of human life is not the state of blessedness reached when the vision of God is attained, but is pre-existent, God himself. There is no logical repugnance in the supposition that God should so have ordered things that human beings would perish at death like other animals. If so, their desire to know God directly would never be satisfied; and they would never gain complete happiness. Yet God would exist for all that. And although human beings could not attain their ultimate end through their own operation, in knowing and loving God, they could, like the rest of creation, participate in the divine perfection according to their nature, which although intellectual, is finite and corpo-real. They could understand enough of the moral life and of the physical world—including that it is created by an infinite first cause—to deserve to be called the paragon of animals. Nothing created, not even the knowing and loving of God by created beings, increases the amount of goodness that exists. If God alone existed things would be as good as they now are. God has no need to create anything (cf. *SCG* I, 81, 2–4; *ST* I, 104, 3c.). A created world in which human beings at best gain the human happiness Aristotle describes would not be repugnant to practical reason.

St. Thomas, if I have reconstructed his position correctly, held that, from the point of view of human beings, things are unimaginably better than philosophy gives them any reason to hope. To those who agree with the great scientist and (humanly speaking) good man, William Kingdon Clifford, that it is a moral duty to dismiss any opinion that cannot be demonstrated, St. Thomas did wrong in accepting the Christian revelation without scientific or philosophical demonstration. I do not think he did. Nor do I think that, in order to justify disagreeing with Clifford, we must resort, like William James, to arguing that, when a proposition cannot be demon-strated to be either true or false, we are entitled to believe whatever makes for ben-eficial results in practice.[23] On this topic, however, I cannot here say much.[24] Assuming that a divine creator is not a philosophical impossibility, if such a creator should reveal himself to intellectual creatures (as in the alleged revelation of the Torah to Moses), I do not see how authenticity of that revelation could be *philosophically* dem-onstrated. As long as we cannot see God directly, he can only reveal himself by signs; and, from the point of view of philosophy, signs are intractably ambiguous. A theory here is certainly needed. And no doubt philosophy has something to contribute to developing one; but such a theory could not strictly be a part of philosophy.

If my argument is sound, St. Thomas held that Aristotle was mistaken when he maintained that the ultimate end of human life is what *he* called *eudaimonia*. Apart from revelation, the ultimate end is God, and the image of God in every human being. Naturally, like all living things, human beings also seek, by such means as they think permissible, the *telos* that is theirs by nature—*eudaimonia*. But even though, by grace, they so act in this life as to attain their ultimate end in the next, they may nevertheless fail to attain anything Aristotle would have described as *eudaimonia*. Of course, what Aristotle accounted a failure, St. Thomas did not. He saved Aristotle's thesis that the ultimate end of human life is *eudaimonia* by two drastic amendments. First, he rein-terpreted *eudaimonia* as what he called *beatitudo*: the total satisfaction of the desires of an intellectual creature by a vision of God's essence unmediated by any intermediary *species intelligibilis* or concept. Second, he denied that human beings could either attain *beatitudo*, or even learn what it really is, except by grace. *Beatitudo*, so understood, is not only a far greater thing than Aristotle ever thought *eudaimonia* to be, but it is in principle attainable by all human beings, no matter what their birth or fortune in life. Saved in this way, of course, the thesis ceases to be a philosophical one.

A final thought. In view of his theory of its ultimate end, Aristotle could not but conclude that human life is a failure for most of us, and a tragedy for many of the best of us. In doing so, he was sagacious as well as candid. By contrast, the efforts of two of the best of his successors, Kant and Sidgwick, to reach a conclusion more cheerful than his, were at best excusable. St. Thomas's way of making Aristotle's teaching cheerful, while it would have been as foolish to the Greeks as St. Paul's theology was, has the merit of being inexcusable.

Notes

© 1985 Marquette University Press. Published with permission.
The texts of the two works of St. Thomas I used throughout are:

(i) *Summa contra gentiles*. Editio Leonina manualis. Turin and Rome: Casa Editrice Marietta, 1946. Abbreviated as "*SCG.*"

(ii) *Summa theologiae*. 60 vols. London and New York: Blackfriars, in conjunction with Eyre and Spottiswoode and McGraw Hill, 1963–76. (General Index issued in 1981 as vol. 61.) Abbreviated as "*ST.*"

Responsibility for translations is mine. However, in *Summa contra gentiles*, of which I quote only from parts I and III, I follow fairly closely the renderings of Anton C. Pegis and Vernon J. Bourke in the edition in five volumes republished by the University of Notre Dame Press in 1975. Most of my renderings of *Summa theologiae* take those of the Blackfriars edition as their point of departure, but are usually more literal.

1. John Duns Scotus, *De primo principio*, text rev. and trans. Evan Roche O.F.M. (St. Bonaventure, New York: The Franciscan Institute, 1949), chap. 2, concl. 5 (pp. 116–19). Although I should have been helpless without Fr. Roche's version, I have made bold to depart from it, hoping that my revised version would be more intelligible when read aloud. Scotus's text, from which I have translated excerpts, is as follows: *Probatur: quia finis non est causa nisi inquantum ab ipso tamquam a priore essentialiter dependet esse finiti. Patet, quia quaelibet causa est sic prior inquantum causa. Non autem dependet finitum quantum ad esse a fine ut sic priore, nisi inquantum finis ut amatus movet efficiens ad dandum illi esse, ita quod efficiens non daret esse in suo genere nisi fine causante in sua causalitate. Nihil ergo causat finis, nisi quod efficitur ab efficiente qua amante finem.*

Hic corollarium sequitur non tacendum, quod falsa imaginatio est de fine, quod illud est causa finalis entis, quod est operatio ultima vel objectum, quod per illam operationem attingitur. Si intelligatur quod tale inquantum tale est causa finalis, falsum est, quia illud consequitur esse; nec esse finiti dependet essentialiter ab illo inquantum tale, sed praecise illud, propter quod amatum ab efficiente, efficiens facit aliquid esse, quia ordinatum ad amatum, illud inquantum tale est causa finalis facti.

2. *Summa theologiae* I–II, 1, 8c.

3. Ibid., I–II, 100, 6c.

4. Sir David Ross, *Kant's Ethical Theory* (Oxford: Clarendon Press, 1959), p. 51.

5. Cf. David Hume, *Enquiries into the Human Understanding and into the Principles of Morals*, ed. L. A. Selby-Bigge, 2d ed. (Oxford: Clarendon Press, 1902), pp. 221–22, 272–79.

6. In "Is Thomas Aquinas a Natural Law Ethicist?" *Monist* 18 (1974): 52–66, Vernon J. Bourke surveys the corpus of St. Thomas's ethical writings, and usefully comments on differences between them. He confesses that, as a result, "the theory of right reason seems to me to take precedence [in St. Thomas's work] over the theory of natural law" (p. 66). This concedes too much to antirationalist conceptions of law. To St. Thomas, I suspect, Professor Bourke's distinction would be without a difference.

7. Henry Sidgwick, *The Methods of Ethics*, 7th ed. (London: Macmillan, 1907), p. 411.

8. Ibid., p. 121.

9. Jerome B. Schneewind, *Sidgwick's Ethics and Victorian Moral Theory* (Oxford: Clarendon Press, 1977), chap. 13, is the best treatment of these topics. Cf. my review essay, "A New Sidgwick?" in *Ethics* 90 (1980): 282–95, esp. 288–89 and 294–95.

10. Sidgwick, *Methods of Ethics*, p. 508.

11. Ibid.

12. Ibid.

13. Ibid., p. 509.

14. Immanuel Kant, *Kritik der praktischen Vernunft* (Riga: Hartnoch, 1788), pp. 198–99 (Ak. ed., vol. 5, p. 114), trans. L. W. Beck.

15. Ibid., p. 202 (Ak. ed., p. 113), trans. Beck.

16. Ibid., p. 205 (Ak. ed., p. 114), trans. Beck.

17. Ithaca, New York: Cornell University Press, 1970.

18. Wood, *Kant's Moral Religion*, p. 226.

19. Aristotle, *Nicomachean Ethics* I, 1101ª18–22; quoted by St. Thomas, *ST* I–II, 3, 2 *ad* 4.

20. Bertrand Russell, *The Analysis of Mind* (London: Allen and Unwin, 1921). Cf. C. D. Broad, *Examination of McTaggart's Philosophy*, vol. 1 (Cambridge: Cambridge University Press, 1933), p. li.

21. Russell, *Analysis of Mind*, pp. 65–68.

22. In pointing out the limits of Aristotle's conception of *eudaimonia* as the end of human life, I do not think that I have asserted anything that Aristotelians who are also Thomists would deny. But they do not assert it—or not as stridently as I do. Cf. Henry B. Veatch, *Rational Man* (Bloomington: Indiana University Press, 1962), pp. 177–79; and *Aristotle* (Bloomington: Indiana University Press, 1974), pp. 103–11, 124–27.

23. William James, in his essay "The Will to Believe," originally published in the *New World*, June 1896, quoted Clifford at length in developing his alternative view. The version I have used is that in William James, *Essays in Pragmatism*, ed. Alburey Castell (New York: Hafner, 1948).

24. See chapter 1, "Philosophy and the Possibility of Religious Orthodoxy," in this book.

SIX

The Scholastic Theory of Moral Law in the Modern World

lthough no more than one religion can be true, it is now generally accepted that there may be honest mistakes about whether a given religion is the true one. Yet neither scholastic philosophers nor most plain men have yet been brought to agree that there may be honest fundamental mistakes about morality. Differences about morality are socially divisive, because many plain men consider that the state ought to enforce morality by legislation, if it can do so without infringing its citizens' moral rights. I remember that the church in which I was brought up as a child in Australia provoked great hostility by supporting legislation to close all liquor bars, in order to make it difficult to commit the sin of drinking alcohol. Since there are more drinkers than would-be divorcers, that hostility was much greater than that aroused toward the Catholic Church in New York by the opposition of some Catholics to changes in the divorce laws. Such examples remind us that the question I propose to discuss: "How can what belongs to common morality be distinguished from what belongs to the way of life of a particular religion?" is, if nothing else, a timely one.

Yet it is not merely timely. St. Thomas himself recognized that only some precepts of the divine law (the revealed positive law of God) are also precepts of the natural law (the law of reason "whereby each one knows, and is conscious of, what is good and what is evil"[1]). Those precepts of the divine law that are not precepts of natural law are not binding on non-Christians. Undoubtedly, when the Church has been powerful, its members have been tempted to impose religious duties on non-

Christians in the name of morality; and when it has been weak, to draw back from denouncing moral wrongs on the plea that the wrongdoers are outside the Church's jurisdiction. Yet the scholastic theory of natural law provides a foundation for distinguishing the duty to obey the moral law, which for Christians is both moral and religious, from purely religious duties that fall outside common morality. It is therefore worth inquiring whether the scholastic theory may become common ground for Christian and non-Christian philosophers. If St. Thomas was right, there is no reason why it should not.

1. The Natural Law and Contemporary Analytic Philosophy

My first thesis, then, is that the scholastic theory of natural law, in particular, St. Thomas's version of it, may have something to offer contemporary non-Christian moral philosophy.[2] There are two reasons for dismissing this thesis as a fantastic absurdity. The first is derived from a cardinal doctrine of modern ethical theory, the second from a cardinal doctrine of scholasticism.

The vast majority of analytic philosophers would accept the doctrine of the autonomy of ethics as fundamental. Following A. N. Prior, that doctrine may be formulated as follows: "the claim to deduce ethical propositions from ones which are admitted to be non-ethical"[3] is fallacious. It is true that this doctrine has recently been questioned;[4] but I do not think that it has been shaken. If the scholastic theory of natural law should imply that ethics is not autonomous, it could have no serious influence on analytic ethical theory. Yet St. Thomas himself appears to imply it, by deriving the first precept of the natural law, *bonum est faciendum et prosequendum, et malum vitandum*, from a nonethical statement about the nature of good, *bonum est quod omnia appetunt.*[5]

Fortunately for my thesis, what St. Thomas said need not be interpreted as denying the autonomy of ethics. He certainly did not mean that we all ought to do and promote whatever we in fact seek; for he admitted that many of us seek what is evil. His statement that *good is that which all things seek* must be understood as meaning that good is that which all things *by nature* seek; and, since man is a rational animal, applied to man it means that human good is that which all men seek *by virtue of their nature as rational animals.* Evildoers choose to do and to promote what is opposed to what they seek by virtue of their rational nature; they affront their own reason. Now I do not think that any analytic philosopher would deny that the words *"quod omnia appetunt,"* so understood, express an ethical concept. The objection to my thesis from the analytic side therefore fails: the scholastic theory of natural law is not incompatible with the autonomy of ethics, or at least is not obviously so.

The objection from the scholastic side goes deeper. The scholastic philosophers were theologians too, and every great scholastic system is Christian: that is, its purely philosophical part is presented as not merely incomplete and incompletable by philosophy alone, but as finding its completion in revealed theology. It is, therefore, legitimate to doubt whether the theory of natural law is intelligible to philosophy alone. Partly for this reason, Miss G. E. M. Anscombe has expressed the view that the scholastic theory of moral law is theological in essence, and that the part of scholastic moral theory that is philosophical is the Aristotelian theory of the cardinal virtues.[6] And it cannot be denied that St. Thomas defines natural law theologically: having explained that a rational creature is subject to divine providence in a higher way than a brute, in that it partakes of the divine reason, he lays it down that "such participation of the eternal law in a rational creature is called natural law."[7] The eternal law, being "the very Idea of the government of things existing in God the ruler of the universe,"[8] is studied by theology rather than by philosophy.

Yet from the fact that St. Thomas, in a theological work, defines natural law theologically, it follows neither that it cannot be defined philosophically, nor that a philosophical definition would be incomplete, as, according to St. Thomas, any account of the natural end of man that neglected divine revelation would be incomplete. Although this is not stated in terms by St. Thomas, it is implied by his assertion that "all men know . . . the common principles of the natural law."[9] It is also presupposed in his derivations of the various precepts of the natural law, in none of which does he make any appeal to revealed theology. Nor does he explicitly draw upon natural theology, except in deriving precepts having to do with divine worship.

At this point, St. Thomas can be instructively contrasted with Kant. In an excellent Thomist textbook of Ethics I found the following:

> The distinctive thing about the rationally free agent is not, as Kant thought, that he is a law unto himself. Man is not the ultimate source or principle of the moral law. Rather, human reason is subject to the laws of reality, which come from the divine reason.

These remarks exhibit a misunderstanding precisely opposite to the misunderstanding that St. Thomas has no strictly philosophical conception of natural law. Kant defines the moral law philosophically. After defining an objective principle as "valid for every rational being,"[10] he goes on to say that if there is to be a moral law for men, i.e., a categorical imperative, "it must be such that from the idea of something which is necessarily an end for everyone because it is an *end in itself*, it forms an *objective* principle of the will."[11] I take it to be patent that Kant is not saying that a rational being is a law unto himself: such a being must indeed determine for himself what the law is, but he must do so according to *objective* principles. And those objective principles are valid for every rational being because they have an objective foundation in "something which is necessarily an end for everyone because it is an end in itself."

Writing as a philosopher, Kant defined the moral law without reference to God. Yet he held, as a theologian, that the moral law is derived from the divine reason. In the *Groundwork* he was at pains to point out that the divine will cannot be said to be subject to the objective principles of the moral law as to imperatives, because it is "already of itself necessarily in harmony with [them]."[12]

Kant and St. Thomas differ about what the fundamental principles of the moral law are, although not as much as many believe; but they do not differ in any significant way about the relation between what St. Thomas would call the "natural law" and what he would call the "eternal law." From the point of view of moral philosophy, the natural law is a set of precepts the binding force of which can be ascertained by human reason; from the point of view of theology, it is that part of what God eternally and rationally wills that can be grasped by human reason as binding upon human beings (Kant would say, upon all rational beings). Just as in theology Kant may agree with St. Thomas that the moral law is a participation of the eternal law in a rational creature, so in moral philosophy St. Thomas may agree with Kant that in determining what the precepts of the natural law are, theological considerations are out of place.

On this point, what holds of Kant also holds of contemporary analytic philosophy.

2. Scholastic Derivations of the Precepts of the Natural Law

If nonscholastic philosophers have much to learn from what scholastic philosophers have accomplished in the theory of natural law, why have they not done so? Prejudice and ignorance are part of the explanation. But they are not the whole of it. My second thesis is that, despite what has been accomplished, no adequate scholastic *philosophy* of natural law has yet been elaborated. That, too, must enter into any satisfactory explanation of why nonscholastic philosophers have neglected the scholastic achievement. It should also be mentioned in any explanation of why explicit natural law arguments are rarely found convincing by non-Catholics.

I shall try to establish my second thesis by examining St. Thomas's derivation of a precept of the natural law that is not very controversial: the precept that lying (*mendacium*) is evil and to be avoided. St. Thomas defines a lie as speech contrary to the speaker's mind,[13] and he holds lying so defined to be prohibited by the natural law for the following reason:

> . . . since words are naturally signs of thoughts, it is unnatural and wrong for anyone by speech to signify something he does not have in his mind. (*Summa theologiae* II–II, 110, 3)

This argument plainly presupposes an unstated principle, namely, that if an activity has a natural end, then it is unnatural and wrong voluntarily to engage in that activity in such a way as to prevent the attainment of its end. Both this presupposition, and St. Thomas's explicit premise, that the natural end of speech is to signify what the speaker thinks, may be questioned.

What is meant by the "natural end" of a process? The concept is Aristotelian, and it is too fundamental to be usefully defined. Natural processes go on of themselves, as natural substances come into being from other natural substances, without the help of any artificer. Living things, the best specimens of natural substances, are generated, grow, and decay in characteristic ways. It is usual to speak and think of them as tending to grow to maturity, and as resisting decay. In general, Aristotle would say of such things that their natural end is to achieve the state of maturity characteristic of their species. Similarly, of the parts of a thing which has a natural end, Aristotle would say that their natural end is to contribute to the efficient functioning of the whole: thus, the natural end of an eye is to enable its possessor to see. The same also holds of processes that go on in natural things: if they contribute to the efficient functioning of the thing in which they occur, as most of them do, then their natural end is to make that contribution. It makes no difference whether those processes are voluntary or involuntary. Thus the natural end of the involuntary process of breathing is (on Aristotelian principles, although Aristotle did not know it) to convey oxygen to the blood, and to expel carbon dioxide from the lungs; and the natural end of the voluntary process of eating is to convey food to the digestive organs.

It cannot be too strongly insisted upon that Aristotle neither personifies nature nor endows it with *conscious* purpose. Conscious purposes are found in nature, in intelligent beings; but most natural ends or purposes are not conscious. Art imitates nature, but nature is not an artificer.[14] "[T]hose things are natural which, by a continuous movement originated from an internal principle, arrive at some completion: the same completion is not reached from every principle; nor any chance completion; but always the tendency in each is towards the same end, if there is no impediment."[15]

I will not question that there are, in Aristotle's sense, natural things and natural processes. However, the use in ethics to which Aristotle and St. Thomas put the concept of a natural end presupposes more than that. Above all, it presupposes that it is wrong to frustrate nature. This presupposition must, of course, be qualified. When a cow eats grass, it prevents that grass from completing its natural growth; and when a man slaughters and eats or sells the flesh of a cow, he prevents that cow from completing its natural growth. Hence, St. Thomas lays it down that the subrational part of nature is for the use of the rational part.[16] This, if I understand it correctly, is an ethical and not a physical principle. From the point of view of physics, the flesh of cattle is no more naturally food for man than is the blood of man food for mosquitoes. But, although he allows man's right to use nonrational natural things for his own purposes, St. Thomas denies that he may voluntarily engage in any natural activity, if he does so in such a way as to prevent that activity from arriving at its natural end. If you voluntarily engage in eating, you must not increase your capacity to eat by resorting, as some Romans did, to the vomitorium; for that would prevent the activity of eating from arriving at its natural end of digestion.

A second presupposition, which has important moral consequences, is that natural things and processes have only one end, or have one that is pre-eminent. Aristotle seems to have thought this obvious. "Nature," he declared in the *Politics*, "is not niggardly, like the smith who fashions the Delphian knife for many uses; she makes each thing for a single use."[17] Eating both nourishes and gives pleasure; but Aristotle would consider it obvious that the pre-eminent natural end of eating is nourishment, not pleasure.

We are now in a position to decide upon the validity or otherwise of St. Thomas's demonstration that lying is wrong. In my opinion, neither its premise, that the natural end of speech is to express what is in the speaker's mind, nor its presupposition, that it is wrong voluntarily to engage in a natural activity and to prevent that activity from arriving at its natural end, is evident upon reflection. Let me take each in turn.

It is simply not true that speech is related to its alleged end of expressing what is in the speaker's mind in the way in which eating is related to nourishment, or the eye to seeing. If eating is not completed by digestion, the body has been interfered with in some way; and an eye in which there is no sight is either defective or damaged. But, from the point of view of natural science, a lying speech act is not, per se, either defective or interfered with. If speech acts have a natural end, in Aristotle's sense, it is to express whatever thought the speaker chooses to express.

It is, indeed, possible to argue that veracity must be the norm for speech acts. As Professor J. M. Cameron has observed in his Terry Lectures, "Lying could not be the norm for purely logical reasons, since the point of telling a lie is that it should be taken to be the truth and this could not happen unless truth-telling were the norm."[18] But it does not follow that the natural end of a speech act is to conform to that norm; for a thing tends towards its natural end provided there is no impediment, and a lying speech act does not in the least tend toward truth. Nor, conceding that veracity is the norm for speech, does it appear to follow that every speech act ought to conform to that norm. If people wish to communicate by speech, then logically they must normally tell the truth—but not always. And this logical necessity does not appear to me to be a moral obligation. It holds for liars and truth-tellers alike.

St. Thomas's presupposition that it is wrong voluntarily to engage in any natural activity in such a way as to prevent it from arriving at its natural end, is equally vulnerable. If St. Thomas considers that rational beings have the right to interfere with and even destroy subrational natural things for their own purposes, why should he think it wrong per se for them to interfere, for their own purposes, with the natural activities in which they engage? I am aware that, in asking this, I shall appear to some to be frivolous and wanting in natural piety. But any philosopher who wishes to argue as St. Thomas does should take account of the fact that I am by no means alone. In the sagacious and lucid introduction to his translation of the third and fourth books of Aristotle's *Politics*, Richard Robinson has stated my objection more sharply than I:

> Once we have explicitly asked ourselves why we should do anything just because nature does it, or why we should aid nature in her purposes, we see that there is no reason why we should. Let nature look to her own purposes, if she has any. *We* will look to *ours*.[19]

3. Strengths and Weaknesses in the Scholastic Theory of Natural Law

It does not follow from the objections I have urged against St. Thomas's discussion of lying that his theory of the natural law is false. St. Thomas's definition of the natural law, and his statement of its first precept, neither of which I desire to question, are logically separable from his derivation of further precepts from the first precept. Indeed, I make bold to say that one reason why the scholastic theory has had less influence outside Catholic circles than it merits, is that it is assumed to be a seamless unity, and that little is known of it but arguments like St. Thomas's against lying. It is widely believed that if you reject such arguments (that against artificial contraception is, of course, the best known) then you must deny that there is a natural law: that is, you must abandon the conception of the moral law as a matter of human reason.

If my objections to St. Thomas's discussion of lying are just, then St. Thomas was mistaken in looking to Aristotelian natural philosophy for a way of specifying the goods that the natural law bids us seek, and the evils it bids us avoid. But nothing in his definition of natural law obliged him to make that mistake. Nor did anything in Aristotle's *Ethics* do so. I am inclined to conjecture that he was led to make it by his belief in creation: accepting Aristotle's views about natural teleology, and believing that the natural world was created by God, it may have seemed reasonable to treat the ends of natural things and processes not only as divinely appointed, but as divinely sanctioned. Yet, as we have seen, St. Thomas himself invoked the doctrine of the subordination of the weaker and less perfect in nature to the stronger and more perfect,[20] to justify man's interference with *some* natural processes.

I do not wish to give the impression that the only part of the scholastic theory of the natural law that I think strong is its foundation, or that I wish to level the edifice erected by the scholastics on that foundation. The treatment in scholastic philosophy of specific moral questions is every whit as important as the treatment there of first principles. Indeed, if one looks for exact and detailed inquiry into the more notorious moral difficulties, there is almost nowhere to go in contemporary philosophy except to the writings of the neoscholastics.

4. Prospect

My final thesis is that in order to correct the weakness in the scholastic theory of natural law I believe myself to have detected, it is necessary to re-examine, without theological preconceptions, the philosophical problem of how to derive specific moral precepts from the first precept of the natural law. I venture to suggest a possible way of doing so.

St. Thomas's recognition of subordination in nature, and his doctrine that "man is the end of the whole order of generation,"[21] suggests that he might have accepted Kant's principle that "man, and in general every rational being, exists as an end in himself, not merely as a means for arbitrary use by this or that will."[22] The principle is, in my opinion, self-evident. It must not be interpreted as implying that man is not ordered towards anything higher, as St. Thomas held that he is ordered to God, but rather as implying that if he is so ordered, it must be in a way consistent with his nature as an end. This is, of course, amply acknowledged in Christian theology.

Kant's principle, which I take to be implicit in the work of St. Thomas, furnishes a way of specifying good and evil. Let me sketch how it might be applied to the case of lying. According to it, any act by the nature of which a rational being is used *merely* as a means is evil; and hence, by the first precept of the natural law, is to be avoided. But, in ordinary conditions of free communication, to tell another something that you do not believe is to use him merely as a means. By arrogating to yourself the right to misinform him merely because for some reason you so choose, you treat him merely as a means to your ends. Hence in ordinary conditions of free communication, lying to others is unconditionally prohibited.

In conditions of violence, as for example in the classic case of a would-be murderer who demands with threats to be told in which direction somebody he is pursuing has made off, the situation is otherwise. By employing or threatening violence, the questioner has already treated the person questioned merely as a means. He has no right to be told anything, and the person questioned is entitled to protect himself, and the pursued quarry, by a lie. (It is a question whether the word "lie" should be used in such a case. Perhaps the qualification, "in conditions of free communication," should be added to St. Thomas's definition.)

In the cases I have considered, our principle yields results that conform to common sense, and to the moral tradition generally, although in the latter case, under the influence of St. Thomas's argument, scholastic philosophers are apt either to be absurdly rigorous, or to explain away the justified lie by postulating improbable speech conventions (e.g., the so-called broad mental reservation). But there are innumerable difficult cases. For example, what is it permissible to do when you are obliged to keep a secret, and find yourself in a situation, probably by your own fault, in which you will reveal the secret whether you answer a question truthfully or refuse to answer it? Any principle by which such cases are other than difficult might be dismissed on that ground alone. I submit that Kant's principle both exhibits their difficulty, and yet contains resources for dealing with them. It is instructive, armed with that principle, to work through the moral cases in a good manual of casuistry.

Lest I should appear to be recommending the absorption of scholastic moral philosophy into Kantianism, may I repeat that I am pleading for a fresh and purely philosophical approach to the problem of deriving the specific moral precepts of the natural law, and that one of my reasons for suggesting that Kant's principle might be invoked in such derivations was that I took it to be implicit in St. Thomas's thought. Other suggestions ought also to be explored. Far from desiring that scholastic moral philosophy be absorbed in Kantianism, I hope that the influence of scholasticism may help us to free what is true in Kant's moral philosophy, which is a great deal, from the eccentric moral opinions Kant fallaciously drew from his principles.

That the existing scholastic theory of natural law has an important contribution to make to any rational theory of morality is beyond question. A thoroughly reconsidered and purely philosophical theory of natural law could do even more. It could provide the foundation of that rational moral consensus which is the necessary cement of a pluralist society.

Notes

From *Proceedings of the American Catholic Philosophical Association* (Volume 40: "Scholasticism in the Modern World"). © American Catholic Philosophical Association 1966. Printed with the permission of the American Catholic Philosophical Association.

1. Gloss on *Rom.* 2:14, quoted by St. Thomas, *Summa theologiae* I–II, 91, 2.

2. In the original version of the essay, this section begins with the following paragraph. Ed.

The non-scholastic philosophers I shall have in mind throughout this paper are those working in the tradition variously labeled "analytic," or "linguistic," or even "empiricist." I shall not define it, beyond saying that it is the tradition now dominant in non-Catholic professional philosophy in North America, the British Commonwealth and northwestern Europe except for France and Germany. The reason why I have this sort of nonscholastic philosophy in mind, and not existential philosophy, which is dominant in France, Germany, and southwestern Europe, and strongly represented in other countries, is that existential philosophy concerns itself with the nature of authentic moral choice, rather than with the question of the rightness or wrongness of what is chosen. To it, the theory of the natural law is at best an irrelevancy and at worst bad faith. In analytic philosophy, on the other hand, no question is more anxiously debated than how the rightness or wrongness of an act can be established.

3. A. N. Prior, *Logic and the Basis of Ethics* (Oxford: Clarendon Press, 1949), p. 95.

4. E.g., by John Searle, "How to Derive 'Ought' from 'Is,'" *Philosophical Review* 73 (1964): 43–58; Max Black, "The Gap Between 'Is' and 'Should,'" ibid., 165–81. G. J. Warnock's verdict on the matter is of interest: "the antinaturalist thesis . . . while probably true, has really no great importance for moral philosophy. It is a thesis . . . about the 'general theory' of evaluation . . ." *Contemporary Moral Philosophy* (London: Macmillan, 1967), p. 68.

5. *Summa theologiae* I–II, 94, 2.

6. "Modern Moral Philosophy," *Philosophy* 33 (1958): 1–19. In Miss Anscombe's position, I can find no place for natural law; she makes all law positive, i.e., either divine or human.

7. *Summa theologiae* I–II, 91, 2.

8. "[I]psa ratio gubernationis rerum in Deo sicut in principe universitatis existens" (*Summa theologiae* I–II, 91, 1).

9. *Summa theologiae* I–II, 93, 2.

10. Immanuel Kant, *Groundwork of the Metaphysic of Morals*, trans. H. J. Paton (New York: Harper and Row, 1964; originally published in 1948 by the Hutchinson University Library under the title *The Moral Law, or Kant's Groundwork of the Metaphysic of Morals*), p. 88 (2d German ed., p. 51n).

11. Ibid., p. 96 (2d German ed., p. 66).

12. Ibid., p. 81 (2d German ed., p. 39).

13. This is far more satisfactory than St. Augustine's "a false statement uttered with intent to deceive," for reasons explained by St. Thomas (*Summa theologiae* II–II, 110, 1 *ad* 1, 3). Yet variants of St. Augustine's definition still turn up in contemporary analytic philosophy. E.g., C. D. Broad, *Five Types of Ethical Theory* (London: K. Paul, Trench, Trubner, 1930), p. 209.

14. Aristotle, *Physics* II, 199^{b}25–31.

15. Aristotle, *Physics*, trans. R. P. Hardie and R. K. Gaye, II, 199^{b}15–19.

16. St. Thomas Aquinas, *Summa contra gentiles* III, 22, 8.

17. Aristotle, *Politics*, trans. Benjamin Jowett, I, 1252^{b}1–5.

18. J. M. Cameron, *Images of Authority* (New Haven: Yale University Press, 1966), p. 27. Professor Cameron does not use this premise in the way I object to. He argues only that mendacity could not count as a moral *virtue*.

19. *Aristotle's Politics Books III and IV*, trans. with introduction and comments by Richard Robinson (Oxford: Clarendon Press, 1962), p. xxiii.

20. "... quaedam etiam perfectiora et virtuosiora ex quibusdam imperfectioribus et infirmioribus [nutrimentum habent]" (*Summa contra gentiles* III, 22, 8).

21. *Summa contra gentiles* III, 22, 7.

22. *Groundwork*, p. 95 (2d German ed., p. 64).

SEVEN

Teleology and Consistency in Theories of Morality as Natural Law

This paper resembles a carnival monster: a great papier-maché head, in which controversial conclusions about the teleological foundation of the conception of morality as natural law are drawn from confessedly indirect evidence, supported by a ridiculously unimpressive body and legs in which those conclusions are tested by investigating how any theory of natural law can meet the fashionable contemporary charge that it cannot be consistent. Still, however grotesque my monster, its topic is timely.

Its first part, in which I present my unorthodox view of St. Thomas Aquinas's theory of natural law, is the one most directly and deeply indebted to the philosopher we are met to honor—Henry Veatch. As I look back on the quarter of a century in which I have known him, it is impossible to disregard the numerous topics on which he has had no choice but to try to set me right, or to escape acknowledging that on most of them, including some nonphilosophical ones in comparison with which nothing philosophical matters much except the fundamentals of all thought whatever, after stubborn resistance I have tamely succumbed. It would be agreeable to my self-esteem to call to mind some matter of philosophical importance in which Henry has capitulated to a view of mine; but in confessing that I cannot, I must also confess that, on the matters on which we persist in differing, I wish I were more confident that my future will be less ignominious than my past.

I

In several recent articles Henry Veatch has powerfully upheld the position taken in *For an Ontology of Morals* that any true moral theory must, like Aristotle's, be eudaimonistic, and primarily concerned with virtue rather than with law.[1] In doing so he has sided, although in his inimitably original way, with the main body of Thomist philosophers. Of course neither he nor any other Thomist has ever denied that the Jewish and Stoic conception of moral law is an integral element in Christian ethics, nor has he ever pretended that Aristotle anticipated that conception—here some other Thomists have been less accurate. And finally, he has never failed to recognize that, unlike Aristotle's, St. Thomas's ethics is in part a revealed moral theology, in which neither the greatest virtues nor the highest states human beings can attain are discoverable philosophically. Moral philosophy is therefore at best only a part of ethics. And certain notions that have recently been agitated in the philosophical journals, for example that of a sanctity that is purely moral, are therefore strictly unintelligible.[2]

It has been said that the best is the enemy of the good; and I believe that in a Christianized Aristotelian eudaimonism, in which eudaimonia is identified with the intellectual good, the beatific vision gets in the way of our grasping certain essential truths about the everyday moral good, even though it is perfectly compatible with them. Aristotle has told us why.[3] The being whom to see is the supernatural end of all rational creatures, the only thing that will satisfy the longing they have by virtue of being rational, is nevertheless not a natural object of the human intellect. Our philosophical habitation is in the physical world of animate and inanimate creatures, so far as we can arrive at intelligent beliefs about it by reflecting on what is offered to us in sensation. The Christian faith, and the Jewish faith too, tell us that in the end there is no eudaimonia for human beings unless they are of good will. But, since no merely philosophical theory of eudaimonia can be true, no moral theory of good will that rests on a purely philosophical theory of eudaimonia can be well founded; and philosophical experience supports Kant's contention that building on such a foundation is always disastrous.

Perhaps there is a hint of this in Aristotle's famous statement of what eudaimonia, the human good, is: namely, "activity of soul in accordance with virtue, and if there are more than one virtue, in accordance with the best and most complete... in a complete life" (*Eth. Nic.* I, 1098ª16–18). The familiar Kantian objection to this begins from Aristotle's ready concession that "external goods" such as friends, riches, political power, good birth, good children, and even beauty are necessary to eudaimonia, because "it is impossible, or not easy, to do noble acts without the proper equipment" (*Eth. Nic.* I, 1099ª31–1099ᵇ7), and from his acknowledgment that virtues (which are dispositions to actions of certain kinds) are acquired by practice (*Eth. Nic.* II, 1103ᵇ14–25). Henry Veatch rightly reminds us that Aristotle does not contend that "a life of virtue" is "an absolute guarantee of happiness" but only that "a good man, while he may not be completely happy under circumstances of adversity, is at least happier under such circumstances than the nonvirtuous man would be."[4] Kant primarily objected, however, not to this (although he might fairly have complained that it dodges the problem of adverse circumstances brought about by refusing to act viciously), but rather to Aristotle's implicit doctrine that the radically unfortunate (for example, gifted persons born to slavery in the Hellenic world of the fourth century B.C.) cannot live a humanly decent life at all because they lack the external goods necessary for the good actions that must be done if the virtues are to be acquired.

Yet is there a serious philosophical alternative to Aristotelian eudaimonism? The usual Thomist answer is that there is not; and Henry Veatch has put the reason for it in a nutshell: namely, that if we reject eudaimonism we abandon teleology for deontology, and "the deontologist invariably tries to ... maintain that our moral obligations may be seen ultimately to be rationally justifiable just in themselves, and without any appeal to any prior notion of the good or of an end."[5] Although Kant's remark that it is necessary to purge moral theory of "whatever ... is derived from the special predisposition of humanity, from certain feelings and propensities, and even, if this were possible, from some special bent peculiar to human reason"[6] may seem to lend force to this objection, I think it can be conclusively shown to be false. Kant explicitly grounded his deontology upon a teleology, although a teleology of a distinctive kind. The soundness of that teleology is indeed controversial, but not its existence or its fundamental character. But that is not all. After briefly setting out the nature of Kantian teleology and its function in his moral theory, I shall proceed to argue that, if we scrutinize the structure of St. Thomas's theory of natural law, we shall find that the teleology underlying it is not a Christianized version of eudaimonism, but an anticipation of the very same teleology Kant was to arrive at a little more than five hundred years later.

Let us begin with Kant. His objection to taking eudaimonia as the end by reference to which the moral law can be determined differs from, but is equivalent to, the objection I have already made to identifying it with the human good. In the actual circumstances of human life, Kant repeatedly points out, it may not be possible for a human being to attain natural this-worldly happiness, yet it must be possible for every human being to observe the moral law. And the same point can be made about every other material or psychological state of affairs the production of which can be proposed as an end: circumstances can make its production impossible, but as long as free human action (i.e., the condition of either moral or immoral action) is possible, then the observance of the moral law is possible. Hence, Kant reasoned, "in the idea of a will that is absolutely good ... there must be a complete abstraction from every end that has to be produced."[7] What has concealed Kant's teleology from most recent philosophers (from Henry Sidgwick and Sir David Ross, for example) is that it is not a teleology of producible ends, and they can conceive no others.[8] However, in view of *Summa theologiae* I–II, 2, 8, where the question "Is man's happiness realized in any created good?" is answered by a quotation from St. Augustine, "As soul is life for flesh, so God is the blessed life for man" (*De Civ. Dei*, xix, 26), it is surprising that the concept of a nonproducible good should be unfamiliar to any Thomist. The end on which the moral law depends, according to Kant, "must ... be conceived, not as an end to be produced, but as a *selbständiger Zweck*"[9]—as an independently existing end with which we are confronted. And the primary demand that such an end makes on us, as rational beings who recognize it as an end, is that we not act against it, and hence that "in all our willing we never rate [it] merely as a means, but always at the same time as an end."[10]

One reason why Thomists have failed to perceive the concept of a nonproducible end in their own moral tradition has been their misunderstanding of the place in that tradition of what St. Thomas called "the first principle in practical reason" that "good is to be done and pursued, and evil avoided," a principle which in turn depends on the identification of good as "what all things seek": *bonum est quod omnia appetunt*.[11] On the face of it, this suggests that human action is a matter of producing—of doing things that can be done, and of pursuing things that can be obtained on one hand, and of bringing about states of affairs in which things that can be avoided are avoided. But appearances deceive. As Germain Grisez has pointed out in his brilliant paper "The First Principle of Practical Reason,"[12] that principle, as St. Thomas conceives it, is the principle of all rational action as such, moral or immoral; and what it says, in effect, is that rational action is by its very nature *sub ratione boni*. "[I]f 'good' denoted only moral goods," Grisez wrote, "either wrong practical judgments could in no way issue from practical reason or the formula we are examining would not in reality express the first principle of practical reason."[13] Since most rational action is directed to the production either of producible goods or of states of affairs in which evils are avoided, the terms in which St. Thomas expressed his principle harmlessly suggest production, but they do not imply it. As it stands, St. Thomas's principle tells us that if we believe (as Kant did) that reducing a self-existent end to a mere means is something that is rational to avoid—an evil—that will be a *rationale* for avoiding it. Whether or not it is in fact rational to avoid such conduct is something that awaits investigation.

Where, if anywhere, does St. Thomas carry out such an investigation? Not in the treatise *De lege* in *Summa theologiae*, although he lays the foundation for it in the article *Quae sint praecepta legis naturalis?* (I–II, 94, 2) in which he introduced the first principle of practical reason. And not in the elaborate investigations of the theological and cardinal virtues of the second part of Part II of *Summa theologiae*, although in that part a great deal is said about the more specific precepts of morality. Rather, the cardinal exposition of natural law is where a Christian biblical scholar might have been expected to put it: in the treatise on Mosaic law (*De lege veteri*) where he takes up the Pauline theme of what fragment of the Mosaic law coincides with natural law. But that portion of *Summa theologiae* has not hitherto attracted much attention from moral philosophers.

Let us, however, look at the foundation laid in I–II, 94, 2. St. Thomas begins by inquiring what are the goods to which human nature as such inclines, because human reason "naturally apprehends as good all those things to which [man] has a natural inclination." Three kinds of thing fall into this class: first, the good which a man has in common with any substance whatever—his own existence; second, the goods which he has in common with all other animals—heterosexual intercourse, the rearing of offspring, and the like; and third, the goods proper to him as rational—which include a due relation to God, and such relations with his fellows as are necessary for living with them in a civil society.

Taken in conjunction with the first principle of practical reason, this list of human goods (and a corresponding list of evils) provides us with a series of moral precepts which are not only self-evident (*per se nota*) but are recognized in practice by all civilized human beings. "[W]ith regard to common principles of reason, whether speculative or practical, truth and rectitude are the same for all, and are equally known." However, St. Thomas recognized that, even with regard to common principles, a given person's knowledge may be depraved "by passion, or by bad custom or native proclivity (*ex mala habitudine naturae*)." His example of the third of these was the Germans of Julius Caesar's time, who saw nothing wrong in robbery.[14]

The fundamental common principles (*principia communissima*) of the natural law cannot, according to St. Thomas, be eradicated from the human heart.[15] Unless there is some depraving force they will assert themselves. But it is quite otherwise with the secondary, more specific precepts that are derived from them. They are not written in every heart. About them, honest errors are made, and in consequence honest differences of opinion are found.

Well, what are the *principia communissima* of natural law? While this is not explicitly answered in I–II, 94, it is in *De lege veteri*, the authority appealed to being that of Jesus commenting on Moses, not that of Aristotle. The *prima et communia praecepta* of the Mosaic law, *all* the precepts of which are declared in some sense to belong to natural law,[16] are identified as *Thou shalt love the Lord thy God* and *Thou shalt love thy neighbor*; and it is further laid down that all the precepts of the Mosaic decalogue "are related to these as conclusions to *principia communia*."[17]

What is loving one's neighbor in the sense in which the second of these two precepts commands it? I was long persuaded by what amounted to a scholarly consensus that it would have been anachronistic to interpret it in a sense anticipating Kant. However, the only non-Kantian interpretation proposed is that loving your neighbor is promoting in him the goods necessary to human flourishing, and never acting against them.[18] And there are two reasons against it. First, it is difficult to find a sound argument for it on the basis of St. Thomas's first principle of practical reason. While it follows from that principle that action in pursuit of any good necessary to human flourishing is rational in the sense of being *sub specie boni*, it in no way follows that acting against those goods is always wrong (for example, when full human flourishing is impossible, and one is confronted with a choice of evils). And second, it implausibly entails that the scriptural analogy between loving God and loving your neighbor is remote. Loving God presumably means treating him as the independently existing end of all your actions. You can, indeed, try to make the world better for God's sake; but you simply make a fool of yourself if you imagine that if you succeed you will make God's situation better. And that the analogy between loving God and loving your neighbor is not remote follows from the intimate relation between them authoritatively (for Christians, at least) laid down in St. John's first epistle (4:20): "he that loveth not his brother whom he hath seen, how can he love God whom he hath not seen?" His neighbor is the image of the unseen God, and the love he reasonably elicits is an image of the love God reasonably elicits. If the love God reasonably elicits is the will to treat him as the ultimate independently existing end of any action whatever, it is hard not to infer that the love your neighbor reasonably elicits is the will to treat him as an independently existing end in any action that concerns him.

That St. Thomas's theory of natural law in certain respects anticipates Kant's metaphysics of morals is confirmed by comparing what both found to say about motivation. Both recognized the existence of a state of a rational being in which it cannot will evil: Kant called that state holiness, and described a holy will as one that necessarily wills according to reason.[19] The only actual holy will he mentions is divine: the will of "the Holy One of the gospel."[20] St. Thomas indeed went further. The divine will is holy in Kant's sense, but, by divine grace, every human being can also attain a holy will through the beatific vision, which will ultimately be granted to all who avail themselves of the means of grace.

St. Thomas and Kant were agreed that it is possible for human beings to will either according to what they perceive to be requirements of reason or according to the promptings of other inclinations (desires, passions, even hatred of the human condition itself). The objects of such requirements and inclinations *all* confront us *sub ratione boni.* To gratify a natural desire, to avoid or reduce the power of what we perceive as harmful, and to rise above the limitations of our present condition are all in themselves rational things to attempt, but not when they have such further characteristics as preventing others from gratifying desires for elementary necessities, or avoiding or harming what will otherwise prevent us from doing wrong.

If I am not mistaken, St. Thomas also agreed with Kant that reason unconditionally requires that we treat God and the rational creatures that are his images as what Kant called independently existing ends (*selbständige Zwecke*). Kant's remark that "morality and humanity, inasmuch as it is capable of morality, alone have dignity"— where dignity is identified with intrinsic worth—seems to make essentially the same point as St. Thomas's "because to subsist in rational nature is of great dignity, every individual of rational nature is called a 'person.'"[21] To reject this is to deny the ground on which the natural desires of rational creatures are held to have a different and more fundamental significance for practical reason than those of irrational animals. The story is told that Voltaire, when a thief who had picked his pocket justified himself by saying "A man must live," replied, "I don't see the necessity." St. Thomas and Kant were at one that Voltaire was wrong: confronted with a person whose life can be preserved only by consuming some superfluous property of yours, his dignity as a person—an individual of rational nature—imposes a categorical obligation on you to relieve him. But only as an independently existing end. It would not be a categorical obligation to provide for his needs if you could unless he were such an end.

Finally, Kant's observation that *Achtung,* the consciousness of an immediate determination of the will by an imperative of reason, "is properly the representation of a worth that abashes my self-love (*meiner Selbstliebe Abbruch tut*)"[22] seems to me to be an enlightening (although of course unwitting) gloss upon a much discussed passage in St. Thomas.[23] There, in the course of showing that human beings first sin mortally when, beginning to have the use of reason, they discern a due (*debitum*) end according to their capacity but fail to direct their lives according to it, St. Thomas remarked, "At that time the first bit of thinking it falls to a man to do is to deliberate about his own self."[24] T. C. O'Brien here rightly warns that "There is no need . . . to posit the disjunction; either God is somehow chosen as final end, or self is."[25] The point appears rather to be that, deliberating on one's own self, one both discerns one's own dignity as an individual of rational nature, and at the same time recognizes that, if an individual of rational nature is a *finis debitus*, then there are rational constraints on what one may do to gratify one's desires and passions.

II

St. Thomas, I have argued, understood the second of his *prima et communia praecepta* of natural law, "Thou shalt love thy neighbor," as Kant did; namely, as equivalent to "Thou shalt treat all rational beings (for every rational being you encounter is, in the relevant sense, your neighbor) always as independently existing ends." The ground I have so far given has been that only so understood can that *praeceptum* generate the specific precepts of the Mosaic decalogue as a common principle generates a specific conclusion. If it is understood simply as "Thou shalt promote the various goods necessary to thy neighbor's flourishing" it will not absolutely exclude (say) murder and bearing false witness, as the decalogue does; for there may be situations in which the consequence of a murder may be that more lives will be saved than lost, and of an act of perjury that more truth will become known than otherwise would have. The connection of the *prima praecepta* with the specific precepts of the decalogue in turn shows that in that part of St. Thomas's first principle of practical reason which prescribes that good is to be done and pursued, "good" cannot be confined to what is necessary for human flourishing (*utile*), but must also include what practical reason demands of us out of respect for the dignity of rational beings (*honestum*). And I have also found passages in St. Thomas's treatment of practical reason in relation to morality that appear to bear out this interpretation.

This argument is indirect, but unavoidably so; for St. Thomas has not provided us with the only evidence that would enable us directly to confirm or disconfirm it: namely, an explicit derivation of the *prima et communia praecepta* of the Mosaic law in accordance with the first principle of practical reason.

St. Thomas's omission to provide such an explicit derivation has tempted some interpreters to the fatal course of reconstructing what his conception of natural law was from his general discussion of it alone, without considering what he wrote about the Mosaic law at all. The gist of what is written about the secondary precepts of natural law in the general discussion is simply that from the principle that it is true and right that we act according to reason (which I take to be equivalent to the first principle of practical reason itself) it follows as a proper conclusion that goods held in trust are to be restored; but "the principle is insufficient (*deficere invenitur*) the more one descends to particulars," as is shown by the fact that the conclusion drawn from it, although generally true, admits of exceptions—as when what is held in trust would, if restored, be used against one's country.[26] On this, James F. Ross has commented that to St. Thomas "The common principles of natural law are not, therefore, universally general truths applied by universal instantiation to individual cases but are *policies* which must be realized where possible (wherever reason permits) and must *not* be encrusted with qualifications."[27]

When we turn to the treatise *De lege veteri*, however, we find that the precept that goods held in trust are to be restored is presented as a conclusion from the precept of the decalogue "Thou shalt not steal";[28] that every precept of the decalogue is described as "knowable straight off from the first common principles with a little thought";[29] and that the precepts of the decalogue are *omnino indispensabilia* as embodying the divine intention, from which it follows that they allow of no exceptions.[30] The precepts of the decalogue are therefore, contrary to Ross, "universally general truths." However, they are insufficient for deciding many particular cases, because the more we descend to particulars, the more questions arise as to whether those particulars do or do not fall under the general precept. To determine whether they do or do not, additional premises are needed, which are not implicit in the general precepts themselves. In the case in question, whether the goods of enemies of one's country that have been left in trust are to be restored, some premise is required which defines what an enemy's property rights are. The precept "Thou shalt not steal" is rightly said to "fail" (*deficere*) to settle this, but such failure is in no sense a defect.

The precepts of the decalogue, therefore, are applied to particular cases, not by "universal instantiation" but by the mediation of additional premises which lay down whether or not certain more specific cases fall under their terms. What St. Thomas calls "secondary precepts" of the natural law are not written in every heart because these mediating premises are not. And that is why the secondary precepts we use are often only approximate, and admit of exceptions. However, it does not follow that moral theorists should not try to discover mediating premises by means of which exception-free secondary precepts can be deduced. Indeed, when St. Thomas spoke of precepts not expressly included in the decalogue "which are found by the diligent inquiry of wise men to be in accordance with reason," and which are "contained in [the precepts of the decalogue] as conclusions from principles,"[31] was it not presupposed that the more diligent the inquiry, the fewer would be the exceptions to those secondary principles?

This outline of the structure of natural law as St. Thomas conceived it may well seem to you to be out of date in scholarship and moral style alike. In refusing to abandon part at least of its moral style, namely that according to which any adequate theory of right reason must certify as "imperatives" such "derivative obligations" as "not to murder, not to steal, not to commit adultery, not to bear false witness, etc." I am content with the support of Henry Veatch.[32] And, despite the readiness of respected scholars to abandon natural law as inessential to St. Thomas's moral theory, their own scholarly integrity must in the end forbid it.

The following remarks, by Vernon J. Bourke, a scholar and philosopher to whom all students of St. Thomas are indebted, are representative of this readiness.

> While the notion of natural law does play a part in Aquinas's teaching on morality, it does not seem to me to be a central role. Indeed there are many reasons why it might be better, today, to stop talking about natural moral law, both in the context of Thomistic philosophy and in the broader context of contemporary ethics. What I now advocate is the position that right reason (*recta ratio*) is the key theme in the ethics of Aquinas.[33]

Whether the role of the notion of natural law in St. Thomas's ethics is "central" or not is a vague and unprofitable question. If one wants to determine whether or not St. Thomas was "a natural law ethicist" it seems to me that there are two questions that matter: (1) Did he think that certain kinds of action are permissible or impermissible by their very nature? and (2) If so, did he think that their permissibility or impermissibility is to be ascertained by procedures implicit in his discussion of natural law? To these questions there are straightforward answers. That he did think that certain kinds of action are permissible or impermissible by their very nature is obvious: the *Secunda secundae* is full of questions of the form "*Utrum X sit peccatum?*" "*Utrum Y sit licita?*" where only the natures of X and Y are in question. And in answering these questions, when he is invoking neither revealed divine commandments nor human positive law, the procedures he follows are those implicit in his discussion of natural law. That is why students have always gone to the treatment of such questions in the *Secunda Secundae* for examples of arguments on points of natural law. It does not matter that in these treatments the phrase "natural law" is seldom used. As Senator Ervin observed in the Watergate hearings: if you draw a good picture of a horse, you needn't write "horse" underneath it.

None of this contradicts Bourke's assertion that "right reason (*recta ratio*) is the key theme in the ethics of Aquinas." But the question is whether an ethics of right reason involves a morality of natural law—a strict deontology. St. Thomas, I contend, unmistakably held that it does.[34]

III

Besides being corroborated or weakened by the indirect evidence of how its secondary precepts are derived from its primary common principles, and of how those principles are established in accordance with the first principle of practical reason, theses about the nature of the teleological foundation of St. Thomas's theory of natural law may also be tested by comparing what they imply about why its secondary precepts cannot be inconsistent with one another with what St. Thomas found to say about implicit objections that they are.

In carrying out this test, the only objections examined will be implicit, because St. Thomas had a far clearer grasp of what a consistent set of secondary precepts of natural law would be than any of his contemporaries known to me. According to any natural law theory of morality, moral precepts are commands of practical reason. And St. Thomas clearly perceived that no set of precepts can be a set of commands of practical reason unless (1) any conjunction of what is commanded by members of the set is also commanded by practical reason, and (2) whatever is commanded by practical reason can be carried out. It follows that precepts of natural law cannot come into conflict *simpliciter*; for they could do so only if situations were possible in which obeying some of them would make it impossible to obey others, that is, only if there were a conjunction of what is commanded by precepts of natural law that cannot be carried out, even though, by (1) and (2), all such conjunctions are commanded, and whatever is commanded can be carried out.[35]

St. Thomas, however, saw clearly what some moral theologians did not, that not all moral conflict is moral conflict *simpliciter*. It is perfectly possible for human beings to find themselves in situations in which they cannot obey some precepts of the natural law without disobeying others, not because the natural law is inconsistent or inapplicable to the actual human situation, but because they have already violated it.

St. Thomas described a person in such a situation as "*perplexus secundum quid*": he is, in the idiom of today, in a moral conflict, not simply speaking, but by reason of a special circumstance for which he is to blame. Logically, as St. Thomas saw, to conclude that a set of precepts is inconsistent because it can give rise to moral conflict *secundum quid* would be as absurd as to conclude that a set of axioms is inconsistent because it generates a contradiction when combined with the contradictory of a theorem that follows from it. A set of precepts is consistent if anybody to whom it applies can obey it in all situations to which it applies; but there is no assurance that disobeying one of its members will not entangle him in situations in which he cannot avoid disobeying others. "It is not *inconveniens*," St. Thomas drily observed, "that a person in mortal sin be perplexed."[36]

Although distinguishing moral conflict *simpliciter* from moral conflict *secundum quid* disposes of unsophisticated accusations of inconsistency brought against the natural law as traditionally understood by numerous theologians in the Dark Ages[37] and numerous academic philosophers today, it cannot dispose of objections that the natural law gives rise to moral conflict *simpliciter*. Such charges are made, and they are acknowledged to be serious.

Among contemporary Thomists, the objection of this sort that is most discussed is that natural law, as traditionally conceived, is inconsistent in forbidding murder, but permitting killing in self-defense, killing enemy combatants in a just war, and capital punishment. The alleged contradiction is not direct (murder is defined as killing the materially innocent, and an assailant threatening life or limb is not materially innocent), but arises from the usual non-Kantian interpretation of the ground on which murder is held to be contrary to natural law, namely that life itself is a good intrinsic to persons—rational individuals—and so has a dignity in virtue of which it should be respected and protected. On the same ground one's own life is to be defended against murderous attack. But a moral conflict *simpliciter* appears to follow if one can only save one's life by defensive measures that will cause the assailant's death. For, on one hand, one is forbidden to kill one's murderous assailant; and on the other hand, one is forbidden not to defend oneself—and the only effective defense is to kill one's assailant.[38]

St. Thomas's solution of the casuistical problem "whether it is licit to kill another in defending oneself" is as controversial as it is celebrated.

> Nothing forbids there being two effects of one act, of which only one is in intention, and the other is beyond intention. However, moral acts receive [their] species according to what is intended, and not, be it added, from what is beyond intention, which is *per accidens* as appears from things said above. Therefore, from the act of somebody defending himself two effects follow: one indeed is the preservation of his own life, but the other is the killing of the attacker. It is because of this, that the preservation of his own life is intended, and an act of this kind does not have the character of an illicit one, since it is natural to anybody that he preserve himself in being as far as he can. Yet any act proceeding from a good intention can be rendered illicit if it is not proportioned to its end. And so if anybody to defend his own life uses more violence than is needed, it will be a wrong. If indeed it repels violence with moderation, a defense will be licit; for according to the laws [the *Decretals of Gregory IX*] *it is licit to repel force by force with the moderation of a blameless guardianship....*
>
> But because it is not licit to kill a man except by public authority for the common good, as is clear from things said above [II–II, 64, 3] it is illicit that man intend to kill man in order to defend himself, with the exception of one who has public authority, who intending to kill a man in self-defense refers it to the public good, as appears in a soldier fighting against enemies, and in an officer of the court fighting against robbers.[39]

That this passage should commonly be received as showing that St. Thomas took it to be always wrong directly to attack human life is extraordinary, and only a little less so that it should be interpreted as "an enunciation of the principle of the double effect as we understand it today, and as an application of that principle to the lawfulness of killing in self-defense."[40]

What it does show, plainly and unmistakably, is that St. Thomas held that human life may licitly be *intentionally* taken by those with public authority acting for the common good. Since homicide in the line of duty by soldiers and officers of the court is perfectly licit when intentional, St. Thomas would have held it to be an error to seek to justify it only when *praeter intentionem*. The long and honorable line of philosophers who, like Grisez, have taken St. Thomas to maintain "the inviolable dignity of human life as a natural law principle," and have proceeded to treat his theory of justifiable killing by private persons in self-defense as fundamental to whatever is sound in his entire theory of justifiable homicide, have stood his theory on its head.[41] The foundation of St. Thomas's theory of justifiable homicide is his theory that public authority is justified in killing for the common good; his theory of justifiable killing in self-defense, far from being its foundation, has to do with a special exception to the prohibition of private persons from usurping a function of public authority. His reason for holding that private persons may not intentionally kill even in self-defense is set out in II–II, 64, 3:

> to kill a wrongdoer is licit inasmuch as it is ordered to the safety (*salutem*) of the whole community, and so it pertains to him alone to whom is committed the charge of keeping the community safe.... But charge over the common good has been committed to rulers holding public authority, and so to them alone is it licit to kill wrongdoers, but not to private persons.

In II–II, 64, 7 St. Thomas did no more than point out that, in saving his own life, which he is "more bound (*plus tenetur*)" to do than to save another's, a private person may *praeter intentionem* do what an officer of the court would do intentionally in the course of duty, without usurping a function reserved to public authority. Not only is it not true that those having public authority are permitted to kill grave wrongdoers *praeter intentionem* because private persons are, it is on the contrary true that private persons would not be permitted to do it *praeter intentionem* if those having public authority did not have the duty to do it *in intentionem*.

At a symposium in honor of Henry Veatch it is unnecessary to dwell on the point that the common good, as St. Thomas conceived it, is not the good of the many as opposed to that of the few, but, since human beings are social, a good willed in every act of will for a particular good.[41] That they live in a peaceable and law-abiding society is a good robbers and murderers will, and of which they do, take advantage. "Hence," St. Thomas reasoned, "if any man is dangerous to the community, and corruptive of it because of some sin, he is killed *laudabiliter et salubriter*, so that the common good may be preserved."[42]

Grisez has found this unsatisfactory for three reasons: that, except for the muddle that only wrongdoers endanger the common good, it would justify killing the innocent; that killing wrongdoers is not necessary to preserve the common good; and that it depends on the false Aristotelian doctrine that the good of individuals is less "godlike" than the good of the social whole of which they are parts.[43] Now, while I concede that St. Thomas's use of the Aristotelian notion that individuals are related to their communities as parts to wholes prevented him from expressing his point exactly, it seems to me that his recognition that the good of the community to which an individual belongs matters morally only to the extent that it is genuinely common to its members invalidates in advance morally objectionable conclusions drawn by preferring social goods that are not common to the good of individuals. And I contend that the point St. Thomas was trying to express is that an individual who wills gravely to wrong his fellows, by attacking the human dignity that is the independently existing end of all rational human activity, attacks a fundamental good common to himself and them, and so makes a good life for himself as well as for them impossible.

But is it not evil in itself (*malum secundum se*) to kill any human being whatever, even one who acts in this way? Not at all, St. Thomas answered.

> By sinning a man turns his back on the order of reason; and so falls away from human dignity, inasmuch as he is indeed naturally free and existing for himself, and in a certain way falls into the servile condition of the beasts, so that from himself he is rather ordered to what is for the good of others.... And so although to kill a man remaining in his natural dignity is evil in itself, yet to kill a sinner can be good. Just as to kill a beast. For an evil man is worse than a beast, and does more harm, as Aristotle says.[44]

Although this is inexactly expressed—Grisez rightly points out that self-degradation, "even if it is conceived as a kind of existential suicide, cannot alter one's human nature or detract from one's inherent dignity as a human person"[45]—it can reasonably be interpreted as anticipating something like the following:

> By sinning a man turns his back on the order of reason, which requires him to respect himself and all other rational beings as ends in themselves. In so doing he degrades himself to a condition like that of the beasts, who act in natural instinct, without conceiving either ends in themselves or means. If in this degraded state he hinders other rational beings from following the order of reason, they may forcibly hinder his doing so, without infringing his dignity as a rational being. And, since the order of reason ordains that civil societies be established, so that laws enabling all to follow the order of reason may be made and upheld, the public authorities in such societies may suppress actions violating the law by lethal force if necessary, and may impose punishments for lawbreaking proportionate to the offense, without infringing the dignity of lawbreakers as rational beings. To put a murderer to death by due process of law does not infringe his dignity as a rational being, provided his death is "kept entirely free of any maltreatment that would make an abomination of the humanity residing in the person suffering it."[46]

That this is the substance of what underlies St. Thomas's treatment of homicide in *Summa theologiae* II–II, 64 seems to be an inescapable conclusion when articles 2, 3, and 7 are read in order. It follows that the first principle of natural law, *Thou shalt love thy neighbor,* cannot be construed as implying *Thou shalt treat the goods essential to thy neighbor's well-being, for example life, as inviolable.* St. Thomas, like Kant, held that what follows from the principle about the inviolability of the goods necessary to your neighbor's well-being is that they are inviolable if he "remains in his dignity," that is, if he does what his dignity requires, but not otherwise.

The preceding investigation of whether my thesis that the teleology underlying St. Thomas's theory of natural law is substantially identical with the Kantian one can be tested by examining how St. Thomas treated charges that its precepts are inconsistent, while complex in detail, has been simple in design. It began with his own clarification of what it would be for the precepts of a system of natural law to be inconsistent: briefly, they would be so if and only if situations to which they would apply should be possible in which they would be in conflict *simpliciter*—conflict *secundum quid* would not count. It then turned to his treatment of homicide, because it contains the article (II–II, 64, 7) that is widely believed to show both that he held a certain good necessary to human well-being, namely life, to be an inviolable end, and also that he resolved the apparent conflict between the duty not to take life and the permissibility of defending one's own life at the cost of taking another's by anticipating the modern theory of the double effect. According to that theory, while it is illicit intentionally to take a human life, it is licit to take one *praeter intentionem* if the loss of that life is an unintended effect of any course of action by which you can preserve your own life. There is no conflict *simpliciter*, because acts are assigned to species according to their intentions; hence the species of the acts performed in such cases is *preserving one's own life*, and not *taking the life of another*.

In developing a consistent natural law theory of homicide along these lines, Grisez has persuasively argued that public authority acting for the common good cannot licitly take human life except on a ground analogous to that on which private persons can: namely, community self-defense. And even then it may not intentionally do so.

> As in self-defense, a soldier on a battlefield can shoot straight at an enemy soldier, intending to lessen the enemy force by one gun, while not intending to kill. Similarly a military camp or a factory producing military goods can be bombed. But an enemy hospital or non-military area cannot be justly attacked. The enemy soldier may not be killed if he can be inactivated otherwise, or if he has surrendered.[47]

Despite my difficulties with the theory of the double effect,[48] I find this theory of natural law intellectually attractive, especially in its conclusions about the conditions under which it is licit to engage in war at all, and about the means by which it is licit to wage it.

The question before us, however, is not what is the best theory of natural law, but what was St. Thomas's. Grisez takes the theory of the double effect developed from II–II, 64, 7 both to render consistent the interpretation of the natural law principle *Thou shalt love thy neighbor* as laying it down that the various goods necessary to human well-being are to be promoted wherever possible and never acted against, and also to be indirect evidence that at some deep level of his thought St. Thomas himself endorsed that interpretation. Hence he leaves himself no choice but to dismiss St. Thomas's explicit recognition of the permissibility of intentional killing by public authority for the common good as an irrational accommodation to contemporary prejudice.[49]

On the other hand, if instead of assuming that St. Thomas's natural law framework took human life as such to be an inviolable good, we infer what his framework was from how he defended the consistency of the precepts to which it gives rise, we shall not take it to be an aberration that, like Kant five hundred years later, he not only expressly affirmed that public authority has the duty intentionally to take human life when only so can internal law and order and external peace and justice be protected, but also defended the consistency of doing so on the ground that human life as such is not inviolable. True, his reason for declaring that to kill a sinner can be good is defective because of its uncritical reliance on the Aristotelian conception of civil society as a whole of which human beings are parts. However, if this defect is corrected on Kantian lines, his treatment of homicide can be accepted as a philosophically coherent whole, superior in a number of specific details to Kant's.[50] By contrast the entire structure of II–II, 64 is in conflict with the "framework" on which Grisez maintains that it is erected.[51]

Notes

From *The Georgetown Symposium on Ethics: Essays in Honor of Henry Babcock Veatch*, edited by Rocco Porreco. © University Press of America 1984. Reprinted with the permission of the University Press of America.

1. Especially "Telos and Teleology in Aristotelian Ethics," in Dominic J. O'Meara, ed., *Studies in Aristotle* (Washington, D.C.: Catholic University of America Press, 1981); and "Variations, Good and Bad, on the Theme of Right Reason in Ethics," *The Monist* 66 (1983): 51–70.

2. Cf. Susan Wolf, "Moral Saints," *Journal of Philosophy* 79 (1982): 419–39.

3. Aristotle, *Physics* I, 184^{a}10–21.

4. Henry B. Veatch, *Rational Man: A Modern Interpretation of Aristotelian Ethics* (Bloomington: Indiana University Press, 1962), p. 179, commenting on Aristotle, *Eth. Nic.* I, 1100^{b}23–1101^{a}8.

5. Veatch, "Right Reason in Ethics," p. 68.

6. Immanuel Kant, *Grundlegung zur Metaphysik der Sitten* (2d ed., Riga, 1786), pp. 59–60 (Ak. ed., p. 425). Here and hereafter I have drawn upon the translations of L. W. Beck, James Ellington, and H. J. Paton.

7. Ibid., p. 82 (Ak. ed., p. 437).

8. For classical examples, see Henry Sidgwick, *The Methods of Ethics*, 7th ed. (London: Macmillan, 1907), p. 390; Sir David Ross, *Kant's Ethical Theory: A Commentary on the "Grundlegung zur Metaphysik der Sitten"* (Oxford: Clarendon Press, 1954), p. 51. Henry Veatch has described as "sharp and decisive" a remark in R. P. Wolff, *The Autonomy of Reason: A Commentary on Kant's "Groundwork of the Metaphysics of Morals"* (New York: Harper and Row, 1973), p. 131: "[A] categorical imperative cannot 'directly command a certain conduct without making its condition some purpose to be reached by it,' for that is the same thing as saying that it commands an agent to engage in purposive action with no purpose" (quoted by Henry Veatch in "Right Reason in Ethics," p. 55). It is perfectly understandable that Kant's critics should take the word of professedly sympathetic commentators *after* Paton and Beck that Kant drew no distinction between engaging in purposive action and engaging in action to produce some end believed to be producible, but it is inexcusable that such commentators should give their word that he drew none. For the necessary corrections of Wolff see Marcus G. Singer, "Reconstructing the *Groundwork*," *Ethics* 93 (1982–83): 566–78. Singer appropriately concludes: "To be sure, the *Groundwork* needs inter-

pretation. But it is not in need of this sort of *transformation*, in which it is divorced from the whole of Kant's developing and developed philosophy" (p. 578).

9. Kant, *Grundlegung*, p. 82 (Ak. ed., p. 437).

10. Ibid.

11. "*Bonum est faciendum et prosequendum, et malum vitandum*" (*Summa theologiae* I–II, 94, 2. I have used the Latin-English edition published in 61 volumes by Blackfriars, London, between 1964 and 1981.)

12. First published in *Natural Law Forum* 10 (1965): 168–96. Its substance is readily accessible in Anthony Kenny, ed., *Aquinas: A Collection of Critical Essays* (Notre Dame: University of Notre Dame Press, 1976), pp. 340–82.

13. Grisez, in Kenny, ed., *Aquinas*, p. 368.

14. St. Thomas, *Summa theologiae* I–II, 94, 4. Two articles later, this is inconsistently referred to as a *praeceptum secundarium*.

15. Ibid., I–II, 94, 6.

16. Ibid., I–II, 100, 1.

17. Ibid., I–II, 100, 3 *ad* 1.

18. Germain Grisez, "Toward a Consistent Natural Law Ethics of Killing," in *American Journal of Jurisprudence* 15 (1970): 65–66, 90–96, splendidly exemplifies this approach, with respect to the good of human life itself. Henry Veatch appears to take a similar line in "Right Reason in Ethics," p. 67–68.

19. Kant, *Grundlegung*, pp. 39, 86 (Ak. ed., pp. 414, 439).

20. Ibid., p. 29 (Ak. ed., p. 408).

21. Compare Kant, *Grundlegung*, p. 77 (Ak. ed., p. 435) with St. Thomas, *Summa theologiae* I, 29, 3 *ad* 2. (The latter should be taken together with "*persona significat id quod est perfectissimum in tota natura*" (I–II, 29, 3c.)

22. Kant, *Grundlegung*, p. 16n (Ak. ed., p. 401 n. 2).

23. St. Thomas, *Summa theologiae* I–II, 89, 6c. In Appendix IV to vol. 27 of the Blackfriars edition, its editor, T. C. O'Brien, comments on it at length (pp. 125–33).

24. "*sed primum quod tunc homini cogitandum occurrit est deliberare de se ipso*" (*Summa theologiae* I–II, 89, 6c.).

25. In the Appendix cited in note 23, p. 128.

26. St. Thomas, *Summa theologiae* I–II, 94, 4c.

27. James F. Ross, "Justice Is Reasonableness: Aquinas on Human Law and Morality," *Monist* 58 (1974): 90.

28. St. Thomas, *Summa theologiae* I–II, 100, 4 *ad* 2.

29. Ibid., I–II, 100, 3c.

30. Ibid., I–II, 100, 8c.

31. Ibid., I–II, 100, 4c.

32. Veatch, "Right Reason in Ethics," pp. 65–66.

33. Vernon J. Bourke, "Is Thomas Aquinas a Natural Law Ethicist?" *The Monist* 58 (1974): 52.

34. In both Sections I and II I have made use of hitherto unpublished material presented in a paper, "Morality and Natural Law in the Philosophy of St. Thomas Aquinas," read at a symposium devoted to St. Thomas's ethical theory on October 11, 1974, at Aquinas College, Grand Rapids, Michigan, as part of a celebration of St. Thomas's 700th anniversary.

35. My formulation of the presuppositions (1) and (2), by reference to which natural law theorists hold any putative set of moral precepts that generates moral conflict *simpliciter* to be inconsistent, derives from an analysis by Bernard Williams, in a paper "Ethical Consistency" in *Problems of the Self* (Cambridge: Cambridge University Press, 1973), pp. 166–86, esp. 179–80.

36. St. Thomas distinguished perplexity *simpliciter* from perplexity *secundum quid* in several places: *Summa theologiae* I–II, 19, 6 *ad* 3; II–II, 62, 2 obj. 2; III, 64, 6 *ad* 3; and *Quaest. disp. de veritate*, 17, 4 *ad* 8. G. H. von Wright, in *An Essay on Deontic Logic* (Amsterdam: North Holland Publishing Co., 1968), p. 81 n. 1, has pointed out (with acknowledgments to P. T. Geach) the importance of St. Thomas's distinction, but he appears not to have been heeded.

37. E.g., St. Gregory the Great, *Moralium libri sive expositio in librum b. Iob*, xxxii, 20 (in Migne, *Patrologia Latina*, vol. 76, pp. 657–58). St. Gregory, holding a command theory of morality, and so not accepting the presuppositions of a natural law theory, simply argued that the moral law gives rise to moral conflicts. But his argument can be used against the theory that morality is natural law, and St. Thomas's reply suggests that it was.

38. While I have constructed a possible theoretical position, and do not attribute it to anybody, I have kept in mind Germain Grisez's subtle and powerful argument in "Consistent Natural Law Ethics," pp. 64–96, esp. pp. 65–66, 73–74, 87–91.

39. St. Thomas, *Summa theologiae* II–II, 64, 7c. My translation is as close to the original as I could make it. The passage is thoroughly discussed, and more elegantly translated, by Grisez, "Consistent Natural Law Ethics," pp. 73–75, 87–91. The concept *"praeter intentionem,"* as St. Thomas uses it, is clarified and illustrated by Joseph M. Boyle, Jr., *The Thomist* 42 (1978): 649–65.

40. Joseph T. Mangan, S.J., "An Historical Analysis of the Principle of Double Effect," *Theological Studies* 10 (1949): 49. This important paper, while it establishes that *Summa theologiae* II–II, 64, 7 "is the historical beginning of the principle of the double effect as a principle" (ibid., p. 61), is less successful, in my opinion, in showing that it ought to have been.

41. St. Thomas, *Summa theologiae*, I–II, 19, 10c.

42. Ibid., II–II, 64, 2c.

43. Grisez, "Consistent Natural Law Ethics," pp. 67–69.

44. St. Thomas, *Summa theologiae* II–II, 64, 2 *ad* 3.

45. Grisez, "Consistent Natural Law Ethics," p. 69.

46. The final sentence is from Immanuel Kant, *Metaphysik der Sitten*, 2d ed. (Königsberg: F. Nicolovius, 1798), vol. 1, *Rechtslehre*, p. 229 (Ak. ed., p. 333). I have used John Ladd's translation.

47. Grisez, "Consistent Natural Law Ethics," pp. 91–92.

48. See my *Theory of Morality* (Chicago: University of Chicago Press, 1977).

49. E.g., "[W]orking in a natural-law framework that assumes that human life is inherently a good to be protected and respected, Aquinas is precluded from defending capital punishment and killing in warfare on utilitarian grounds. Yet as a theologian, Aquinas was confronted with a tradition which justified capital punishment and took warfare for granted" ("Consistent Natural Law Ethics," p. 72).

50. While remembering that Kant's treatment of homicide in *Metaphysik der Sitten* has a number of details best explained as lapses into dotage, it is hard to imagine St. Thomas

even in his dotage deviating into such cant as "If legal justice perishes, then it is no longer worthwhile for men to remain alive on this earth" (*Metaphysik der Sitten*, vol. 1, p. 227, Ak. ed., p. 332)—as though in human history legal justice has not many times perished and been restored.

51. In part III, I owe a great deal to Professor Joseph M. Boyle, Jr., of St. Thomas University, Houston, for allowing me to read unpublished work of his, and for criticism in correspondence. While there was no time to send him the present paper before submitting it for publication, I trust to his professionalism to correct my errors in Thomistic scholarship.

EIGHT

Moral Absolutism and the Double Effect Exception: Reflections on Joseph Boyle's "Who Is Entitled to Double Effect?"

Most *Catholic moralists*, especially those who have to do with the practice of medicine, have long accepted that some moral prohibitions are not absolute, but admit exceptions when what is putatively prohibited because of a bad effect has a counterbalancing good effect. In recent years their doctrine has attracted much interest and some favor among secular non-Catholics. Moralists influenced by Kant, however, tend to resist "double effect" exceptions as superfluous. The issues are confusing, because not only are theories of the double effect exception various, but so also are theories according to which it is superfluous. Joseph Boyle's illuminating exploration of some of the theories in the field, both Catholic and non-Catholic, and his exposition and persuasive defense of a particular Catholic theory of it, disentangle some of my own perplexities;[1] and in what follows, I shall try to disentangle some others.

I pass over the double effect exception in nonabsolutist moral theories, like those of Philippa Foot and Warren Quinn,[2] and confine myself to its place in absolutist ones, that is, to ones in which "there are exceptionless moral norms prohibiting inflicting certain kinds of harms on people" (p. 486).

1. Actions, Intended and Unintended: The Case of Craniotomy

Boyle would agree, I believe, that the human actions that are subject to moral judgment are changes or persistences in an agent's bodily or mental state brought about by his will, or "voluntarily," in the technical sense of that word. Hence refusing to bring about such a change is as much an action as bringing one about.[3] An agent *voluntarily* causes an effect of such a voluntary change or persistence if and only if he believes that it can have that effect, not necessarily that it must. And he *intentionally* causes an effect he voluntarily causes if that effect is either the end for which he causes it, or among "the precise steps [he] takes to achieve" that end (p. 479).

What you intend is therefore what you *plan* to do, whether as your end or as among the means by which you plan to accomplish it. You do not intend something you will to do if you will it neither as your purpose nor as contributing to your purpose, even if you foresee that carrying out your plan will cause it. A good test of whether or not you intend a particular foreseen effect of an action is to suppose that, by some fluke or miracle, the action does not have the effect you foresee, and to ask whether you then consider your plan carried out and your purpose accomplished. Boyle contends that, if intended effects are conceived as planned, the distinction between them and unintended side-effects is clear in principle, although there will be borderline cases.[4] Confusion arises when unintended effects are conceived, not as planned, but as causally more remote from the change or persistence in the agent's body that causes them than are intended effects.

Some Catholic moralists resist Boyle's analysis on the ground that no effect of an action can be a side effect if any step the agent takes to bring about his end is a sufficient condition for it. For example, Stephen Theron argues as follows that killing a foetus, while an unintended side effect of a hysterectomy performed to prevent its mother from being killed by her uterine cancer, is an intended effect of a craniotomy performed to prevent its mother from being killed by the blockage of her birth canal.

> If I could remove the cancerous womb without causing death I would. But I can't credibly say, if I could do the craniotomy...without causing death I would. For the *point* of th[is] act is to cause death, and that is why it is killing, whereas the point of removing the cancerous womb and foetus is to save life, and that is why it is not killing, even though it causes death. The craniotomy may also have the point of saving life, but that is through its aim of killing. The hysterectomy has the point of saving life through its aim of removing a womb.[5]

Presumably Theron's reason for asserting that the "aim" of craniotomy is killing is that the "precise step" in it by which the foetus is made removable from the birth canal is the crushing of its skull, which is a sufficient condition of its death. By contrast, none of the precise steps by which a cancerous womb is removed kills the foetus: it is killed by the removal itself.

Boyle implicitly rejects reasoning like Theron's for two reasons. First of all, an action, whether it is a voluntary change of the agent's state or a voluntary persistence in the same state, is inescapably the causing of *all* the effects of that change or persistence. Since, in the normal course of nature, hysterectomy and craniotomy both cause the death of the foetus concerned, a hysterectomy is as much a killing as a craniotomy, even though the foetus is not killed by any "precise step" in carrying it out. And second, since the point of crushing the foetus's skull in craniotomy is not to kill it, but to make it removable from the birth canal, its death is no more the point of the operation than is the death of a foetus the point of hysterectomy. Despite his bold tone, Theron has no credible answer to the question Boyle would presumably ask: "Why can a surgeon performing a craniotomy not 'credibly say' that, if he could crush the foetus's skull in a way that would neither kill nor irreparably injure it, he would?"

2. How the Effects of an Action and the Scope of Intention Are Limited by Intervening Actions

The moral implications of the above conception of human action vary according to the conception of cause and effect with which it is associated. Both Catholic and Kantian moral absolutists, and in general all moralists who accept the freedom of the will in a noncompatibilist sense, limit an action's effects, and a fortiori what its agent intends to bring about in doing it, to those that follow from it in the course of nature and the ordinary operation of social institutions, and not from the free reactions of others to it. (Thus, actions in the ordinary course of business, for example, those of postal officers in delivering a letter that has been mailed, are not counted as free reactions.) The principle on which they do so is that a free reaction to an action is a "new action" ("*novus actus*"), the effects of which are its effects, and not those of the action to which it is a reaction. It follows that a *novus actus interveniens* terminates not only the effects of the original action, but also what its agent intentionally brings about in doing it. And it also follows that what an agent plans or intends can extend beyond what he plans or intends to bring about. He may intend that others react in a certain way to what he does; but he cannot intend to bring it about that they do, because bringing that about is not in his power.

These distinctions are the foundation of both Catholic and Kantian views of the treatment of action in face of threats, whether by radically unjust legal authority or by private criminals. History offers numerous and horrible examples of somebody powerful and evil commanding somebody else to do something morally abominable (e.g., to choose patients for lethal or radically injurious medical experiments) under the threat that otherwise he will have something even more abominable done. Sophie's predicament in William Styron's novel *Sophie's Choice*, is an example: she is told that if she does not choose one of her two children to be sent to the gas chamber, both will be sent. Although the case is fictional, the records of the concentration camp crimes of the Nazis contain numerous similar ones, many of them even more vile. Yet, as most Jewish writers on the Nazi genocide have concluded, such cases, although agonizing for the victims, are not morally problematic. Given that it is absolutely morally prohibited to collaborate in certain irreparable wrongs, as it will be in any absolutist moral system, that others will react to your refusal to collaborate by doing some graver wrong cannot be a morally relevant reason for your not refusing. By not refusing you will collaborate in a wrong for which there are no amends. Yet you cannot plead that if you refuse, you will cause that graver wrong; for you will not cause it. Nor can you plead that, in failing to refuse, you intended only to prevent the graver wrong, and that your collaboration was the unintended side effect of trying to prevent it; for even if the threatener refrained from doing what he threatened, you did not prevent him from doing it: that is, you neither caused nor could have caused his not doing it. Your belief that you intended to is at best self-deception.[6]

3. Boyle's Revisionary Theory of the Double Effect Exception

Having got rid of the irrelevancy of harms caused by new intervening actions, we may now turn to Boyle's revisionary theory of double effect exceptions. It is as follows.

Catholic moral absolutism absolutely prohibits intentional invasions of the human goods that are fundamental; and, as a rule but not absolutely, it also prohibits even unintentional invasions of these goods. Since Catholic morality accepts the Pauline principle that it is absolutely prohibited to do evil that good may come of it, it makes no end obligatory that can only be brought about by absolutely prohibited means. Hence none of its absolute moral prohibitions are such that they can be observed only by violating some other. However, situations may occur in which whatever one does will have unintended side effects that it would be absolutely prohibited to bring about intentionally. For example, a surgeon may be confronted with a situation in which he must either refrain from saving a mother's life or kill her child by craniotomy. In both cases he will cause the death of what, on the face of it, is a materially innocent life: something he is absolutely prohibited from doing intentionally. If he operates with the end of saving the mother's life, he must unintentionally take her child's; and if he refuses to operate with the end of avoiding killing the child, he will refrain from saving the life of its mother. Yet he is not absolutely prohibited from doing either of these things unintentionally. That is the ground of the "double effect exception." Unintentionally invading a fundamental human good is not prohibited when its end is to avoid some other proportionate invasion of such a good (see pp. 486f.).

For a reason that I shall examine below (in section 5), Boyle's reasoning holds only if the conflicting plans between which the agent must choose are independent. A physician morally considering whether a craniotomy should be performed is not making a cost-benefit choice between the mother's life and the foetus's: his purpose is to save the mother's life, if he can, by all morally permissible means; and he has concluded that, to accomplish it, he must extract the foetus from her birth canal, which he can do only by crushing its head, which in turn will kill it. In maintaining that such a plan is morally permissible, Boyle assumes that the foetus's death is unplanned and unintended, and not a cost deliberately paid. A physician whose purpose is to save the foetus's life could likewise plan to save its life, with the mother's death as an unintended side effect. Since under either plan the intended good and unintended harm are the same—saving a human life and causing a human death—it would, according to Boyle's analysis, be morally permissible to carry out either.

4. Kantian Moral Absolutism, and Its Reason for Dispensing with the Double Effect Exception

Consider now a Kantian moral absolutism[7] founded on the fundamental principle that, in every voluntary action, every rational being must always be treated as an end, and never as a means only.[8] Two sorts of absolute prohibition follow from this principle: prohibitions of voluntarily doing anything that fails to treat any rational being (including yourself) as an end;[9] and prohibitions of voluntarily omitting to form and act on rational plans of life to perfect yourself and to promote the happiness of others as far as you permissibly and reasonably can. What you can permissibly do is determined by the prohibitions of the first sort; and, given your capacities, what you can reasonably do to perfect yourself is limited by what you can reasonably do to promote the happiness of others, and vice versa. Since absolute prohibitions of the latter sort prohibit only failing to form and act on some plan of self-perfection and beneficence, and not failing to do the specific actions required by any particular plan, the prohibitions of specific actions they entail are "imperfect," that is, conditional upon the plan adopted.

Since Kantian moral absolutists deny that absolute prohibitions of voluntary actions derived from their fundamental principle can come into conflict, they are predisposed to dismiss double effect exceptions as superfluous. Obviously, prohibitions entailed by reasonable plans of self-perfection and beneficence cannot conflict with prohibitions of the first sort, because they are conditional upon their observance; nor can they conflict with one another, because plans generating such conflicts are defective and must be revised. But can prohibitions of the first sort themselves come into conflict? That they are all derived from a single substantive principle does not show that they cannot, because that principle may itself be inconsistent; and since it is not logically formalizable, it cannot rigorously be proved consistent. However, Kantians contend that it has never been shown that treating a rational being as an end in some given way can either fail to treat that being as an end in some other way, or fail to treat any other rational being as an end.

Here Boyle would presumably object, "But how does an absolutist Kantian morality treat cases in which a choice must be made between killing a baby by performing a craniotomy, or its mother by not performing one? Both are voluntary actions, and presumably both are absolutely prohibited: one as voluntarily killing an innocent, and one as voluntarily and unnecessarily allowing an innocent to die. Unless it is revised to allow double effect exceptions, is not Kantian morality, if interpreted as absolutist, inconsistent?" Although he was never to my knowledge confronted with this objection, Kant would have met it by invoking what he called "the universal principle of *Recht.*"

That principle, that "Every action is *recht* that in itself or in its maxim is such that the freedom of the will of each can coexist together with the freedom of everyone in accordance with a universal law,"[10] he considered to follow immediately from his fundamental principle of morality; and he inferred from it that "if a certain use of freedom is itself a hindrance to freedom according to universal laws (that is, is *unrecht*), then the use of coercion to counteract it ... is consistent with freedom according to universal laws; in other words ... is *recht*," or, in other words, that "*Recht* is united with the authorization to use coercion against anyone who violates *Recht*."[11] Hence, in all situations in which an innocent's lawful freedom is threatened or obstructed by another, even nonvoluntarily, if that threat or obstruction can be removed only by invading that other's fundamental good, it is not only permissible to invade it, but impermissible not to.

In requiring this invasion, Kantian morality claims to be no less absolutist than Catholic morality, as Boyle presents it. However, what is absolutely prohibited, according to it, is not intentionally causing or allowing certain fundamental harms, but voluntarily causing or allowing invasions of lawful freedom. Because of this difference, it does not need double effect exceptions in order to permit invasions of the fundamental good of those who, voluntarily or not, threaten or obstruct somebody's lawful freedom. Catholic morality does, because, as presented by Boyle, it lacks a counterpart of Kant's subordinate principle that "*Recht* is united with the authorization to use coercion against anyone who violates *Recht*." That is why situations that to Kantian moralists demand that a violator of *Recht*, perhaps a nonvoluntary one, be coerced, confront Boyle's Catholic moralists with inescapable choices between unintentional causings of fundamental harms, which they legitimate by recognizing double effect exceptions. However, except when the unintentional harms between which choices must be made are not proportionate, as killing and (say) knocking unconscious are not, the doctrine of double effect cannot guide choice. Hence in treating cases in which there is a violator of *Recht*, even a nonvoluntary one, Kantian theory seems to me superior, especially as in many of them Catholic moralists will in fact recommend what it requires.

Although it is seldom discussed, and Boyle passes over it, Kantian moralists recognize a second large class of cases in which choices must be made between unavoidable fundamental harms: those in which an agent's violation of morality creates a situation in which whatever he does causes such a harm: for example, a surgeon has negligently promised to perform urgent operations at two different places at the same time, and when he finds out, it is too late to find another to do either. In such cases, both Catholics and Kantians agree that the least harm possible be chosen (*minima de malis eligenda*), but there is no double effect exception. If your own wrongdoing has put you in a situation in which you cannot avoid voluntarily doing evil, you are doubly guilty, both for putting yourself in that situation and for the evil you do in it. That evil is not absolutely unavoidable, as it must be in genuine double effect cases: it is conditional upon your having done what you could and should have refrained from doing.

5. How Extensive Is the Class of Unavoidable Fundamental Harms?

Kantian moralists freely acknowledge that there are two kinds of situation in which causing fundamental harms cannot be avoided: those in which only so can somebody's lawful freedom be safeguarded; and certain of those brought about by the agent's own wrongdoing. In situations of the former kind, they deny the need for double effect exceptions, on the ground that what is absolutely prohibited is not intentionally invading fundamental goods, but failing to safeguard lawful freedom; and in situations of the latter, they deny their validity, on the ground that the agent could have avoided being in them. If fundamental harms are unavoidable only in situations of one of these kinds, then the Kantian doctrine that double effect exceptions are superfluous seems to me to merit serious consideration by Catholic absolutists, at least if they agree with Boyle about the nature of human action.

Boyle, however, intimates that the class of unavoidable fundamental harms is much more extensive than that.

> Any action which has as a side effect the sort of harming of someone which it is plausible to think absolutely prohibited if brought about intentionally is covered by the Doctrine of Double Effect, and this class of actions is very extensive indeed. . . . (p. 492)

Is it? The answer turns on how extensive is the class of unavoidably harmful side effects. Boyle argues that it is very extensive, because plans of at least three common kinds involve such side effects, namely: (i) plans to deflect harms from some to others; (ii) plans for allocating scarce resources; and (iii) plans to reduce harmful processes occurring in patients when the treatment of one such process involves neglecting or even exacerbating the other. If he were right about plans of these three kinds, Boyle would have made out his case; but Kantians contend that he is not. They dismiss (i) as bogus; and although they accept (ii) and (iii) as genuine plans, concerning (ii) they deny that a harm is caused by so allocating resources that it cannot be prevented, given that no other allocation would be more effective; and concerning (iii) they deny that a harm that is a chosen cost is a side effect, because what is chosen is intended.

The most familiar examples of kind (i), plans to deflect harms from some to others, are invented "trolley cases," in which different individuals or groups have been tied, like the legendary Pauline, to different forks in a railroad down which an unstoppable trolley is approaching. Who among them will be killed depends on which fork it takes; that depends on whether the points at the fork remain as they are or are switched to the other fork; and that, finally, depends on some unfortunate who has one and only one choice: to switch the points (to deflect) or to leave them as they are (not to deflect).

Because prima facie their principle forbids deflecting harms from one set of innocents to another as reducing the latter to mere means to the good of the former, Kantians were apt to be discomposed by being mocked as upholding A. H. Clough's satirical commandment:

Thou shalt not kill; but need'st not strive, / Officiously, to keep alive.

Needlessly, however. They did not deny that to allow somebody to bleed to death by not applying a tourniquet to an accidentally severed artery is just as wrong as to cut his throat; and they should not have been ashamed to assert that it is wrong for a physician to endanger other innocents by recklessly speeding with help to a patient with a severed artery, even though, by refusing to endanger them, he might allow his patient to bleed to death before he brought help. There is nothing objectionable in the variant of Clough's commandment:

Thou shalt not kill; but must not strive, / By wrongful means, to keep alive.

Hence they should have declined to rush to judge imaginary trolley cases. If there has ever been an actual one, I am ignorant of it. A pilot or a truck driver steering his crashing vehicle to cause the least possible harm does not choose between definite innocents he will harm: he tries to harm none at all. Nor is it hard to see why the literature on the subject avoids real cases. Trolleys crossing points are all too easily derailed, for example by setting the points in midposition between the two forks; and, unless time is very short, those tied to the tracks (why on both forks?) can be released—helpers will multiply with each release. If it is stipulated that time is very short, how can any reliable judgment be made of what the situation is? And if such a judgment cannot be made, would not switching a railroad's points be culpably reckless? Kantian moralists are entitled to dismiss as bogus any imaginary deflection case that is not presented as comprehensively as a real one would be in any report of it that was credible. The more comprehensively such cases are described, the more morally relevant information is apt to emerge; and judgments made in the absence of morally relevant information are worthless.

As Boyle points out, plans of his kind (ii), those for allocating scarce resources, structurally differ from those of kind (i) in that they are plans to save some at the price of *letting* others suffer. But that does not go far enough. On a Kantian analysis, all such cases fall under the "imperfect duty" of benevolence. We each have an absolute duty to do what good we reasonably can, with whatever resources are at our command; but none of us are morally obliged to do more than we reasonably can. Although sometimes several allocations of resources will be equally reasonable, choosing and sticking to one rather than another until a better becomes available does not deny to *anybody* help that can reasonably be given: *all* are helped who reasonably can be. It would be as silly as it would be monstrous to describe a fireman who intentionally follows a reasonable procedure by which he rescues as many people trapped in a burning building as he can rescue, as *causing* the deaths of those he does not, because he could have chosen another reasonable procedure by which some of those rescued would have been different. In intentionally acting on any plan that is as good as possible, he cannot save some whom he can save on another equally good; but that is not a good reason for not acting on it.

Here I believe I am generalizing Boyle's own objection to Baruch Brody's doctrine that intentionally letting some people die is intentionally killing them: namely, that the intention from which it follows that some people are not given lifesaving treatment may not be that they die, but that scarce medical resources may be put to the best use (p. 490). My only complaint is that he does not pursue its implications. The important questions scarce resources raise in medical ethics are about what allocations are reasonable, given that the end is to do as much good as possible, while treating all concerned as ends in themselves. If different allocations are equally reasonable, it is reasonable to choose one of them and stick to it until it is found how to improve upon it. Yet any reasonable plan for allocating scarce resources will set a limit to what can morally be done. A physician who chooses such a plan and sticks to it neither fails to help those he would have helped on the plans he rejects, nor causes the harms they suffer. They are caused by the scarcity of resources, not by how they were allocated; for they could not have been allocated better.

Plans of Boyle's kind (iii) are those in which different kinds of harm to one and the same person are allegedly side effects of different courses of action between which a choice must be made: for example, between relieving a terminally ill patient's severe pain by analgesics that will probably shorten his life, and refraining from probably shortening his life by leaving his pain untreated.

> In both cases the side effects of taking the action will include the probability of death, but the side effects of the alternatives are also bad, and include some which it is plausible to think [it] would be absolutely impermissible to inflict intentionally. (p. 491)

In other words: when it is morally prohibited either intentionally to fail to relieve the patient, or intentionally to make it more probable that his life would be shortened, it is legitimate for a physician either to plan to relieve his pain, with the unintended side effect of probably shortening his life, or to avoid probably shortening his life, with the unintended side effect of not relieving his pain. Whichever harm is thus unintentionally caused is excused by a double effect exception.

Physicians mindful of the common-law doctrine of informed consent, which Catholics as well as Kantians approve, will object that such choices are not theirs, but their patients', and that rational patients will each make them by deciding whether or not the benefit of relief of their pain is greater than the cost of a probable shortening of their lives. That is, they will each make cost-benefit calculations; and, in planning arising from such calculations, each will be confronted with a future in which he must endure one or another of two proportionately harmful processes, and must choose *either* that one be treated at the cost of accelerating the other, *or* that one not be accelerated at the cost of the other's not being treated. Such choices will be intentions that one harmful process be treated or not accelerated at the cost of accelerating or not treating the other. And just as you do not unintentionally part with your bus fare in spending it on a glass of beer, so when you deliberately pay the cost of incurring or increasing one harm to yourself in order to obtain the benefit of avoiding or reducing another, you do not pay it unintentionally. In both cases, since paying the cost is as much part of the plan as gaining the benefit, it cannot be excused as an unintended side effect.

Two conclusions follow. First, no moral system that prohibits *both* not procuring a benefit *and* paying its cost can be rescued from inconsistency by the doctrine of double effect, because costs cannot be paid voluntarily but unintentionally. Nor does Catholic morality, as Boyle presents it, need such rescue; for, since it regards as untreatable any condition of which the effective treatment is morally prohibited, its prohibition of not intentionally treating certain conditions *if they are treatable* cannot require intentional resort to any morally prohibited treatment. Second, any moral absolutism that mistakenly regards an individual's planning to obtain benefits as independent of the costs by which he plans to obtain them, and allows payments of costs to be excused as unintended side effects, can be transformed into a form of good-maximizing consequentialism. Boyle will disarm his theory against such a transformation, unless he repudiates treating costs as unintended side effects.

6. Summing Up

Although he has established that the doctrine of double effect is indispensable in any absolutist theory of morality, like his Catholic one, in which intentionally invading certain fundamental human goods is absolutely prohibited, Boyle seems to me to have exaggerated its importance even in such moralities; for it applies only to cases in which plans to observe one prohibition are made independently of plans to observe another. Kantian moralists must concede not only that Boyle's theory is impressive, but that the practical code that he fallibly derives from it is in the main sound. However, they believe that Boyle himself has succumbed to a danger in the doctrine: that of invoking it in cases in which, on his own theory, it is superfluous or misplaced. Thus it is superfluous in cases in which evils that cannot reasonably be avoided are mistakenly treated as effects of reasonable plans for using scarce resources; and it is misplaced in cases of an individual's choosing to obtain a benefit at the cost of incurring a harm, where incurring the harm cannot be an unintended side effect.

Notes

From *Journal of Medicine and Philosophy*, 16, no. 5 (1991). © Kluwer Academic Publishers 1991. Reprinted with kind permission from Kluwer Academic Publishers.

1. J. Boyle, "Who Is Entitled to Double Effect?" *Journal of Medicine and Philosophy* 16 (1991): 475–94. Subsequent page references in the text refer to this article.

2. P. Foot, *Virtues and Vices* (Berkeley: University of California Press, 1978), pp. 19–32; W. Quinn, "Actions, Intentions and Consequences: The Doctrine of Double Effect," *Philosophy and Public Affairs* 18 (1989): 334–51.

3. A fuller exposition and defense of my views about the nature of human action may be found in A. Donagan, *Choice: The Essential Element in Human Action* (New York: Routledge and Kegan Paul, 1987). Although Boyle's approach, in which he largely follows Grisez, differs from mine, they seem to me to coincide with respect to causation and intention.

4. This analysis of action is largely the work of Germain Grisez. It has been adopted by his collaborators John Finnis and Boyle himself. It coincides in many respects with contemporary analytic theories, especially that of Donald Davidson. How it may be put to work in moral theory may be studied at length in the admirable and inevitably controversial treatment of the (now) apparently successful U.S. policy of nuclear deterrence in J. Finnis, G. Grisez, and J. Boyle, *Nuclear Deterrence, Morality and Realism* (Oxford: Clarendon Press, 1987).

5. S. Theron, "Two Criticisms of Double Effect," *The New Scholasticism* 58 (1984): 76. Theron is criticizing my endorsement (A. Donagan, *The Theory of Morality* [Chicago: University of Chicago Press, 1977], p. 159) of an analysis by Germain Grisez anticipating Boyle's, but he does not refer to Grisez directly.

6. Theron's bewilderment at my refusal to call martyred Christians suicides betrays either ignorance that actions do not cause voluntary reactions to them, or oblivion that the martyring of Christian confessors is a voluntary reaction by others to their confessions of faith (Theron, "Two Criticisms," p. 75).

7. Boyle expressly recognizes that an absolutist interpretation of Kant is possible (p. 493), although he mistakenly concludes that mine is not for a reason examined in note 9 below.

8. Although my understanding of Kant's absolutism is not that of all Kantians, as Boyle's of Catholic absolutism is not that of all Catholics, it is revisionary only in taking the second of Kant's three formulas of the categorical imperative, the formula of the end in itself, to be fundamental, and not equivalent, as he himself believed, to the first, the formula of the universal law of nature. The reasons I have given for this in *The Theory of Morality* still seem to me sound.

9. Boyle interprets my version of Kantian morality (in *The Theory of Morality*) as absolutist only in name, on the mistaken ground that it absolutely prohibits only the causing of certain harms *at will* while permitting it in an indefinite set of conditions, arrived at by an "enormously complex and intuitive" procedure (p. 493). Of course *I* think my procedure neither intuitive in any sense in which Boyle's for arriving at his list of fundamental harms is not, nor more complex than that of any other moral theory that seriously claims to be complete in outline, including his. But, however that may be, he is flatly mistaken about what I tried to do. I began by determining the kinds of action it is impermissible to do at will only as the first step to specifying the kinds it is impermissible to do under any circumstances. E.g., observing that falsehood at will is absolutely prohibited was my first step toward specifying what lying is (viz., falsehood in free communication, when it is not expected under some convention, e.g., of courtesy); and I concluded that lying is absolutely prohibited.

10. I. Kant, *Metaphysik der Sitten*, 2 vols. (Königsberg: Nicolovius, 1797), p. 230. Page references are to vol. 6 of the Prussian Academy's edition of Kant's works. The translation used is by J. Ladd, *Kant: The Metaphysical Elements of Justice* (Indianapolis: Bobbs-Merrill, 1965). I have departed from Ladd's translation only in leaving the noun "*Recht*" and cognate expressions untranslated.

When juxtaposed with their absence from absolutist moral theories like Kant's, the paucity of the cases in which the doctrine of double effect is indispensable in theories like Boyle's suggests another possibility. Perhaps the doctrine of double effect, which notoriously did not become explicit until very late, is an intruder in the Catholic moral tradition; and perhaps Kant was not mistaken in failing to discern any fundamental difference between Catholic and Lutheran views of common human morality, and in imagining that his theory captured the essence of both.

11. Ibid., p. 231.

NINE

Common Morality and
Kant's Enlightenment Project

*I*s there any prospect that all societies and cultures in the world will one day accept the same morality? No. Is there any prospect that their mores or ways of living will become much more alike? Yes, provided that the socialist and "third world" societies adopt market systems of economics, as it now appears that they will.

How can societies have much the same mores and yet not the same morality? The thinkers of the eighteenth-century Enlightenment, who laid the foundations of twentieth-century social and political science, were in a position also to lay the foundations for an adequate twentieth-century moral philosophy because they saw that the answer to this question must throw light not only on what morality is, but also on how its content is determined. Whether they did what they could have done, however, is disputed. Adam Smith's admirers do not contend that his *Theory of the Moral Sentiments* has the authority of his *Wealth of Nations*. And although not a few philosophers maintain that the greatest of the Enlightenment philosophers, Immanuel Kant, not only correctly identified the foundation of morality in his pioneering *Grundlegung zur Metaphysik der Sitten* but also demonstrated in his late and uneven *Metaphysik der Sitten* the structure of the specific moral systems that can be built on that foundation, others deny it.[1]

I maintain that Kant succeeded in what he set out to do, and, incidentally, that the view of morality he worked out can hope for widespread acceptance in a peaceable and free multicultural world. He succeeded because of a connection he divined between religion and the new social sciences. He recognized, as many Christians do not, not only that the principles of his own country's Christian morality, which he revered, are presupposed by the Christian faith in all its branches, and so are not its product, but also that the Christian faith can be preached to all nations only because those principles depend on what is common to all human beings, no matter what their race or society. In addition, he perceived that the new Enlightenment social sciences depended on a related presupposition: that social and political differences are to be explained historically, as humanly intelligible responses to different physical and social conditions.

Morality, as Kant presents it, is traditional Christian morality demystified and universalized. It does not presuppose the truth of the Christian faith, but is presupposed by it. It does, however, presuppose an Enlightenment view of human society, and it entails liberal views of both economics and politics. Kant maintained, rightly in my opinion, that the human race has little prospect of a decent, peaceable, and prosperous future unless substantial bodies of opinion everywhere come to accept this morality. In what follows I outline its structure and explain the reasons Kant gives for its various features, interrupting exposition to examine objections to it that have been found plausible. I do not, however, follow the order of Kant's exposition in any of his writings, and I disregard the blind alleys into which he was sometimes diverted.

1. What Morality Is and Why It Matters: Sociological Preliminaries

What is morality? Kant's tacit point of departure is a sociological fact: while all societies, and many groups within them, impose a set of customary dos and don'ts on their members' conduct, many but not all societies recognize a smaller set of dos and don'ts, usually more vaguely defined, that measure the conduct of human beings everywhere. The concept of morality is the concept of such a smaller set of dos and don'ts. One mark of a civilized society is that its members share this concept, for only because they have it do civilized people acknowledge that human conduct everywhere is properly judged by standards accessible to members of societies other than their own, whose opinions they are not entitled to ignore. The concept of morality is therefore inseparable from the concept of a potential community of all human beings, de jure membership of which gives rise to duties that are more fundamental than those arising from de facto membership of particular societies, although they are compatible with them.

While all civilized persons agree that there are requirements on human conduct as such, they do not agree about what those requirements are. In part that is because they do not agree about what human beings are. Some opinions about what human beings are, such as that members of certain races are not fully human, can be disregarded as demonstrably false. Others that cannot be so disregarded—for example, the Hindu doctrine that all living beings are transmigrating souls in a world governed by a morally nonneutral law of Karma, who are in some lives rational and in others not—morally divide those who hold them from those who hold contrary doctrines. Since in this paper it is impossible to discuss these differences, I can only give notice that here a doctrine contrary to the Hindu one will be assumed: namely, that each animal, human or not, is a living being distinct from every other, and that what happens to human animals depends solely on their interaction with a morally neutral natural environment, with their fellow humans, and with whatever supernatural beings (gods or demons) there may be. This doctrine is common both to the major mono-theistic religions (Judaism, Christianity, and Islam) and to nontheistic naturalism. I believe it to be true, but I shall not try to show that it is.

Although those who assent to these assumptions about human beings and the natural world they inhabit can and do disagree about morality, their disagreements are not as a rule expressed in differences of conduct. The extent of their disagreements is therefore often concealed. Thus a Chinese Maoist and a Chinese Christian may both refuse to practice or countenance abortion except when the mother has been subjected to constraint or her health is endangered. Yet the sameness of their conduct in this respect is not agreement in morality: the Maoist believes that the Chinese Communist state will not flourish unless Chinese parents have all the children they can, and that its claims are superior to all others; the Christian, while believing that China's population is excessive and should be limited by all legitimate means, also believes that killing freely conceived unborn children who are not endangering their mothers is murder. With respect to abortion, the mores of a Maoist China and of a Christian China would be much the same, but not their morality.

It is fortunate for us as human beings, even though it may confuse us as phi-losophers, that nonmoral reasons abound for disapproving of most kinds of action of which anybody disapproves for moral reasons. As Henry Sidgwick pointed out over a century ago,[2] generalizing an observation already made by Kant,[3] the mores of a society of moral egoists, who believe it to be everybody's sole duty to do whatever will maximize his or her own happiness, would be much the same as those of a society of utilitarians, who believe it to be everybody's sole duty to maximize the general happiness, or even as those of a society of "intuitional" moralists, who believe them-selves to intuit the soundness of the roughly Christian moral tradition of Victorian England. Although moral pluralism—the doctrine that those who accept one view of morality can nevertheless recognize a contradictory view of it as equally acceptable—is absurd, every sane person, theist or atheist, egoist or Kantian or utilitarian, can agree that living in a peaceable and law-abiding society is a good which it is a moral duty to promote, and that violence to persons, fraud, breach of contract, and invasions of freely chosen family relations and of justly acquired property are evils contrary to that good. In other words, as Kant and Sidgwick saw, those who thus agree may hold different views of morality. Most of us prefer not to think about this, and only think about it when it is thrust upon us by exceptional cases. We can agree to disagree about morality only because our moral disagreements do not as a rule give rise to different mores.

Up to a point even actions of kinds believed to be morally wrong can be tolerated. Liberals who believe it to be morally wrong to advocate totalitarianism of any form also believe themselves morally obliged to safeguard the legal right of totalitarians to commit the moral wrong of urging their vicious opinions on others. Yet the range of moral tolerance is limited. In many cases, those who condemn actions of a certain kind as morally wrong also believe themselves morally obliged both to prevent others from doing such actions and to refuse to do them even though the law of the land requires it. Nearly all of us believe ourselves to have both obligations with respect to murder. Hence, if we believe it to be murder to procure an abortion or to kill in an unjust war, we cannot in good conscience either stand idly by while others procure abortions or accept lawful induction for military service in what we believe to be an unjust war. Thus the internal peace of any society is imperiled in those exceptional cases in which a strong body of opinion within it denounces actions of a certain kind as morally intolerable, and another strong body affirms that any human being has the right or even the duty to do actions of that kind.

Because popular moral outrage is commonly ugly, cruel, and misdirected, the Enlightenment philosophers considered it a moral duty to combat socially divisive moral errors. And because many of the most cruel and misdirected actions for the suppression of moral wrong have been done in the name of one religion or another, they believed that establishing moral truth would tend to eliminate religious superstition. Enlightenment moralists like Kant, who were not hostile to religion as such, hoped to purify established religion of superstition. Others, however, held that religion is necessarily superstitious. Of those others, most hoped to establish a morality for human beings as such, independent of all religion; but some became moral nihilists, and attacked morality itself as, along with religion, an imposture. By a *coincidentia oppositorum* of which religion affords other examples, the superstitious deny any place within their religion for a universal human morality on the same ground as the one on which moral nihilists dismiss the Enlightenment project: that there are no requirements on human beings simply as human. Both deny that anything universally human underlies the mores of any religious or social-political community. The superstitious maintain that one particular religious community is sanctioned by divine power, and morally nihilistic free spirits deny it, but except in that one special case, both agree that all systems of mores are to be studied with disenchanted objectivity as expressions of nondivine social power.

Since requirements on conduct vary in kind, moralists may simply be disregarded unless they make plain what kind of requirement they take a moral one—one governing human conduct as such—to be. The proposition that human beings in the United States are legally required not to commit murder could be disregarded if those who put it forward could not explain what kind of requirement a legal one is, and how it requires whatever it does. As Wittgenstein once remarked, the first question raised by uttered sentences of the form "Thou shalt..." is "And what if I do not?" Legal requirements derive from social institutions exercising coercive force, but not all requirements are coercively enforced. In logic we are taught the law of noncontradiction, which can be expressed as a requirement: "Thou shalt not affirm both a sentence and its contradictory." If you ask, "And what if I do?" a sufficient answer is that if you make such a double affirmation you will both assent to a sentence and dissent from it. Of course you can persist and ask, "And what if I do that?" If you ask it, it would be idle to answer you; a peaceable response would be to flee your approach. If you do not in practice recognize requirements on what you, as human, may affirm in your thinking, your fellows cannot communicate with you. But other than thinking, are there any such requirements on what human beings, as human, may do?

2. *The Truth-Conditions of Moral Propositions: Kant's Innovations*

Asking what a requirement on human conduct as such might be is another way of asking "Under what conditions is it true to say that human beings as such are required to conduct themselves in a certain way in a certain situation?" When we know those conditions, we shall also know what we are disregarding if we disregard them.

Among Christians the answer most commonly given assimilates moral requirements to legal ones. All human beings are regarded as subjects of a divine sovereign, whose laws they are required to obey on pain of divine judgment and punishment. The divine law has been promulgated in the canonical Scriptures—in particular, the Mosaic decalogue as set out in *Exodus* 20:1–17. The defect of such an answer was made clear once for all by Plato in *Euthyphro* 10a–11a. If human beings are required not to commit murder, say, only because God has forbidden it in divinely revealed law, and if God has not so forbidden it because they are independently required as human beings not to commit it, then they are not required as human beings not to commit it. They have an overwhelmingly strong reason not to, for it would be insane to break the law of an all-knowing and all-powerful sovereign; but that is not a moral reason—a reason binding upon them as human, as distinct from subjects of a divine sovereign.

Although they all accepted Plato's objection to identifying morality with divine positive law, the Enlightenment philosophers diverged in their views of what it is. Those in the empiricist tradition concluded that the only requirements on the conduct of human beings must arise from certain of their feelings, which were sometimes obscurely attributed to a moral "sense." The most persuasive theory of this kind I have encountered is John Stuart Mill's in the brilliant third chapter of *Utilitarianism*, "Of the Ultimate Sanction of the Principle of Utility."[4] The objection to all such theories is that having some particular capacity for feeling, or some particular sense, even if having it is normal in human beings, is not essential to them as rational animals. If Mill was right, then abnormal human beings who do not *feel* approval, in the strict psychological sense, for promoting the happiness of sentient creatures generally, lack the internal ground for conducting themselves morally (that is, according to the principle of utility), which Mill himself considers ultimate. They may do so in response to external sanctions—for example, they may desire not to forfeit the approval of others—but they have no internal sanction, no reason as human beings, for it.

Because of this, Kant, along with most Enlightenment nonempiricists, concluded that the requirements of morality must arise not from feeling but from reason, to which human beings necessarily have access as rational animals.[5] St. Thomas Aquinas and other medieval scholastics anticipated them, along with many Protestants.[6] According to Aquinas, God's commands proceed from God's reason: the eternal reason by which he has created all things and governs them. Morality (or natural law, as Aquinas called it) is therefore only derivatively a set of divine commands; primarily, it is a set of requirements that reason itself imposes on human conduct, that reason being found infinitely and perfectly in God and derivatively and finitely in human beings. It may therefore be defined as *"quaedam participatio legis aeternae in rationali creatura."*[7] God's eternal law provides for each creature according to its nature; and since human beings are by nature rational animals, it provides that they are to conduct themselves according to requirements of reason. Hence, in thinking out how, as rational beings, they are required to conduct themselves, they are participating in God's legislation for them. They are capable, if they seriously set about it, of understanding why the divine law for them as human, as revealed to Moses, is as it is.

What, then, is it for rational animals to be required as rational to conduct themselves, except in their thinking, in this way rather than that? Perhaps because it is as unpretentious as it is deep, Kant's answer has been widely misunderstood.[8] It depends on distinguishing two functions of reason and noticing an implication of that distinction. Reason has both the theoretical function of investigating what is true and what is false and the practical function of investigating what, in this situation or that, is to be done or not to be done. The results of successful investigations of the former kind are propositions whose contradictories are false; those of the latter kind are intentions to act the alternatives to which are irrational. Kant observed that propositions about the irrationality of proposed alternative intentions are true or false, even though those intentions themselves are not. Although evident when pointed out, many philosophers have failed to see it. And since there are theoretical propositions about the rationality of acts of practical reason, Kant saw that the problem of what the propositions of moral theory are saying—what their truth conditions are—is solved: they are propositions about whether it is rational or not, in a certain kind of situation, to act in a certain kind of way.

Kant's distinction between theoretical and practical reason presupposes that there are requirements of reason on human conduct, just as there are on theoretical thinking. If so, they will presumably resemble the requirements of logic on theoretical thinking. But are there any? Hume denied it: only passion can move us to act, he maintained; reason cannot. Against him, Kant's first observation about practical reason is that there are requirements to which it undeniably gives rise: namely, those of technology or skill. Human beings wish to bring about a multitude of ends, and they therefore investigate how this or that end can be brought about most efficiently, that is, most cheaply, or with least sacrifice of other ends. A completed investigation into means and costs yields both a theoretical and a practical conclusion: the theoretical one that a certain means is the most efficient and least costly way of bringing about a wished-for end; and the practical one that, unless the intention to bring about that end is abandoned, it is irrational not to adopt that means. Such a practical conclusion, as Kant points out, is conditional or "hypothetical": if the means is not adopted, abandon the end, and if the end is intended, adopt the means. One or the other must be chosen, on pain of irrationality.[9]

The procedure by which Kant reaches this theoretical proposition about practical reason deserves study. As he himself noticed, it closely resembles that by which the rules of classical logic are established: a process of showing that they can be rejected only by assenting to and dissenting from the same proposition.[10] Rejecting the cheapest and most efficient means to an end resembles dissenting from the consequent of a hypothetical proposition while assenting both to it and to its antecedent. However, as Kant also noticed, moral requirements are not conditional upon whether an end is in fact adhered to; they require everyone in certain situations to act for the sake of certain ends. Hence rejecting a moral requirement, if there is such a thing, does not resemble assenting to a conditional proposition and its antecedent and dissenting from its consequent; it is not analogous to self-contradiction.

Unfortunately, Kant's own treatment of conditional requirements has led some philosophers to refuse to recognize any proposition in moral theory unless denying it can be shown to involve something resembling logical falsehood.[11] Skepticism of that sort is absurd even in philosophy of mathematics, and there is no reason to countenance it in moral theory. Rebutting it, however, does call for accuracy and candor in setting out the lines on which Kant shows that acting for certain ends is required of human beings as rational.

Doing so takes us to his second observation about practical reason: that, unless there are ends it unconditionally requires its possessors to make their own, it can require no conduct of them as its possessors.[12] Are there such ends?

From the Greeks to the present, it has been widely held that human beings as such naturally seek happiness. Kant acknowledges not only that they do but that it is rational for them to do what they reasonably judge will promote their natural end. On the face of it, a presumptive morality of rational egoism would follow: that, other things being equal, it is irrational for any human being not to do whatever actions he or she rationally judges will contribute more to his or her happiness than any available alternatives might. That is Sidgwick's first "method of ethics." Appearances, however, deceive. The conditions of any human being's happiness are, according to Kant, opaque to reason. No one can hope for anything more reliable than "counsels of prudence." Hence, since the principle of rational egoism cannot be rationally applied, it cannot require any actions of human beings as such.[13]

Is any end of action both sanctioned by reason and such that it can be rationally applied? If so, what is it? The ground of Kant's answer to this question is his third and perhaps most important contribution to the theory of practical reason. It is a distinction between two kinds of end. In drawing it, he was anticipated by scholastics,[14] although his contemporaries and successors ignored or misunderstood what he had done. His point of departure was that both the Greek and the modern conception of an end as something to be brought about by action—as something "producible" (*bewirkender*)—is incomplete. In general, an end (*telos, Zweck*) is something for the sake of which something is done. It is true that some ends are producible; "happiness" may serve as a name for one's success, in a complete life, in getting produced whatever producible ends he or she wishes for. Producible ends, however, presuppose existing beings for whose sake they are produced; that is, every producible end presupposes a "self-existent" (*selbständiger*) end. Overlooking this, most philosophers have been blind to the self-existent ends that lie behind the producible ends people have. If they had not been blind to them, Kant implies, they might have perceived that each human being necessarily regards himself or herself as "a self-existent end, and can recognize that all others necessarily so regard themselves, on the same rational ground."[15] Unfortunately, he does not expressly say what he took that rational ground to be. Can we reconstruct it?

Kant suggests that he believed that ground to be that human beings necessarily conceive of themselves as social creatures of a sort that is unique among terrestrial animals.[16] Termites, ants, and bees are social creatures, but their social behavior is programmed, not adopted as the result of rational discussion and agreement. Non-rational animals can have no part in institutions such as law and compensation or punishment for actions contrary to rationally accepted norms; not even those who contend that gorillas, chimpanzees, or whales are rational contend that those species participate in such institutions or could do so. Human beings—the only terrestrial animals known to be rational—cannot live full human lives except in communities in which their conduct is regulated by commonly accepted laws and by a variety of other institutions and private arrangements. For them, treating one another as full members of the same community is the same as treating one another as self-existent ends: as existing beings for whose sake those laws, institutions, and arrangements exist. It is true that throughout human history there have been many human political societies, that most human beings are members of only one such society, and that in most such societies most members have not been full members. But normal adult rational beings cannot rationally think of themselves, or of one another, as unfit for full membership in some political community, for they cannot rationally think of themselves as unfit by nature for taking a full part in the life of such a community. Hence, to the extent that any of them are excluded from such membership, they cannot rationally think of their exclusion except as a misfortune to be explained by private interest or prejudice, not by reason.

Requirements on the conduct of human beings as such, Kant observes, "[do] not rest at all on feelings, impulses, and inclinations; [they] rest merely on the relation of rational beings to one another, in which the will of a rational being must always be regarded as legislative, for otherwise it could not be thought of as an end in itself."[17]

In short, no normal human adult can seriously deny any of the following four propositions:

1. My own conduct is determined by my will, in the light of my own thinking about what to do;
2. The conduct of every other mature rational being is determined in the same way;
3. Among terrestrial beings, human beings are unique in that their significant behavior is conduct that is so determined;
4. Among all beings whatever, rational beings are unique in that only they can discuss how to coordinate their conduct according to agreed rules, in which each would be regarded as a self-existing end, and how to enforce those rules.

It follows from these propositions that among terrestrial beings, only humans can form the concept of an end in itself, can govern their conduct according to their conclusions about what beings, if any, fall under that concept, and can form communities the members of which recognize that they are required so to govern their conduct. From this, Kant proceeded to a fourth proposition about practical reason: that anyone who asks the question whether beings of any sort are marked off from those not of that sort as ends in themselves may rationally answer that among terrestrial beings only human ones are so marked off. "Morality," Kant concludes, "consists in the relation of every action to that legislation through which alone a realm of ends (*ein Reich der Zwecke*) is possible. This legislation, however, must be found in every rational being."[18]

3. Objections to Kant's Doctrine that Practical Reason Requires Its Possessors to Think of Themselves as Ends in Themselves

Objections of two sorts are directly made to Kant's doctrine that practical reason requires its possessors to think of themselves as ends in themselves. Some are skeptical; others deny that rationality, an abstract concept, can ground requirements on the concrete actions of flesh-and-blood human beings.

The simplest skeptical objection to Kant's doctrine is that it is logically possible to assent to all four of the propositions that are its grounds and still deny it. Yet skeptical cavils of this sort are dismissed in other fields. Even in mathematics axioms are accepted because of considerations that are dialectical (that is, in which alternatives are explored) and holistic (that is, in which account is taken of all the evidence—the apparently adverse as well as the apparently favorable). Such a process always leaves open the possibility that an accepted axiom will be replaced by another, although for the present it would be methodologically silly not to work with it. It is perverse to demand that moral philosophers dispose of skeptical doubts that no one takes seriously elsewhere.

Kant has drawn attention to a set of facts that not only distinguishes rational beings from all others but also requires them to distinguish how they treat one another from how they treat everything else, at least in the respect that it is only one another's conduct they can attempt to change by rational argument. The same set of facts also implies that, if any nonrational being were in fact an end in itself, neither it nor any other such being could act upon that consideration. It would be cruel and thus wrong for any rational being to kill an antelope for food by setting hungry wild dogs onto it when he or she could shoot it; but no ecologist would allow that wild dogs act cruelly or wrongly in killing prey in the painful way they do. Outside the realm of rational beings, nothing treats anything, even itself, as an end in itself. No nonrational animal killed by a predator thinks of itself as wronged because no nonrational animal thinks at all. It seems to me to follow that there is no good reason why rational beings should recognize anything but one another as an end in itself. If so, the only serious question that remains is whether there is any reason why they should recognize one another as such ends. Was not Kant right in thinking that it matters that a communal life according to mutually accepted reasons is possible for them, but only if they so recognize one another? In this practical case, is not reasoning from *posse* to *esse* sound?

Such reasoning is dialectical (it takes account of skeptical objections), practical (it considers whether or not to accept a certain reason for acting or not), and holistic (it purports to set forth all the facts about acting for ends relevant to what rational beings might recognize as an end, together with the implications for communal life both of recognizing one another as ends and of not doing so). It implicitly acknowledges that the practical conclusion to recognize each rational being as an end in itself is not such that the reasoning for it cannot be rejected without assuming some logically impossible proposition. On the other hand, Kant maintains that no one in his right mind can reject the reasoning for it. He confidently leaves each reader to reach his or her own verdict.

Alasdair MacIntyre has developed a disguised variant of the skeptical objection from the undeniable fact that Enlightenment moralists, even those who describe themselves as Kantian, have not in fact accepted one another's conclusions.

> If those who claim to be able to formulate principles on which rational moral agents ought to agree cannot secure agreement on the formulation of those principles from the colleagues who share their basic philosophical purpose and method, there is once again *prima facie* evidence that their purpose has failed, even before we examine their particular contentions and conclusions.[19]

To me the differences between Enlightenment moralists seem to be what might have been expected from philosophers who are in substantial agreement about morality but who differ in intellectual formation and temperament. Why should Kantian moralists agree completely about Kantian moral philosophy any more, say, than Thomist natural

theologians about Thomistic natural theology? And why should not the stricter Kantians take comfort from fellow travelers like John Rawls, just as the stricter Thomist
natural theologians, confronted with Ockhamists and fideists, take comfort from
fellow-travelers like Francisco Suarez?

"Yet are you not troubled by the fact that most moral philosophers who have
read Kant are not Kantian in any sense: for example, they do not agree with Kant
that practical reason requires its possessors to regard one another as ends in all their
actions?" I agree only to the extent that I am persuaded that they have understood
Kant's thought as, I believe, most Kantians today do: for example, his distinction
between producible and self-existent ends. The Kant whom most Kantians defend is
not the Kant whose doctrines are described in anti-Kantian polemics from Hegel to
MacIntyre. Does not the utilitarian slogan "Each for one, and none for more than
one,"[20] suggest that utilitarians who grasp Kant's distinction between self-existent and
producible ends will have difficulty in rejecting it—and whatever follows from it?

Of those who understand Kant's conception of rational beings as self-existent
ends, which in fact reject it, and on what grounds? I leave Nietzsche's abusive and
antihuman rhetoric to those with a taste for it; it seems to me to disqualify itself as
reasoning.[21] However, there is a tradition traceable to Hegel according to which
grounding morality on human rationality "homogenizes" human beings and so exalts
a tendency in modern mass society to "undermine the communities or characteristics
by which people formerly identified themselves and put nothing in their place."[22] The
mistake of all such objections derives from an error that pervades much Hegelian
criticism of non-Hegelian philosophy: the error of believing that abstracting a property
of something, and examining what follows from having that property, implies that
that thing has no other properties.

It is perfectly true that Kant rejects the "communities or characteristics by which
people formerly identified themselves"—and distinguished themselves from other people—as grounds for morality, but he did so not to deny that human beings are
community-forming creatures or that they have characteristics in common with some
but not all others that affect which communities they choose to join, but to determine
the rational limits on the kinds of community they may aspire to form or join and
the kinds of distinguishing characteristics they may cultivate. Far from homogenizing
human beings, Kantian doctrine assumes that they cannot be homogenized. At the
same time, it rejects as contrary to practical reason any political community that claims
to determine the producible *tele* or ends their members must devote their lives to
bringing about, as Hegel and his followers admire the ancient Greek *polis* for doing.
Kant differs from Hegel and his post-Hegelian critics in his freedom from the illusion
that human beings will ever be completely at home in any society there ever has been
or ever will be on earth, and hence from the illusion that decent members of a society
in which ethical truth is fully recognized cannot be alienated from it or from their
fellows. Hegel's idealization of the Greek *polis* is as indefensible as his delusion that,
while the elected bourgeois legislatures of France and Britain neither did nor could
concretely embody universal reason, the pre-1848 Prussian monarchy did not but could

have done so. Given the inescapable propensity to corruption of everything human, whether individuals or institutions, alienation that is remediable can be remedied only by intensifying alienation that is not. A moral theory may be true and yet alienation persist after it becomes generally accepted. As Kant more and more came to recognize, his moral theory implies that every human being is a *viator* whose destination is not to be at home in any actual earthly community.[23]

4. How Kant Determines the Content of Morality

If Kant was right in concluding that the existence of morality presupposes that practical reason imposes unconditional requirements on the conduct of its possessors, and that it could not do so unless it recognized certain existing beings as ends, in the sense of beings for whose sake its possessors rationally act, then certain conclusions about the structure of morality follow.

The fundamental requirement that practical reason imposes on its possessors is that they treat one another equally, as beings for whose sake they must act. From this fundamental requirement certain "side-constraints" (the expression of Nozick's) follow on what they may rationally do.[24] The principle of these side-constraints is that no rational being may be used simply as a means to doing something for the sake of anybody else. Hence no possessor of practical reason may interfere in activities of others in which the status of everyone else as an end—their dignity—is respected. Violence and fraud may not be used against those who are not violating the dignity of others even if, on balance, good will come of their use.

However, more than side-constraints follow from the fundamental requirement. One does not treat other rational beings as ends equally with oneself unless one supports their innocent projects as far as one can without disproportionate loss to one's own. That may require one actively to help them as well to protect them from wrongful interference by others. Thus it does not follow that no one may be a means to benefiting another. No rational being may be *simply* a means to benefiting another, but every rational being is required, so far as it is in his or her power, to be a means for the good of others. Yet the benefits anyone confers on anyone else must be in a system of social relations in which those who confer them are ends equally with those on whom they are conferred. Contractual exchanges of benefits between equals are among Kant's models of social interaction in which no party is treated as a mere means. Models of its negation are enforced exchanges of benefits between slaves and masters and bargains driven with the unfortunate to which equals would not have agreed.

Despite the familiar charge that Kantian morality is individualist and nonsocial, Kant insisted in the first volume of *Metaphysik der Sitten*, the *Rechtslehre*, that much of what makes life civilized is possible only in a political society.[25] A good will exercised outside a civil society is as good as a good will exercised in one, but it realizes many fewer moral possibilities. Since practical reason requires us to benefit one another, without any of us being reduced to mere means to others' ends, it also requires us to join with our fellows in setting up a political society if we do not live in one, and, if we do, in supporting the one in which we live. Outside political societies neither peace nor prosperity are possible: there is no way of resolving honest differences of opinion about what is due to each from each and no way of compelling compliance with the enforceable parts of morality by those tempted to flout them.

Since all human beings are equally one another's ends, each of us has duties to himself or herself as well as to others. And since, subject to the requirements of practical reason, rational beings each pursue their own happiness as they conceive it, it is rational for normal human adults to be self-supporting, either as individuals or as members of freely formed families, and for nonadult children to be supported primarily by their parents. Yet even in communities of farming families it would be irrational if there were no communal arrangements for looking after the unfortunate: young orphans, widows with young children, the disabled, and the aged. In more complex industrial societies it would be irrational if, besides such arrangements, there were not also others to ensure that those seeking work could find it on terms that respected their dignity as self-existent ends.

Given that each normal adult rational being is primarily required to support himself or herself, one would be irrational both in pursuing one's own well-being as one conceives it and in supporting others in pursuing theirs, if one did not plan to do both effectively. One is not required to take every opportunity either to improve oneself or to help others; everyone has so many opportunities of both kinds that one must choose among them. What is required is that one give short measure neither to oneself nor to others. For most people, the stronger temptation is to give short measure to others, but Dickens's Mrs. Jellyby reminds us that for some the opposite is the stronger temptation. Both in improving oneself and in supporting others' pursuit of happiness, reason requires not that one act in any specific way in any specific situation, but that one make and act upon rational plans.

In making such plans, one must plan to observe the side-constraints imposed on one's actions by the requirement that in all one's intentions every rational being must be regarded as a self-existent end. One may not violate a side-constraint either to improve oneself or to help others because the ground of plans to do both is that every rational being, oneself included, must be treated as a self-existent end in all of one's actions. This is the ground of St. Paul's dictum—which has so puzzled utilitarians and other consequentialists—that even for the glory of God it would be wrong to do evil that good may come.[26]

5. Objections to How Kant Determines the Content of Morality

The major social problems of Kant's time were the persistence of unfree political, social, and economic institutions and warfare between sovereign states for political ends to which their citizens were assumed to be mere means. Although he wrote under a galling censorship that made the candid publication of his political views impossible, in his treatment of public law in the first volume of *Metaphysik der Sitten* he disguised a powerful argument for a liberal republican society as an analysis, heavily indebted to Rousseau, of the nature of all political societies, including the Prussia of his day.[27] A year before publishing this penetrably disguised manifesto of political liberalism, denouncing aggressive war as a means to any morally legitimate political end,[28] he had already ensured that in the illiberal and nationalist Europe that emerged from the Napoleonic wars he would be ridiculed as a mere theorist, ignorant of how society works, and too arrogant to confess it. He would also be despised as an ideologist of capitalist individualism by left-wing intellectuals who blamed warfare and political repression not on illiberalism but on market liberalism. Objections of both sorts continue to be made.

The most persistent objection to Kant's determination of the content of morality is to its deductive structure. Does not a system in which propositions about specific requirements of practical reason are deduced, with the aid of specificatory minor premises, from first principles, presuppose that those principles are self-evident, independent of the precepts derived from them? Is not Kant's system, in short, "foundationalist?"[29] Would it not be viciously circular unless its principles were "established on grounds that do not presuppose the acceptability of some or all of the system derived from [them]?"[30]

No, it would not be. This objection rests on a misunderstanding of the purpose, in any field, of putting a body of thought into deductive form, or even into axiomatic form, in which all undemonstrated propositions must be expressly stated in advance. In mathematical logic a theory is put into axiomatic form primarily to make it possible to test it by ensuring that what is claimed to follow from it, true or false, does so rigorously. The result of Frege's attempted axiomatization of arithmetic was to show that one of his axioms was false. Yet a deductive system like Kant's system of morality is not axiomatic. In it specific requirements are deduced from a single moral principle (that it is irrational of possessors of practical reason not to treat themselves and each other as self-existent ends), but this occurs by way of an indefinite number of non-moral specifications of kinds of failure to treat others as self-existent ends—a number that is constantly being augmented, and of which any may be revised or even repudiated. Yet a deductive system of this sort can be tested much more rigorously than the clouds of unsystematic "intuitions" that are all most moralists will commit themselves to, although less so than an axiomatic system.

If a deductive system makes intelligible a considerable body of hitherto unsystematic beliefs, without implying anything to which serious objection can be offered, then it is rational to accept provisionally deductions from its principles about which no one hitherto has had any opinion at all; and it is a secondary purpose of deductive systems to provide such reason for accepting its derivative propositions. In morality as in law, deductive systems are refined as new consequences are drawn from them and found wanting, but it is intelligible that a stage will be reached at which it is reasonable to suppose that all future refinements will be in its nonmoral specificatory premises, not in its principles. Jewish and Christian moralists hold that this stage was reached millennia ago, when the moral parts of the Mosaic Torah were promulgated. Kant agreed with them, although he believed that the biblical formulations of the principles of morality could be improved upon.

Those who object that this is foundationalist fail to distinguish what is systemically fundamental from what is epistemically fundamental. The principles of any deductive system, moral or other, are systemically fundamental: its derived propositions are explained by reference to them, and they are not explained by reference to anything higher. They are not, however, epistemically fundamental; no part of any intellectual system is. Epistemically, a deductive system stands if it has no consequences that must be rejected as false for any reason, if no more comprehensive alternative is equally unobjectionable, and if no equally comprehensive one better explains what it explains. Its principles are accepted on holistic grounds and can always be called in question as new evidence comes to hand, but, as long as there is no reason to question them, the system's derivative propositions are accepted because they follow from its principles.

The propositions by which Kant arrives at his fundamental moral principle—that reason is practical, that practical reason is not confined to means-end or cost-benefit calculations, that there can be no unconditional requirements of practical reason unless there are self-existent rational ends as well as producible ones, and that rational beings are such ends—are offered not as self-evident but as inseparable from a variety of beliefs most of us share or can be brought to share. The very structure of the two morally substantive sections of *Grundlegung*, which is reflected in their titles, "Passage from Common Moral (*sittliche*) Rational Cognition (*Vernunfterkenntnis*) to Philosophical" and "Passage from Popular Moral *Weltweisheit* to Metaphysics of Morals," shows that at every stage his theory grows out of a steadily deepening reflection on common moral thinking.

The second continuing line of objection to Kant's moral theory is to its universality and abstraction. Sometimes it is complained that it is "unhistorical." The charge is vague, but the reply to it need not be. Kant saw the danger to Enlightenment civilization both from nationalist and imperialist wars and from the attitudes that go with them, in which members of one nation-state disregard the dignity of members of others as self-existent ends; he also saw that the only possible remedy was to expose those attitudes as irrational. To reject his exposure, as Hegel did, and to deny content to a morality of humanity, as distinct from the *Sittlichkeit* of this particular *Volk* or that, even if it is not intended to serve the interests of any particular nationalism, is as blind in theory as it is pernicious in practice. Without varieties of community human life is impoverished, but what makes a community different from others, precious though it may be, cannot provide its members with standards by which to judge when its life has gone rotten. Decent human variety presupposes recognition of common human dignity.

What holds for communities holds, even more emphatically, for religions. Every religion has something to learn about human decency from the practice of some other religions. But Kant's Enlightenment morality implies that what any acceptable religion offers is not a distinctive morality but a remedy for the state of those who already have a more or less adequate conception of the morality common to all such religions, but who flout it in practice. Most religions are radically false, and many are morally evil. But if any religion is true, as I believe Christianity is, it will satisfy the test proposed by Jesus: by its fruits you shall know it. Human beings can, if they work at it, tell whether the fruits of a religion are sound or rotten because, as Kant saw, they can find by reflection on their own situation the self-existent ends of all rational action. Christianity, along with some other religions, teaches that, besides the finite self-existent ends we encounter in each other, there is an infinite self-existent end to know whom is perfect happiness. But that cannot invalidate ordinary human moral knowledge; as St. John explained, we cannot love God, whom we have not seen, unless we love one another, whom we have.

Notes

From Gene Outka and John P. Reeder, Jr., eds. *Prospects for a Common Morality.* © 1993 by Princeton University Press. Reprinted by permission of Princeton University Press.

   1. Immanuel Kant, *Grundlegung zur Metaphysik der Sitten*, 2d ed. (Riga: J. F. Hartnoch, 1786), and *Metaphysik der Sitten*, 2d ed. (Königsberg: F. Nicolovius, 1798). Two page numbers are given for all passages quoted or cited from Kant; the first refers to the original edition, and the second refers to the appropriate volume of the Berlin Academy's edition of Kant's collected works (vols. 4 and 6, respectively, for the works cited in this note). For the former, I chiefly follow L. W. Beck's translation in *Immanuel Kant: The Critique of Practical Reason and Other Writings in Moral Philosophy* (Chicago: University of Chicago Press, 1949); for vol. 1 of the latter, J. Ladd, trans., *Kant: The Metaphysical Elements of Justice* (Indianapolis: Bobbs-Merrill, 1965); and for vol. 2 of the latter, James Ellington, trans., *Kant: The Metaphysical Elements of Virtue* (Indianapolis: Bobbs-Merrill, 1964).

   2. In *The Methods of Ethics*, 7th ed. (London: Macmillan, 1907), pp. 162–75, 496–503.

   3. *Grundlegung*, pp. 8–9/397–98.

   4. "If there were not...a natural basis of sentiment for the utilitarian morality, it might well happen that [it] also, even after it had been implanted by education, might be analysed away. But there *is* this basis of powerful natural sentiment...[namely] that of the social feelings of mankind—the desire to be in unity with our fellow-creatures, which is already a powerful principle in human nature, and happily one of those which tend to become stronger, even without express inculcation, from the influences of advancing civilization" (J. S. Mill, *Utilitarianism* [Indianapolis: Bobbs-Merrill, 1957], pp. 39–40).

   5. Although many utilitarians are empiricists and follow Mill, many are rationalists who on this point follow Kant—Sidgwick, for example (see *Methods of Ethics*, pp. 98–104).

   6. See, e.g., John Calvin, *Institutio Christianae Religionis* (1559), 2.8.1.

   7. "A certain participation by rational creatures in the eternal law," St. Thomas Aquinas, *Summa theologiae* I–II, 91, 2; cf. I–II, 100, 1.

   8. For a radical misunderstanding that distorted the development of ethics in analytical philosophy, see G. E. Moore, *Principia Ethica*, 2d ed. (Cambridge: Cambridge University Press, 1922), pp. 126–33.

   9. *Grundlegung*, pp. 40–41/414–15. I owe this analysis of Kant's treatment of techno-

logical imperatives to Thomas E. Hill, Jr., "The Hypothetical Imperative," *Philosophical Review* 82 (1973): 429–50.

10. *Grundlegung*, pp. 44–45/417.

11. They do so with some encouragement from Kant himself, in his attempt to derive the whole content of morality from a principle of universalization. He argues that it is irrational to act on any intention for which it would either be self-contradictory or contrary to your will to intend that everyone in similar situations should act as you intend to (*Grundlegung*, pp. 51–59/420–25, 80–81/436–37). In his practice in *Die Metaphysik der Sitten* Kant abandons his doctrine in *Grundlegung* that the whole content of morality could and should be derived from his universalization principle by not attempting so to derive it. See my "Structure of Kant's Metaphysics of Morals," *Topoi* 4 (1985): 61–72, especially 61–62; and my *Theory of Morality* (Chicago: University of Chicago Press, 1977), pp. 13, 57–59.

12. *Grundlegung*, pp. 64/428, 80–83/436–37.

13. Ibid., pp. 42–43/415–16.

14. Both Aquinas and Duns Scotus anticipate Kant here. See my "Human Ends and Human Actions: An Exploration of St. Thomas's Treatment,'" essay five in this volume, especially sections 1 and 2.

15. *Grundlegung*, pp. 64–66/428–29.

16. Especially in ibid., pp. 73–79/432–36.

17. Ibid., p. 76/434.

18. Ibid., p. 75/434.

19. Alasdair MacIntyre, *After Virtue*, 2d ed. (Notre Dame, Indiana: University of Notre Dame Press, 1984), p. 21.

20. "The greatest happiness principle . . . is a mere form of words without rational signification unless one person's happiness, supposed equal in degree (with the proper allowance made for kind), is counted for exactly as much as another's" (Mill, *Utilitarianism*, p. 76).

21. Curiously, these include Alasdair MacIntyre, who, referring to *Die fröhliche Wissenschaft*, sect. 335, writes that "in five swift, witty and cogent paragraphs [Nietzsche] disposes . . . of what I have called the Enlightenment project to discover rational foundations for an objective morality" (*After Virtue*, p. 113). Of these five paragraphs, this is the one most directly about Kant:

> What? You admire the categorical imperative within you? This "firmness" of your so-called moral judgment? This "unconditional" feeling that "here everyone must judge as I do"? Rather admire your *selfishness* at this point. And the blindness, pettiness, and frugality of your selfishness. For it is selfish to experience one's own judgment as a universal law, and this selfishness is blind, petty, and frugal because it betrays that you have not yet discovered yourself nor created for yourself an ideal of your own, your very own—for that could never be somebody else's and much less that of all, all! (Friedrich Nietzsche, *The Gay Science*, trans. Walter Kaufman. [New York: Vintage Books, 1974], p. 265)

Kant, I imagine, would have been content to observe that Nietzsche's conception of unselfishness is illustrated to perfection by the argument of this passage.

22. Charles Taylor, *Hegel* (Cambridge: Cambridge University Press, 1975), pp. 412–14. The passages quoted appear in the selection reprinted in Michael J. Sandel, ed., *Lib-*

eralism and Its Critics (New York: New York University Press, 1984), pp. 177–97; Sandel's comment (p. 10) suggests that he is more impressed by Taylor's account of Hegel's criticism of Kant than by Taylor's own reservations about it (pp. 179, 191–97).

23. Taylor admirably exposes the unacceptability of Hegel's ethical theory, but he fails to bring out how paradoxical, on his own showing, it is. He argues convincingly that he held that "the last time that the world saw an effortless and undivided *Sittlichkeit* was among the Greeks" (*Hegel*, p. 378), and, just as convincingly, that one of Hegel's historical heroes is Socrates, who "undermined or broke with the *Sittlichkeit* of [his] people" (p. 377). As I think Kant would have said, "The case rests." For those who (like Hegel) continue to idealize the Greek *polis* after reading Plato, I recommend Simon Hornblower, *The Greek World: 479–323 B.C.* (New York: Methuen, 1983).

24. Robert Nozick, *Anarchy, State, and Utopia* (New York: Basic Books, 1974), pp. 28–33.

25. Kant, *Metaphysik der Sitten*, 1:154–58/305–8.

26. See Samuel Scheffler, *The Rejection of Consequentialism* (Oxford: Clarendon Press, 1982), for a recent puzzled attempt to explain why nearly everyone agrees that consequentialism is wrong. Scheffler tacitly assumed that no satisfactory answer was available when he wrote. Kant's name is absent from its index.

27. See especially *Metaphysik der Sitten*, 1:203–12/318–23, 238–44/338–42.

28. Immanuel Kant, *Zum ewigen Frieden* (Königsberg: F. Nicolovius, 1796). This is translated into English as *To Perpetual Peace.*

29. For an example of this criticism, directed against my *Theory of Morality* rather than against Kant, see Jeffrey Stout, *Ethics after Babel* (Boston: Beacon Press, 1988), pp. 129–35. However, Stout's belief that Kant is a foundationalist appears in an aside on p. 169, to which attention is drawn in his index, p. 334.

30. Stout, *Ethics after Babel*, p. 130.

TEN

On Developing a
Contemporary Theistic Ethics

In "Platonism and Naturalism: Options for a Theocentric Ethics,"[1] Robert M. Adams explores how to develop a contemporary theistic ethics that would be Platonic and Augustinian rather than Aristotelian and Kantian. Adams is as balanced and fair as he is timely and provocative. From the moral point of view, my comments on his essay will be Kantian; from the epistemological point of view, they will be neither Kantian nor Platonist—the best description of them I can give is "realist and holist," but those words do not mean the same things to everyone.

The Platonic theocentric ethics Adams explores has six tenets, namely (1) God is a good transcending all others, and other goodness is a participation[2] in God's goodness; (2) God's goodness is final, and so neither instrumental nor beneficial; (3) God's goodness is also beauty: God is the ultimate aesthetic object as well as the ultimate source of morality; (4) in apprehending finite goods as good we glimpse "as in a mirror darkly" the infinite good in which they participate; (5) the object thus glimpsed is loved; and (6) "something about divine goodness is cognitively accessible, at least in part, to people in general." The first three are doctrines about what God's goodness is in itself, no matter how it is apprehended: they are ontological. Of them, (1) and (2) would be asserted by both Kantian and Aristotelian Christians as essential to their theocentric ethics; and (3) can be denied by nobody who accepts the authority of the *Psalms* or *Job.* The second three, however, are epistemological: they are about how finite goods are apprehended, about what accompanies that apprehension, and about to whom that apprehension is accessible. All three have senses in which I think they are true—and in which Aristotelians and Kantians would accept them. But are they the Platonic senses in which Adams asserts them?

Essentially this question can arise as a problem of scriptural interpretation. Consider the passage in the *First Epistle of John*, which presupposes Adams's three Platonist ontological theses, in which we are told that, although "No one has ever seen God; if we love one other, God lives in us..." (4:12), because "those who do not love a brother or sister whom they have seen, cannot love God whom they have not seen" (4:20).[3] John, as I understand him here, says two things. First, our reason for loving our brother or sister is not that we *see* God and so see that our brother or sister is God's image; for we do not see God. And secondly, if we love our brother or sister who is in fact God's image, we not only indirectly love God, but can learn directly to love God by learning, through revelation, that God has made us, and "we are the people of his pasture, and the sheep of his hand" (*Ps.* 95:7).

Nor is that the whole of the matter. The core of the chapter from which I have offered my interpretation is the assertion "In this is love, not that we loved God but that he loved us and sent his Son to be the atoning sacrifice for our sins" (*1 John* 4: 10). You do not "see" God, and a fortiori neither do you see that God loves you, nor do I see that he loves me: we believe it because we accept a long chain of testimony, which includes that of John, whose letter begins, "We declare to you what was from the beginning, what we have heard, what we have seen with our eyes, what we have looked at and touched with our hands, concerning the word of life" (1:1). We began by loving some people, among them ourselves; and by not loving, even hating, some others. Because we were so taught by some tradition or other (perhaps by that of Moses, the prophets, and the apostles) we learned that God loves us, and hence that even those we hate are lovable. We "see" God in one another only to the extent that we believe what is reported about God.

What of the numerous philosophers, from neo-Platonists like Philo and Augustine to the Aristotelians—Muslim, Jewish, and Christian—who all professed to have proved by natural reason the existence of a being with attributes that belong (according to Jews, Christians, and Muslims) only to the God of Abraham, Isaac, and Jacob? I believe they were mistaken. I concede that some of the proofs they offered are internally valid; but all of them have some premise that can be rationally doubted. God does not appear in the world as God, except by deniable signs—even that of being resurrected from the dead. Nor do we need the hypothesis of divine creation as a foundation for the sciences of nature. As a matter of fact, most of the founders of modern natural science seem to have been sincere theists, like most of their contemporaries; and many natural scientists still are, but nothing of permanent scientific value in their results requires the hypothesis of a divine creator. A self-subsistent realm of nature is all natural science need postulate. And that presents a difficulty for any approach to God similar to Plato's approach to the Form of the Good, which depends on finding that nature is not a true realm of being—of objects admitting of scientific *episteme*—but only the realm of phenomena, which are between being and not-being, such being as they have being derived by participation in the inhabitants of the true realm of being, that of the Forms. No monotheist—Jewish, Christian, or Muslim—can deny that the realm of created nature is a realm of being.

Curiously, Adams finds an epistemological difficulty in James Gustafson's non-Platonic theocentric ethics that closely resembles the one I find in his Platonic one. Gustafson's eminence and the distinction of his work, as Adams rightly says, need no certification. The chief points in the ontology underlying Gustafson's ethics seem to me as to Adams certainly true, namely, that ultimately, the end that matters is God, not any human being or all human beings; that nonhuman as well as human creatures can have ethical claims on us by virtue of their relation to God; and that they do so, not merely as things believed to participate in the divine goodness, but as things loved by virtue of doing so. Gustafson then proceeds to infer not only that the claims nonhuman creatures have on us have "to be determined in relation to ... the will of God for all things as that might be dimly discerned" (I, 99),[4] but also that human cognitive-affective powers as a whole enable us, at least dimly, to discern God's will.

Here, like Adams, I distrust my understanding of Gustafson's elaborate and subtle treatment of human cognitive-affective capacities in chapter 7 of *Theology and Ethics*. Gustafson is orthodox in concluding that since intellect, intention, and "radical agency" (that is, free will), as they are ascribed to human beings, can truly be ascribed to God only analogically,[5] the discernment of God's purposes in nature of which human beings are capable is both partial, being confined to a small part of the whole, and dim. It resembles, but is not identical with, a deeply experienced woodsman's discernment of certain things in the course of nature. Such discernment is usually considered to resemble what is sometimes called the "sagacity" of brute animals: it is a matter of perception, memory, and imagination, and the feelings that go with the exercise of those capacities. Just as the woodsman's discernment of nature's course is not simply an anticipation of an ecologist's scientific understanding of it, which depends wholly on systematic causal analysis and theory, so human discernment of God's purposes in nature is not simply an anticipation of what would be good for a given ecosystem. Yet, Gustafson maintains, human beings can sometimes discern God's purposes in nature.

Adams, as a Platonist-Augustinian, voices a deep uneasiness with this which I share: namely, that Gustafson's God seems to be one in whom nature is, rather than a creator transcending nature. If such a panentheism is true, then I am inclined to think that the first modern panentheist, Spinoza, rightly concluded that, while we can truly speak of the intellect and will of God, then God's intellect must be his full understanding of how nature as it is (that is, himself) is completely determined by nature's laws; and his will must be indistinguishable from his recognition that nature cannot be otherwise.[6] In other words, *Deus sive Natura* neither is nor can be anything but itself: it has no ends beyond itself to fulfill, nothing within it can make any difference to what it is, nor is there anything outside it. The rational human attitude toward it is therefore *acquiescentia*: being at peace with what Nature is. It is proper to save whales or elephants from extinction because we care about them. If, *however*, they become extinct because of human actions, even misguided ones, that extinction will no more be against the will of God than when any other species becomes extinct owing to some environmental change, or to a predator exterminating instead of culling a species that supplies its food. If we are simply "in" Nature, what we do is determined by her so far as what happens in her is determined; and if we think that we either cooperate with or oppose Nature, we are deluded by our imaginations. It is as irrational to try to cooperate with Nature as to try to alter her course. Of course, dropping Spinoza's name does not show that Whitehead, whom I take to have influenced Gustafson, was mistaken. However, I am prepared to defend the opinion that, if panentheism is true, then Spinoza was right that human projects for cooperating with God are chimerical, that a theocentric ethics must be an ethics of *acquiescentia*: that is, an analysis of the highest kind of human freedom human beings can attain in view of the laws of human behavior, accompanied by stern advice to be at peace with how things necessarily are, and not to make a fool of oneself by either railing at them or satirizing them.[7]

Setting aside this deep difficulty, like Adams I have a simple epistemological one, namely, that what human beings can discern about God's purposes in nature is a much weaker ground for conclusions about human responsibilities for the nonhuman creation than others that are readily available. I assume that we agree about what I take to be the grounds that Christians have traditionally given, which are human-centered. All the law (the Mosaic Torah) and the prophets hang on the two principles that we are to love God with our whole heart, and our neighbors as ourselves; and the portion that has to do with God is about worship (for example, the prohibition of idolatry, the institution of the Sabbath). As for the world we inhabit, we are told that its fruits and its nonhuman inhabitants are ours, to be used for our good, subject to special revealed laws, such as the dietary laws promulgated through Moses for the Jewish people. Although the question of whether we may exterminate a species if that is for our good is not expressly answered in either the Jewish or the Christian Scriptures, there seems to be no reason to deny that if it were for our good to exterminate the cockroach or the Argentine ant, and if we could (at present we cannot), it would not be wrong to exterminate either. Of course, it must be for our good to do so; and, in general, *Genesis* informs us that God found both the nonanimal and the animal creation "very good." Yet *Isaiah* 11:1–9, in declaring that when the Messiah comes there will be no predation among animals (the lion eating straw like an ox), appears to imply that all is less than well in the animal realm as it is. I agree with Gustafson, Adams, and most educated Americans that "it would be reasonable to make some substantial expenditures and some significant changes in human behavior simply for the purpose of saving the peregrine falcon, or the African elephant, from extinction" (p. 34). However, I also agree with Adams that our wish to save those species is partly sentimental, and that the least disputable reasons for so wishing are that the harm extermination would do, by impoverishing the environment for all human beings indefinitely, would be much greater, perhaps very much greater, than the good extermination would bring to a few people for a short time. To this, Christians traditional enough to believe in original sin may wish to add that, whenever they are moved to "hurt or destroy" (in Isaiah's phrase) any living thing, they have been taught to ask themselves whether they do so from malice—especially when the reasons that spring to their tongues are political and sanctimonious.

To these traditional lines of thought, Adams adds two that are distinctly Platonic. After stating each, I shall comment on it.

The first is that certain natural phenomena, for example the survival of species as distinct from individuals of those species, are discernibly intrinsic goods, because they each participate in the infinite goodness of God. This seems to me substantially correct and an inescapable deduction from what traditional Christianity adapted from Platonic ontology and bequeathed to those of us who would not describe ourselves as Platonists. Here we must remember Adams's caution that "theistic Platonists are, after all, theists. The supreme Good they worship is not an impersonal Form, but an agent" (p. 37). All nonrational species participate in the being and hence the goodness of God. Their good, and even their survival, is a lesser good than the good of rational creatures, but unless their good is incompatible with the good of rational creatures, it has a claim on them. However, I venture one amendment: that not all participated goods should be recognized as ends for action. I shall return to the question of which goods, if any, should be so recognized.

The second line of thought that Adams commends is surprising as well as persuasive: it is a Platonic reason for the place given in Christian ethics to the actual, and in particular to the contingent:

> An abstract and impersonal conception of a transcendent supreme Good would give us little help in seeing a reason to regard actual goods more highly than merely possible goods. It is different, however, if we conceive the supreme Good as personal. Then actual goods can be seen as divine *gifts*, and as such can claim a special respect which lends force to certain rights we claim. We can say, for example, that our bodily organs and our relationships with our children, if we have any, have been given us by God.... And inasmuch as we can say the same about the goods inherent in a system of social relationships in which the medical and parental rights in question are recognized, we have a reason to respect that system and regard those rights as objectively valid. This clearly leaves it open to us to suppose that if we came on creatures, otherwise like us, who lived with evident satisfaction in social arrangements that differed in these respects, we might be persuaded that they had received different gifts, and different rights, from God. (p. 39)

Although this theory of divine gifts seems to me fruitful, I fear that it may invite the unwary to draw invalid inferences. To explain my qualms, I must remind you of the traditional Christian view of the place of human beings in a theocentric universe.

According to that theory, the reason why actually existing things have a claim on us that possibly existing ones do not is that all things produced by action are produced for the sake of beings already in existence. Aristotle recognized this when he distinguished two senses of the expression "that for the sake of which":

That that for the sake of which is found among the unmovables is shown by
making a distinction; for that for the sake of which is both that *for* which and
that *towards* which, and of these one is unmovable and the other is not. Thus it
produces motion by being loved, and it moves the other moving things. (*Metaphysics* XII, 1072^b1–3)[8]

The unmovable *for* which a movable is moved from one state *toward* another must
pre-exist the movement brought about for its sake. Duns Scotus later maintained that
only that *for* which is strictly the end (*finis*) of the movement; the final stage of the
movement—that *toward* which it is a movement—is not properly its *finis*, but its
finitum, that which is ordered to the end. For Aristotle as for Christians, God is the
ultimate end for which all good agents act in their good actions; and Christians, who
believe that God is creator of natural things as well as the end for which they act,
also believe that certain creatures (those who as such participate in the divine goodness) may also be said to be ends *for* which by participation.

Such creatures are not such ends, however, simply because, as divinely created,
they participate in the divine goodness. The survival of every animal species is not as
such a divine purpose; for, by processes involving no human action whatever, nature
as created by God has brought about the extinction of many animal species. Hence,
the scriptural permission to human beings to use animals for their benefit implies
that, if it is genuinely for their benefit (as it will be in very few cases), they may
exterminate a species if they can. What marks out a creature as an end is not that it
is divinely created, but that it is an image of God: that is, that it participates in the
divine attributes of rationality and agency, as not even brute animals do, let alone
plants or inanimate things. If it is objected that rationality and agency are properties
too abstract and empty to make their possessors images of God, it is enough to point
out that all thinking is abstract, and that, far from being empty, the properties of
rationality and agency are rich in what they imply about their possessors. Nothing
can be a rational agent and be incapable of intellectual love, or capable of intellectual
love and not be an agent. Brute animals may love in the sense of desire; but not as
an act of will elicited intellectually. In short, only rational beings, like God, can be
moved by intellectual love of an end *for* which to bring about a change. It is this that
makes them, like God, ends *for* which—what Kant called "ends in themselves."

The reason traditional Christian morality holds moral claims arising from certain
actualities to outweigh claims arising from any possibilities is that it regards all actual
creatures that are images of God, and only those creatures, as being, like God, genuine
ends *for* which, and love of whom has moved God himself, the ultimate end *for* which,
and may move their fellow rational beings, to bring about various changes for their
sake. The only things that are intellectually lovable as ends are actual things capable
of love: God first and then rational creatures.

Like Kant, I speak of "rational" beings rather than "human" ones, because, as
Adams reminds us, twentieth-century Christians cannot escape the possibility that
there are nonterrestrial rational creatures whom they may encounter one day. If there
are, they are as much *imagines Dei* as human beings are. C. S. Lewis did well to prepare

us for the possibility that nonhuman beings may be better than we are—even innocents, who have never lost direct communication with God.[9] They may be, of course,
as bad as or worse than humans. However, our duties to extraterrestrials, whether we
should arrive as strangers on the planets they inhabit or they on the one we do,
are identical in kind with those we have to all terrestrial foreigners. Even with fellow humans, we fail to perform these duties. All habitable nature is for all rational
beings, even though no human society recognizes this in practice even for its own
members.

Given this, what is the consequence for morality? If we see the goods actually
present in the environments we encounter as divine gifts (as I agree with Adams we
should), what is the consequence for morality in that context? His own chief inference
is that we should respect great differences in social relationships as God's different
gifts to different societies ("if we came on creatures, otherwise like us [that is, rational
animals], who lived with evident satisfaction in social relationships that differed from
ours in [respect of the medical and parental rights recognized in them]"). Obviously,
if they are nonmammalian, parental relations and the corresponding parent-child rights
will necessarily be different. But if they are "evidently" satisfied with counterparts of
the Roman institution that a father can put his children to death at will, or of the
Carthaginian one that parents should be prepared to sacrifice at least one child as a
burnt offering to a false god, should we regard the goods inherent in their system of
social relations as divine gifts, through creation, or the providential ordering of their
history?

The strength of Adams's line of thought is twofold: it warns us against the grave
moral and mortal religious error of denying either that every rational animal, terrestrial
or not, is *imago Dei*, or that the history of every society of such creatures is under
divine providence. We must have both the humility to be prepared to learn from
extraterrestrials and the faith to be prepared to teach them; and we must acquire the
capacity, possessed by few or no human beings now, to judge uncorruptly with respect
to which of our beliefs and practices we must alter or promote. Adams rightly denounces the notion that respect for the actual is systematically conservative, although
as a matter of history, it has commonly been so misrepresented. Here I submit a final
Kantian thought: that we can obviate such misrepresentations by drawing our moral
distinctions with an impartial eye on *all* the *imagines Dei* affected by them, and not on
the stability or self-satisfaction of the societies concerned.

Notes

1. Page numbers in parentheses, unless otherwise identified, refer to Robert M. Adams, "Platonism and Naturalism: Options for a Theocentric Ethics," in Joseph Runzo,
ed., *Ethics, Religion, and the Good Society* (Louisville: Westminster/John Knox Press, 1992), pp.
22–42.

2. As Adams notes, since the Form of the Good is not God but imparts to a world that is between being and not-being such being and goodness as it has, "there are obvious problems" about transforming the participation of the world in the Form of the Good in God to its participation in God. How Platonic were the [neo-]Platonists who influenced Augustine?

3. These and the following scriptural citations from *1 John* and Psalm 95 are taken from *The Holy Bible: The New Revised Standard Version* (New York: Oxford University Press, 1989). Ed.

4. This reference to James Gustafson, *Ethics from a Theocentric Perspective*, vol. 1, *Theology and Ethics*, vol. 2, *Ethics and Theology* (Chicago: University of Chicago Press, 1981 and 1984), like all subsequent ones, is to a passage quoted or referred to by Adams.

5. Perhaps I have impertinently excused Gustafson from an unorthodoxy of which he would prefer to be accused. When he declares it "excessive" to apply the analogy of agency to God, I take him simply to deny that God's will is any more like a human will than his intellect is like a human intellect. To deny any analogy whatever would empty the phrase "the will of God" of all sense.

6. I have discussed Spinoza's panentheism in *Spinoza* (Chicago: University of Chicago Press, 1989), pp. 89–102.

7. On Spinoza's doctrine of *acquiescentia* see Donagan, *Spinoza*, pp. 200–6.

8. [*The Complete Works of Aristotle*, ed. Jonathan Barnes (Princeton, N.J.: Princeton University Press, 1984), vol. 2, p. 1694 (trans. W. D. Ross). Ed.] In an earlier version of this paper, the only authority I cited was that of John Duns Scotus, *De Primo Principio*, chap. 2, 4th and 5th conclusions, text rev. and trans. Evan Roche, O.F.M. (St. Bonaventure, New York: Franciscan Institute, 1949). However, Professor Charles Young has since suggested to me that "Aristotle very sketchily distinguishes two senses of 'that for the sake of which' at *Metaphysics* 1072^b1–3 and *de Anima* 415^b2–3. Ross, in his note to *Physics* 194^a35–36 (where the distinction is only mentioned) says that it may have been more fully set out in one of Aristotle's lost dialogues."

9. Especially in the two novels, *Out of the Silent Planet* (London: Bodley Head, 1938) and *Perelandra* (New York: Macmillan Co., 1944), and in occasional papers.

ELEVEN

Alasdair MacIntyre's After Virtue

Alasdair MacIntyre's *After Virtue* has been rightly recognized as a contribution to philosophical ethics of the first importance. It is also of the first importance to members of our society, who are concerned with philosophical ethics not only for its own sake, but also with its implications for the Christian community. Since MacIntyre has followed Keats's advice to Shelley, to "load every rift with ore," the simplifications necessary for commenting on it are more than usually likely to result in blunders. It is therefore particularly gracious of him to have consented to preside over our meeting and—I hope—to put right any blunders with which we, the invited speakers, may unintentionally darken counsel. If a religious community—Christian or other—goes seriously wrong about philosophical ethics, it is likely to go wrong in matters of religious faith also.

Although most of what MacIntyre has to say about Christianity in *After Virtue* is to be found in chapter 13 ("Medieval Aspects and Occasions"), in order to understand it, we must understand his view of morality at the present time and the conclusions about moral philosophy he draws from it. Chapter 2 of *After Virtue* begins:

> The most striking feature of contemporary moral utterance is that so much of it is used to express moral disagreements; and the most striking feature of the debates in which these disagreements are expressed is their interminable char-acter. (p. 6)[1]

In a symposium with Virginia Held and Richard Rorty at the last APA Eastern Division meeting he developed this. In responding to Virginia Held's argument that intellectuals generally should recognize that it is their function to shape moral opinion in society at large, he objected that it falsely presupposes that moral philosophers today either have reached consensus on the principal issues or approximate to it. Moral philosophers today are in a condition of *dissensus* from which they cannot with their present resources extricate themselves. This state of dissensus has an explanation, the clue to which is given at the opening of the third chapter of *After Virtue*: namely, that "[a] moral philosophy . . . characteristically presupposes a sociology" (p. 23).

Any serious moral philosophy must presuppose that its concept of human action, and the various concepts that go with it, can be embodied in "the real social world." It follows that differences about what is sociologically possible have implications for what is serious moral philosophy—and hence for what is possible as morality. And MacIntyre contends that modern intellectuals generally, because their knowledge of human history is not only narrow but distorted, have narrow and distorted views of what is sociologically possible, which cut them off from the sort of sociology they need to put their moral philosophy right. Moreover, just as unhappy families are each unhappy in a different way, so narrow and distorted views of what is sociologically possible are various. They generate a dissensus that is incurable unless it is corrected by a fuller and undistorted understanding of history.

The most elementary sociological fact pertinent to moral philosophy that history discloses to us is that in any human group that deserves the name "society" there are found "coherent and complex form[s] of socially established cooperative human activity" to which certain goods are "internal" (p. 187). Farming is an example of such an activity. Among the goods obviously internal to it are efficiently producing socially needed crops to which the land farmed is appropriate, and preserving the fertility of that land. Given the goods (the *teloi*) internal to farming, it is possible to work out the standards a good farmer meets, and the behavioral dispositions that tend to enable him to meet them. Such behavioral dispositions are the "virtues" of farmers—the "acquired human qualit[ies] the possession and exercise of which [tend] to enable [a farmer] to achieve those goods [internal to farming] and the lack of which effectively [prevent him] from achieving any such goods" (p. 191). Two qualifications must be made here. First, practices are not merely sets of technical skills, because they are activities the *teloi* of which are transmuted by their history. What farming is for—its *teloi*—changes with the history of farming as farmers understand their activity better (cf. pp. 193–94). And second, practices are not institutions, because even institutions for supporting practices (e.g., chess clubs), being also concerned with goods external to those practices, and structured in terms of power and status, tend to corrupt the practices they sustain (cf. p. 194). Two traditional moral virtues—justice (including truthfulness) and courage—are essential if practices are to resist the corrupting power of institutions (cf. pp. 191–93, 194).

This account of the virtues, however, is only the "first stage" of a complete one (p. 196). A disposition that has point and function in a practice, but not in the practitioner's life as a whole, cannot count as a *human* excellence. Now, the claims of one practice may be incompatible with those of another, and the dispositions one requires may be incompatible with those required by another. Moreover, virtues like justice (giving to each his or her due) presuppose something beyond any particular practice: one's due is determined, not by any one practice but by ordering all one's practices. Hence there must be, above the *teloi* of particular practices, a *telos* of human life as a whole. And the traditional virtue of integrity or constancy—of singleness of purpose through a whole life—presupposes that one's life as a whole can have a single unifying *telos* (cf. pp. 201–5).

What can such a *telos* be? MacIntyre's answer depends on conceiving every individual human life as an attempt to live out an intelligible life story, in which what is done by and to that individual will make narrative sense. "The unity of a human life is the unity of a narrative quest" (p. 219). And the *telos* of a life in which that quest is successful will be a particular conceivable version of the good life, one that is intelligible in the light of the traditions of practices to which the person who lives it is heir, and of the circumstances, social and nonsocial, he or she encounters in following or modifying those traditions. It is not too much to say that MacIntyre is prepared to endorse any *telos* an individual may adopt that makes narrative sense.

In doing so, he conceives himself to be imposing a very strict condition indeed. "[T]o think of a human life as a narrative unity is to think in a way alien to the dominant individualist and bureaucratic modes of modern culture" (p. 227). As far as I can tell from his brief but penetrating observations about Jacobin republicanism, Cobbett, and Jane Austen, he has concluded that ever since the seventeenth century western civilization has adopted methods of production and distribution that have excluded virtue-sustaining practices from most of economic life: both craft and professional practices are now marginal. Hence the magnificently misguided effort of the Jacobins to restore the classical tradition of the virtues had to fail: "[Y]ou cannot hope to re-invent morality on the scale of a whole nation when the very idiom of the morality which you seek to re-invent is alien in one way to the vast mass of ordinary people and in another to the intellectual elite" (p. 238). So we must go back to the beginning. "What matters at this stage is the construction of local forms of community within which civility and the intellectual and moral life can be sustained through the new dark ages which are already upon us" (p. 263).

As what might be called "culture-criticism" MacIntyre's argument is impressive. Hence, although I cannot accept his apparent position that modern industrial production is by its very nature inimical to virtue-sustaining productive practices, for my special purpose in these comments—discussing his views about moral philosophy from what I take to be the point of view of Christianity—I shall, for the sake of argument, simply accept his sociology and history. For what matters from a Christian point of view is whether his doctrine about the relation of moral philosophy to sociology is sound.

Morality, as MacIntyre conceives it, must rest on a doctrine of virtue in the Aristotelian tradition; and that doctrine must be sociologically fragile, because virtues can only thrive if they are sustained by traditional practices that are central to social life—a condition that has not been satisfied in the Western world for almost three centuries. Against this, I believe that morality, as Christianity conceives it, rests on a doctrine of moral law in the rabbinic Jewish tradition, which the Stoic tradition in certain respects resembled; and that the Christian doctrine of moral law is sociologically robust, because it is a doctrine for all seasons: for those in which human culture thrives, and for those in which a tolerable human life is impossible.

MacIntyre, of course, perceives that such a thesis can be advanced, but he dismisses it. Why? He expressly recognizes that Christian morality is a rabbinic morality of law: "the Torah remains the law uttered by God in the New Testament as in the Old" (p. 170). And he further recognizes that in "interiorizing" the moral life as at bottom a matter of right willing—willing to obey the "first and greatest commandment" to love God and one's neighbor—twelfth century Christians like Abelard (and eighteenth-century ones like Kant) approached Stoicism (p. 168). But he maintains that such interiorization is not the final Christian position: it is a deviation to which Christians resort only when the society in which they live has ceased to have a shared good that provides it with common tasks (pp. 169–70). Christianity is fully realized only when Christians conceive their lives as having double *teloi*: as citizens of a *civitas caelestis* they are *viatores* whose *telos* is the beatific vision; and as citizens of a *civitas terrena* that acknowledges their dual citizenship, their *telos* is to contribute to its common civic good. Christian morality is a morality of virtues: of the dispositions that must be cultivated if the evils that hinder us from achieving those *teloi* are to be overcome.

Unfortunately I cannot do anything like justice to the subtlety of MacIntyre's treatment of the strain Christianity puts on the Aristotelian tradition. The virtues human beings need as members of the *civitas caelestis*—the so-called theological virtues of faith, hope, and charity—are not Aristotelian. And they compel us to revise our conceptions of the "cardinal" Aristotelian virtues of prudence, courage, temperance, and justice.

I am not aware of disagreeing with MacIntyre's view that an ideal Christian life is a life of dual citizenship, or that virtues are necessary if we are to overcome the evils that hinder us from being good dual citizens. Nor do I believe that Christians like Abelard and Kant who "interiorize" Christian morality are thereby committed to disagreeing with it. Yet I find it impossible to accept *either* his apparent view that Christian morality (as distinct from an ideal Christian life) presupposes a *civitas terrena* compatible with Christianity, *or* his apparent view that the *telos* of the *civitas caelestis*, like the *telos* of an ideal natural human life, presupposes anything like social practices to sustain it.

For the first point one need no more than refer to St. Augustine who worked out the doctrine of the two *civitates*. The *civitas terrena* can indeed, according to St. Augustine, be Christianized; but, *before* Christianity, it did not even satisfy the demands of natural reason.

> Thus in the *civitas terrena* its wise men who live according to man have pursued the goods either of the body or of their own mind or of both together; or if any of them were able to know God, "they did not honor him as God or give thanks to him, but they became futile in their thinking and their senseless minds were darkened; claiming to be wise <"—that is, exalting themselves in their wisdom, under the domination of pride—"they became foolish....">²

When St. Augustine wrote, the greater part of Christian history had been one of contempt, exclusion from normal civic life, and intermittent persecution. Far from having roots in the practices of the *civitas terrena*, Christian morality existed in spite of them. Ultimately, it transformed them.

For the second point, that the *telos* of the *civitas caelestis* does not presuppose anything like social practices to sustain it, we need only consider what it is, and what virtues it requires. Unlike the Aristotelian *telos* of natural *eudaimonia*, the *telos* of the *civitas caelestis* is not a matter of human praxis: it is a gift—intellectual union with the divine essence. And the virtues it requires—faith, hope, and charity—are all interior dispositions of the will. True, the third and greatest of them, charity, gives rise to acts of justice, courage, and the other cardinal virtues. But they are not, as just and courageous, themselves acts of charity. St. Paul authoritatively teaches that though I sell all my goods to feed the poor (distributive justice), and though I give my body to be burned (courage), if I have not charity (i.e., if I am just and brave, but not from charity) those virtuous acts will profit me nothing (*I Cor.* 13:3).

On the other hand, not even social circumstances depriving one of all opportunities for justice, the productive virtues, or courage in any form except sheer endurance can make faith, hope, or charity impossible or pointless. Human beings' situation in the *civitas terrena* cannot disfranchise them in the *civitas caelestis*, or take from their lives narrative intelligibility either as tragedy (for want of knowledge of the means of salvation or refusal to avail themselves of them), or as high or low comedy, depending on the ways they avail themselves of them. MacIntyre recognized this, when he contrasted Aristotle's doctrine that misfortune can frustrate the achievement of the human good with the "medieval" one that, unless "we...become its accomplice" there is "no evil...that can happen" that can exclude us from the supernatural human good (p. 176).

This medieval doctrine, common to Judaism and Christianity, has two implications for moral philosophy. The first is that the Aristotelian tradition was mistaken not only in failing to be aware of the *civitas caelestis* but also in failing to recognize that a life of charity in the *civitas terrena* is a good human life in itself, even if one has no opportunity to acquire and exhibit the virtues internal to the practices sustained by a cultured society. The second and further implication is that although the virtues internal to the practices sustained by a cultured society are not necessary to a good terrestrial human life (although they *are* virtues, and are necessary to a *full* terrestrial human life), a good terrestrial human life nevertheless has necessary conditions. If they do not consist in exhibiting the various dispositions necessary to realizing the *teloi* internal to the practices sustained by one's society, what can they consist in? To answer that question, it is well to look again at the law-morality of Judaism and Stoicism.

The nonceremonial precepts of the Mosaic decalogue, except for that enjoining respect for one's parents, are prohibitory: murder, adultery, theft, false witness, and coveting what belongs to others are all forbidden. Both that injunction and those prohibitions apply in any society in which there are families and property. They are implicit in the virtues necessary for realizing the goods internal to the practices of MacIntyre's virtue-sustaining societies, but their observance does not presuppose the existence either of those practices or those societies. Yet neither Judaism nor Christianity treats the Mosaic Torah as a system of taboos ordained by an unintelligible divinity. What, in Judaism and Christianity, makes the Torah intelligible?

MacIntyre has the right answer, but he does not, so it seems to me, apply it correctly. He writes: "[T]he threefold structure of untutored human-nature-as-it-happens-to-be, human-nature-as-it-could-be-if-it-realized-its-*telos* and the precepts of rational ethics as the means for the transition from one to the other remains central to the theistic understanding of evaluative thought and judgment" (p. 53). In other words, moral law as understood in Judaism and Christianity rests on a doctrine of human-nature-as-it-would-be-if-it-realized-its-*telos*. MacIntyre contends that what he calls "the Enlightenment project"—the attempt to found morality on pure practical reason—had to fail because it has no place for such a doctrine.

What is the *telos* of human nature, as Judaism and Christianity conceive it? The standard quick answer is that of the Westminster catechism: *to know God and enjoy him forever.* The second part of this answer was a comparatively late discovery: no doubt it is implicit in God's transactions with Abraham, but it was not accepted by the Sadducees even in the rabbinic period. Yet from the very beginning it was proclaimed that the *telos* of human nature was to know and love God, and to love the rational creatures made in his image, both fellow Jews and strangers. Quite apart from the possibility of the resurrection of the dead and the beatific vision, beings exist (God and our fellows) whom it is our business to love. And it is our business to love them because of what they are, not because of what we can make of them.

A *telos* of this kind is utterly different from the *telos* of a practice. Unfortunately, the hope of the beatific vision has tended to conceal this. By concentrating on that hope, and by misinterpreting what human beings do in availing themselves of the means of grace as being related to the beatific vision either as certain Aristotelian *praxeis* are related to *eudaimonia*, or worse, as a *techne* is related to its *telos*, many Christians have failed to grasp one of the profoundest ideas of their own faith.

Kant, however, did grasp it. As he wrote in his *Grundlegung:*

> Ends that a rational being adopts arbitrarily as *effects* of his action . . . are in every case only relative; for it is solely their relation to special characteristics in the subject's power of appetition which gives them their value. Hence this value can provide . . . no principles valid . . . for all rational beings. . . . Suppose, however, there were something *whose existence* has *in itself* an absolute value, something which

as *an end in itself* could be the ground of determinate laws; then in it, and in it alone, would there be the ground of a possible . . . practical law.[3]

The *teloi* of the moral law of the Torah are concerned, not with anything we produce, but with beings—ends in themselves, Kant calls them—already in existence: namely, God and our fellow rational creatures.

Do I think, then, that Christians, in reasserting against MacIntyre that Jewish and Christian morality cannot be adequately defended in terms of a revised Aristotelian teleology, but only in terms of its own, must reject his brilliant revision and development of the Aristotelian one? Not at all. But I do think that we must distinguish. In elucidating the moral theology of Christianity and the common human morality that forms part of the Mosaic Torah, Aristotle cannot help much. Moral theology and common human morality are for all seasons: they presuppose no more sociologically than that there are human beings capable of choosing how to act. But Christianity *also* sanctifies the cultivation of terrestrial life. MacIntyre offers us a theory of what distinguishes morality in the great human cultures from the part of it that is common to human life in all conditions. He also reminds us that Christian monasticism preserved for us what we retain of the secular culture of the Hellenic-Roman world, and that doing so was a Christian task. After saying that he has not told the whole story I must add that I think that the part of the story he has told is substantially true, as well as new and timely.

Notes

1. Page numbers in parentheses refer to Alasdair MacIntyre, *After Virtue*, 2d ed. (Notre Dame, Indiana: University of Notre Dame Press, 1984). Ed.

2. *De Civ. Dei.*, XIV, 28 [bracketed material added from Henry Bettenson's translation (Hammondsworth, Middlesex, England: Penguin Books Ltd., 1972), p. 593. Ed.].

3. Immanuel Kant, *Groundwork of the Metaphysic of Morals*, trans. H. J. Paton (New York: Harper and Row, 1964; originally published in 1948 by the Hutchinson University Library under the title *The Moral Law, or Kant's Groundwork of the Metaphysic of Morals*), p. 95 (2d German ed., p. 64).

TWELVE

The Second Edition of Alasdair MacIntyre's After Virtue

In the second edition of his *After Virtue*, Alasdair MacIntyre has added a postscript in which, in "three distinct areas" in which he judged it "most urgent," he offered "a more adequate restatement of positions either central to or presupposed by the overall scheme of [its] argument" (p. 264).[1] The areas he chose are: the relationship of philosophy to history; the virtues and the issue of relativism; and the relationship of moral philosophy to theology. I cannot do better than to approach his book through his postscript to it. In doing so it will become plain why I believe that, for students who have some elementary knowledge of the classics of their subject and of analytical technique, *After Virtue* is the best introduction we have to the serious issues in contemporary moral philosophy.

1. The Relation of Philosophy to History

In his Postscript, MacIntyre presents his view of the relation of moral philosophy to history as a special case of a general theory of the relation of philosophy to history: a general theory, moreover, that is accepted in fields less backward than moral philosophy, such as philosophy of physics. Kant's philosophy, both of morality and of physics, is his palmary example of the antihistoricism he opposes.

Just as what Kant took to be the principles and presuppositions of natural science as such turned out after all to be the principles and presuppositions specific to Newtonian physics, so what Kant took to be the principles and presuppositions of morality as such turned out to be the principles and presuppositions of one highly specific morality, a secularized version of Protestantism which furnished modern liberal individualism with one of its founding charters. Thus the claim to universality foundered. (p. 266)

Contrary to Kantian rationalism—and to any other—not only is

historical enquiry ... required in order to establish what a particular point of view is, but also ... it is in historical encounter that any given point of view establishes or fails to establish its rational superiority relative to its particular rivals in some specific contexts. In doing so, many of the skills and techniques of analytic philosophy will be deployed; and on rare occasions these techniques may suffice to discredit a view. (p. 269)

For the most part, however, analytic technique will not furnish proofs of one philosophical view, or even disproofs of all its rivals. It is only by "considering arguments as objects of investigation in ... the social and historical contexts of activity and inquiry in which they are or were at home, and from which they characteristically derive their particular import" (cf. p. 267), that philosophers can rationally choose between them.

What rendered Newtonian physics rationally superior to its Galilean and Aristotelian predecessors and to its Cartesian rivals was that it was able to transcend their limitations by solving problems in areas in which those predecessors and rivals could by their own standards of scientific progress make no progress. So we cannot say wherein the rational superiority of Newtonian physics consisted except historically in terms of its relationship to those predecessors and rivals whom it challenged and displaced. Abstract Newtonian physics from its context, and then ask wherein the superiority of one to the other consists, and you will be met with insoluble incommensurability problems. (p. 268)

MacIntyre's application of this conception of philosophy in general to moral philosophy specifically may surprise readers of his first edition.

Moral philosophies are ... the explicit articulations of the claims of particular moralities to rational allegiance.... It follows that when rival moralities make competing and incompatible claims, there is always an issue at the level of moral philosophy concerning the ability of either to make good a claim of moral superiority over the other.

How are these claims to be judged? As in the case of natural science there are no general timeless standards. It is in the ability of one particular moral-philosophy-articulating-the-claims-of-a-particular-morality to identify and to transcend the limitations of its rival or rivals, limitations which can be—although they may not in fact have been—identified by the rational standards to which the protagonists of the rival morality are committed by their allegiance to it, that the rational superiority of that particular moral philosophy and that particular morality emerges. *The history of morality-and-moral philosophy is the history of successive challenges to some pre-existing moral order, a history in which the question of which party defeated the other in rational argument is always to be distinguished from the question which party retained or gained social and political hegemony.* And it is only by reference to this history that questions of rational superiority can be settled. (pp. 268–69; emphasis added)

My own reaction to this, as a twentieth century rationalist and (to the best of my belief) a Kantian in moral theory, is that, with a few unfortunately disabling aberrations (e.g., the reference to "incommensurability" on p. 268), it clarifies and articulates a position toward which I now recognize myself as having groped in some of my own writings. If rationalism in its Kantian or any other form entails that any physical or moral—or for that matter, logical—theory could have been developed or can be understood without reference to the state of physical or moral or logical discourse when it was developed, then rationalism in those forms is false. But does Kantian rationalism entail any such thing?

MacIntyre believes that it does. Why? The only reason he has given is that Kant embraced the "thesis that there are principles and concepts necessarily assented to by any rational being, both in thinking and willing" (p. 266). That thesis only entails the anti-historicism to which MacIntyre objects *if it is tacitly assumed that adult rational beings in all circumstances must assent to whatever, so far as they are rational, they would necessarily assent to in any specific circumstances.* But why assume any such thing? A rationalist who assumed it would have to deny that rational beings as such must necessarily assent to the propositions that zero is a number, or that practical reason lays down categorical as well as hypothetical imperatives, if in any culture there is any rational being who cannot be brought to assent to them. That is an absurdity we have no reason to attribute to Kant. He indeed believed that both these propositions are a priori true, and hence that in some sense rational beings as such must assent to them; but he did not deny that ancient Greek mathematicians did not assent to the first, or Scottish empiricists to the second—nor did he deny that Greek mathematicians and Scottish philosophers were rational.

When twentieth century rationalists in moral philosophy (so far as I am acquainted with them) say that "the nature of human reason is such that there are principles . . . necessarily assented to by every rational being, both in thinking and in willing" (cf. p. 266), what they mean is that a rational being capable of grasping the concepts employed in formulating those principles (a matter of education—and hence also of the society to which he belongs) to whom the considerations pertinent to assenting to them and dissenting from them have been presented, will assent to them unless in his reasons for withholding assent he commits some error. They assume in all their thinking Aristotle's distinction between what is intelligible in itself and what is intelligible to "us"—that is, to any particular historically situated human being. I contend that Kant and later moral rationalists (Whewell, for example) anticipated their twentieth-century successors in this.

But did Kant not hold that moral principles are a priori, and does not that imply that any rational being can know them, whatever his historical situation? No. No more than holding that Newton's principle of inertia is a priori committed him to believing that Aristotle committed some mistake in his reasons for holding a contrary position. Aristotle believed that motion was not conserved in part because he lacked some of the concepts Newton employed; and he lacked those concepts in part because his attention had not been drawn to some of the phenomena that prompted his successors to form them. Far from denying that his own philosophy of physics would have been unintelligible to philosophers before the eighteenth century, Kant took it for granted. That, like Aristotle before him, Kant mistakenly believed that some of the physical principles it was rational in his day to prefer to the alternatives available would stand forever does not show that such principles will never be reached. Nor does it show that he did not reach such principles in his moral philosophy.

It would be plausible to believe that what Kant took to be the true principles of morals are products of a historical epoch now past if it were true that those principles generate only a morality that is "highly specific," as MacIntyre contends that Kant's—"a secularized version of Protestantism" (p. 266)—is. We shall return to this. For the moment I confine myself to anticipating what I shall later argue: that Jewish, Roman Catholic, and Protestant morals differ little; that it is part of all three of these faiths in their traditional forms that the moral duties of human beings to themselves and to one another can be presented without direct reference to God or to anything supernatural; and that the features of Kant's moral system that are idiosyncratic or solely of his time are (like such features in the systems of Roman Catholic moralists) not derivable from his principles.

MacIntyre unfortunately combines the true historicist doctrine for which we are indebted to him with what I believe are some serious mistakes about the lessons to be drawn from the history of analytic philosophy. Two such mistakes call for comment. The first is that "the distinctions central to the Kantian project and to its successors" have been subverted by Quine, Sellars, and Goodman (p. 266). I assume that the chief subversions he has in mind are Quine's attack on the analytic-synthetic distinction and Sellars's attack on the myth of the given. To the best of my understanding, I accept both attacks as major achievements of recent philosophy. However, I take them to put the Kantian project in order, and not to subvert it. Kant's incomplete arguments for the three formulas of his categorical imperative are not attempts to exhibit it as analytic; and nothing substantive in them is subverted by replacing his analytic-synthetic distinction by a Quinean one between what is at the core of the totality of the propositions he assented to, and what is at their empirically vulnerable periphery. Nor is anything substantive subverted by treating the core of that totality as subject to revision as the totality is added to or reordered: by denying it the spurious status of a foundational "given."

The second of what I conceive to be MacIntyre's mistakes is his contention that

> what the progress of analytic philosophy has succeeded in establishing is that there are *no* grounds for belief in universal necessary principles—outside purely formal enquiries—except relative to some set of assumptions. Cartesian first principles, Kantian a priori truths and even the ghosts of these notions that haunted empiricism for so long have all been expelled from philosophy. (pp. 266–67)

What is wrong in principle here is that in thrashing out which (if either) of two principles shall prevail in a nonformal field of study such as physics or morals any of the propositions on which the parties to the discussion are agreed must have the status of assumptions—i.e., propositions not to be questioned in the discussion—or that they cannot profitably proceed unless there is some definite set of propositions on which they are agreed.

Nothing in MacIntyre's argument entitles us to assert more than the important truism that, in a discussion about principles, there can be no rational agreement unless those discussing them share enough relevant beliefs. In addition, he makes a serious mistake when he couples Kantian synthetic a priori truths, which are never given, with Cartesian first principles, which are never anything else. Expelling the analytic and the given from physics and from morals leaves the Kantian concept of a priori truth intact. It does not even throw doubt on any of Kant's assertions of the a priori truth of particular principles, although progress in both physics and moral philosophy has. (To MacIntyre's examples from physics, I would add that he was certainly mistaken in believing that it is a priori true that it is morally permissible to act on any maxim that satisfies the test laid down in the first of his formulae of the categorical imperative.)

MacIntyre describes his kind of historicism as, unlike Hegel's, involving "a form of fallibilism; it is a kind of historicism which excludes all claims to absolute knowledge" (p. 270). My contention is that, if absolute knowledge is infallible knowledge, then Kant did not claim to possess what MacIntyre's historicism excludes. Claiming, as Kant did, that certain universal principles are true a priori, and that he had proved them so by transcendental arguments, is not the same thing as claiming infallibility, or "absolute knowledge." All transcendental arguments begin with beliefs taken to be true, and none are stronger than the beliefs from which they begin. MacIntyre has confounded what Kant claims about the principles he tries to establish (that they are universal, necessary, and fundamental to physics, morality, and so forth), and the proofs he offers for them (that they are a priori and so universal and necessary), with something about the epistemic state of the claimant. There is no contradiction in the utterance "I fallibly claim to have demonstrated *a priori* that (say) Newton's second law of motion is a universal and necessary truth of physics." Nor is there any contradiction in parallel claims in moral theory.

2. *The Virtues and the Issue of Relativism*

In replying to a criticism by Robert Wachbroit[2] that his theory is on the horns of a dilemma, because his characterization of the good in terms of the quest for the good, even stipulating that that quest be for goods internal to some set of practices such that pursuing them competently would constitute a full human life, "is compatible with acknowledging the existence of distinct, incompatible and rival traditions of the virtues" (p. 276) <MacIntyre develops a relativism that rationalists can accept and have in fact accepted.> Wachbroit's dilemma is this:

> Suppose that two rival and incompatible moral traditions encounter one another in some specific historical situation where to accept the claims of the one is to be committed to conflict with the other. Then *either* it will be possible to appeal to some set of rationally grounded principles independent of each of the rivals *or* no rational resolution of their disagreements is possible. But if the former, then there is indeed a set of principles to which appeal can be made on fundamental moral issues the rational grounding of which is independent of the social peculiarities of traditions; and if the latter, there is no moral rationality which is not internal to and relative to some particular tradition. (p. 276)

Either rationalism or relativism and scepticism, both of which MacIntyre rejects. But, so Wachbroit argues, in view of the rejection of rationalism that is central to his Aristotelianism, the upshot of *After Virtue* must be relativism and scepticism.

MacIntyre's response, it seems to me, amounts to a sketch of a nondogmatic relativism of the kind which, I have argued, most rationalists from Kant to the present have in fact held in practice, although they have not always expounded it adequately.

> The force of [Wachbroit's] argument [MacIntyre writes] turns on whether [his] ... statement of the alternatives is or is not exhaustive. It is not. For it is sometimes at least possible that one such tradition may appeal for a verdict in its favor against its rival to types of considerations that are already accorded weight in both the competing traditions. (p. 276)

Splendid. But what types of consideration does MacIntyre have in mind? This is what he says.

> If two moral traditions are able to recognize each other as advancing rival contentions on issues of importance, then necessarily they must share some common features. ... It will thus sometimes at least be possible for adherents of each tradition to understand and evaluate—by their own standards—the characterization of their positions advanced by their rivals. (p. 276)

However, it may be rational to decide in favor of one tradition even if its rivals do not concede its superiority.

> [I]t is also the case ... that if in such successive encounters a particular moral tradition has succeeded in reconstituting itself when rational considerations

urged upon its adherents either from within the tradition or from without so required, and has provided generally more cogent accounts of its rivals' defects and weaknesses and of its own than those rivals have been able to supply, either concerning themselves or concerning others, all this of course in the light of the standards internal to that tradition, standards which will in the course of those vicissitudes have themselves been revised and extended in a variety of ways, *then the adherents of that tradition are rationally entitled to a large measure of confidence that the tradition which they inhabit and to which they owe the substance of their moral lives will find the resources to meet future challenges successfully.* [Preceding emphasis mine.] For the theory of moral reality embodied in their modes of thinking and acting has shown itself to be, in the sense that I gave to that expression, *the best theory so far.* (p. 277)

This seems to me to be what moral rationalists have oft thought but ne'er so well expressed.

I believe that Kant would have accepted it, and I have no doubt whatever that Whewell would have. But it does not matter if I am mistaken in this, and if the thought as well as the expression originated with MacIntyre. Even if (as I do not believe) Kant and his followers were moral dogmatists who deluded themselves not only that they had rigorously demonstrated their moral principles from premises that were indubitable, but also that they could not be mistaken about what demonstrations are rigorous or what premises indubitable, *their moral theory is not the same thing as their epistemology of it.*[3]

Notes

1. Page numbers in parentheses refer to Alasdair MacIntyre, *After Virtue*, 2d ed. (Notre Dame, Indiana: University of Notre Dame Press, 1984). Ed.

2. Robert Wachbroit, review of *After Virtue: A Study in Moral Theory*, by Alasdair MacIntyre, *Yale Law Journal* 92, no. 3 (January 1983): 564–76.

3. The third section, discussing MacIntyre's view of the relationship of moral philosophy to theology and promised at the outset, is absent from the existing typescript of this paper. Ed.

THIRTEEN

Ethics and Theology:
Two Lectures

I. The Irrelevance of Theology to Ethics

Many practicing Jews and Christians are disquieted when secular philosophers offer to defend, on purely philosophical grounds, the traditional morality that has been transmitted within their respective faiths. A bit over two years ago I published a book in which just such a defense was attempted; and last spring it moved a clergyman, also a doctoral candidate at a distinguished university, to write to me expostulating that the "ground" of Hebrew-Christian morality "lies in the Hebrew-Christian *Scriptures*, balanced with a reasonable hermeneutic." This did not fail to stir some fellow-feeling; for in the meantime I had accepted the Christian faith and been received into the Church. When an unbeliever I had had no more than a feeble interest in investigating the connection between the Jewish and the Christian faiths and the morality they foster, although its existence is undeniable and I had recognized it. As my beliefs changed, so did my interests; and now that I have thought more about the connection between ethics and theology, my understanding of it, although still less than adequate, is not what it was. In my second lecture I hope to explore some of the principal respects in which theology does matter to ethics. In my first, however, I propose to repeat my earlier offense, and to argue that the ground of Hebrew-Christian *morality* does not lie in the Hebrew-Christian Scriptures: indeed, that it does not lie in the Jewish or the Christian revelation at all.

On what grounds are many Christians disquieted by this? While the same question could also be asked of many Jews, I shall not in these lectures be able to discuss Jewish religious views. For that very reason I am especially concerned to leave no doubt that I hold that, although the ways of life taught by the Jewish and Christian faiths differ, their morality does not. As St. Paul repeatedly implied, what Christians take to be the common moral law binding upon all mankind is contained in the Mosaic Torah.

Of the several grounds on which many Christians have denied that Hebrew-Christian morality can rationally be upheld without presupposing the truth at least of the revelation to Moses, the most profound is that the very concept of a moral law presupposes a divine lawgiver and a divine promulgation of the law given, and that those who imagine otherwise are under an intellectual delusion, which no doubt can be explained anthropologically. In a notorious paper,[1] to which my own intellectual debt can hardly be exaggerated, Professor G. E. M. Anscombe made the point bluntly:

> Naturally it is not possible to have [a law conception of ethics] unless you believe in God as a law-giver; like Stoics, Jews, and Christians. But if such a conception is dominant for many centuries, and then is given up, it is a natural result that the concepts of "obligation," of being bound or required as by a law, should remain though they had lost their root; and if the word "ought" has become invested in certain contexts with the sense of "obligation," it too will remain to be spoken with a special emphasis and a special feeling in these contexts.

Since the middle of the nineteenth century, she maintains, this has in fact happened in Western Europe and North America. Gradually, first the intellectuals and then much of society at large ceased effectively to believe in a lawgiving divinity, although they did not cease to believe that they were under most of the traditional moral obligations. As might have been expected, some of them "look[ed] about for the possibility of retaining a law conception of ethics without a divine legislator."[2] Unfortunately, she goes on to argue, no way of retaining it yet proposed is seriously defensible. The notion that morality is a matter of social norms is not impressive when we remember what social norms can be like. The notion that it is self-legislation is simply absurd: "Whatever you do 'for yourself' may be admirable; but it is not legislating."[3] And, finally, the notion that it is a matter of contract presupposes that there are signs (perhaps certain features of the language used in it) that the members of the society of moral beings have entered into the relevant contracts—a presupposition that awaits elaboration. All things considered, Anscombe recommends atheist moralists to seek their moral norms in human virtues. But if they do, she warns, they "ought to recognize what has happened to the notion 'norm,' which [they] wanted to mean 'law—without bringing God in'—it has ceased to mean 'law' at all."[4] If they can manage it, they would do well to put on their nontheistic *Index Verborum Prohi-*

bitorum all expressions presupposing the law conception of ethics. These include "moral obligation," "the moral ought," and "duty."

This line of thought, which I think profound and partly right, must be sharply distinguished from another that is often carelessly mistaken for it, and which is not profound at all. In my memory I hazily associated this other line of thought with the writings of the English Roman Catholic sociologist Christopher Dawson, whose works the University of Chicago libraries were buying in multiple copies as late as the forties. The essence of Dawson's message is summed up in a few sentences of his *Progress and Religion*, which appeared in 1938:

> The day of the Liberal Deist compromise is over, and we have come to the parting of the ways. Either Europe must abandon the Christian tradition, and with it the faith in progress and humanity, or it must return consciously to the religious foundation on which those ideas were based. . . . [O]ur faith in progress and in the unique value of human experience rests on religious foundations, and . . . they cannot be severed from historical religion and used as a substitute for it, as men have attempted to do in the last two centuries.[5]

The idea Dawson here expressed became familiar in an even more vulgar form in the fifties, when the regular worship of the God of one's choice was urged as a prophylactic against Communism.

It takes only a few minutes of thought to detect the fallacy in such arguments; but unfortunately a few minutes is a long time for thinking. Dawson's argument, for example, could have no force at all unless the "liberal Deists" to whom it was addressed already held the value of human experience to be unique. How otherwise could he hope to shock them into embracing Christianity by disclosing that, in their culture at least, faith in humanity had a Christian foundation? Yet perception of his assumption destroys the force of his disclosure. For if those he addressed held the value of human experience to be unique while at the same time being liberal Deists, then in their case at least faith in humanity had been severed from historical religion. It may have had a religious foundation in the past, but his own argument presupposes that it can exist without that foundation now.

There is not the slightest tincture of this self-refutation in Anscombe's argument. She does indeed accept as a sociological fact that after a religion has died out in a particular society, the morality originally transmitted within that religion may persist. But she offers no explanation of that fact. Nor, having accepted it, does she proceed to argue as though it were not a fact. While she acknowledges, for example, that Kant's rigoristic convictions on the subject of lying were intense,[6] she does not commit the folly of arguing that, since his pietist forebears had condemned lying because they had thought it forbidden by God, Kant himself had either to abandon his convictions about lying, or to return consciously to the pietist foundation on which those convictions were originally based. She freely acknowledges that Kant's convictions have some foundation or other, although a different one from his parents'. Her point is that because that foundation is different, because it is neither divine positive law, nor anything else that can defensibly be described as a genuine law, Kant ought to have desisted from describing his convictions as founded on respect for law.

Anscombe was, in my opinion, wholly right in insisting that the expression "the moral law," and the numerous legalistic expressions that are associated with it, are not mere figures of speech; and that, if we cannot provide a straightforward sense for them, we are not entitled to go on using them. And she was also right, in my opinion, to dismiss the three familiar attempts she mentions to provide a sense for them: that the moral law is a social norm, that it is self-legislated—each human being laying it down as positive law to himself—and that it is a matter of contract. I part with her on one point only, although it is a fundamental one. Her argument presupposes that the three attempts she enumerates to provide a sense for the expression "the moral law"—all of which she rightly dismisses—are the only ones that merit serious consideration. It presupposes, in short, that her enumeration is effectively complete. I think that it is not. I think that Kant elucidated the concept of a moral law in a way distinct from the three she examines and rejects, and that she did not perceive it because, with the help of professed Kantians among her contemporaries, she mistook Kant as holding that moral law is self-legislated positive law. The view Kant in fact held can be traced to the Stoics, and (if he did not himself owe it to the Stoics) to St. Paul.

The Stoic conception of a universal moral law rests on three tenets: (1) that reason has to do not only with what is and is not the case, but also with what rational beings are and are not to do; (2) that the divine law (also held to be the law of nature—but the Stoic conception of nature is far from clear), in its application to human beings, requires them to do what reason requires them to do, and not to do what it requires them not to do; and (3) that human beings, properly instructed, are capable of ascertaining for themselves what reason requires them to do and not to do. Let it now be supposed that, instead of remaining theists until their whole way of thinking was superseded by Christianity, the later Stoics had ceased to believe that God exists, and hence that they no longer thought that there was a divine law, although they continued to believe that reason is practical, that it requires of human beings exactly what the older theistic Stoics had thought it to require, and that human beings are capable of working that out. Would such later Stoics, in losing their belief in divine law, have lost their belief in a moral law? I think not. For, as thinkers influenced by the Stoics pointed out—Cicero is an example—the Stoics found both the ground and content of what they recognized as divine law in ordinary human practical reason. That the findings of ordinary human practical reason were *also* divinely sanctioned had never been considered by the more philosophical Stoics to be among their grounds.

This can be verified, from a Christian point of view, in the writings of St. Paul. In a well-known passage in the *Epistle to the Romans*, he declared that "when the Gentiles, which have not the law [that is, the Torah of Moses], do by nature the things contained in the law, these, having not the law, are a law unto themselves; which show the work of the law written in their hearts, their conscience also bearing witness, and their thoughts the mean while accusing or else excusing one another" (*Rom.* 2:14–15). The inescapable implication of this is that you do not need revelation to work out at least part of what the Torah has revealed as divine law. In a related passage St. Paul also declared that you do not need revelation to know that God exists. Idolatry is a sin because "the invisible things of him from the creation of the world are clearly seen, being understood by the things that are made, even his eternal power and Godhead" (*Rom.* 1:19–20). Since throughout this *Epistle* St. Paul teaches that the God who is thus known will uphold the law that human beings can work out for themselves, he would no doubt have dismissed as artificial the question "Can human beings work out what the moral law is, and yet remain ignorant that it is divinely sanctioned?" It is easy to reconstruct his reasoning. Nobody who cares to find out what the moral law is will be indifferent to the invisible things of God, even his eternal power and Godhead; and everybody who strenuously seeks the truth about both these matters can find it. The supposed class of those who have found out the truth about morality, but remain ignorant of the existence of God, must therefore be empty.

I hope that I do not fail in deference to a sacred author when I submit that in *The Epistle to the Romans* St. Paul was writing about human beings in the cultures known to him: those of the Hellenic-Roman world, of Egypt, of the old Persian Empire, and, of course, of Israel. With respect to those cultures, he was rightly confident of his ability to confute anybody who rejected the main precepts of the moral part of the Mosaic Torah, or who was not a monotheist (whatever lesser powers he might propitiate). So representative a thinker as Cicero would have granted him everything on these matters that he demanded. But he could not have been similarly confident in an exchange with a Hindu or a Buddhist, because their conceptions of nature, of divinity, and of moral agents so radically differ from his that considerations of the kinds he would have advanced would have had no force with them. For example, cosmological arguments for God's existence are unlikely to persuade those who believe that what they see and touch is an illusion; and reasons why one ought to intervene to protect the innocent from violence will have no force with those who believe that an innocent in this life may have guilt to expiate from an earlier one, and that violence occurs only according to the inexorable operation of a morally just law of Karma. Nor did St. Paul foresee a day when, in a culture descended from a Christian one, people holding essentially what he did about the nature of human beings and the world they inhabit, would believe that the natural universe exists independently, and needs no creator God.

That we have experience of a wider variety of cultures than St. Paul is neither to our intellectual credit nor to his discredit. Nevertheless, had he lived today, he could not confidently have assumed that anybody who can find out for himself the truth about morality can also, without revelation, find out that God created the heavens and the earth. Those who today accept the morality embodied in the Mosaic Torah and endorsed by Christianity do so for essentially the same reasons as St. Paul did; but those who accept the Mosaic teaching that the universe was created by God have to answer objections St. Paul had no way of foreseeing. One can observe this in the writings of Kant: for all their technical sophistication, his metaphysics of ethics is no more than a philosophically accurate version of what he himself called "popular moral philosophy (*populäre sittliche Weltweisheit*)"; but his treatment of the existence of God can only be understood in terms of his revolutionary critique of metaphysics itself. I do not suggest that, even today, reason does not enable us to find the true religion and to reject the false ones; but theistic metaphysics is not what it was. Ethics, I maintain, substantially is.

What I have just now been arguing is complicated enough, and perhaps odd enough, for it to be a good idea to sum up its essentials. First, I accept the Stoic and Pauline doctrine that there is a law governing human conduct with respect to human beings that is sanctioned by God because it is required by practical reason, which human beings share with God. Second, I accept the Stoic and Pauline doctrine that, by the use of the practical reason they share with God, human beings can work out what the law is that their practical reason requires them to obey. Third, I contend that, although for sufficiently obvious cultural reasons neither the Stoics nor St. Paul seriously considered the possibility that anybody might accept the second of these doctrines and deny the first, in our day, that cultural possibility has become an actuality. There are many who share, like the late George Orwell, an attitude of mind which he himself ascribed to "the English common people." While "almost ignoring the spoken doctrines of the Church," they hold on to "the one the Church never formulated, because taking it for granted; namely, that might is not right"; and as for what right is, or indeed what Christianity itself is, they tend to define it in words they have forgotten are scriptural, as loving your neighbor.[7] Anybody who adopts such an attitude is in a position to work out what the Stoics, the Jews, and the Christians recognized as the universal moral law, as a requirement of practical reason. And to their doing so, any appeal to the Jewish or Christian revelation, or to theology, would be irrelevant. *That* is the sense in which I contend that theology, natural or revealed, is irrelevant to ethics.

In contending this, I do not at all wish to deny that, within Christian theology, there are necessary connections between propositions about God's knowledge and will and propositions of ethics. However, even these are sometimes exaggerated. If Christianity is true, then among the truths of theology are that God is, in the scholastic sense, the first necessary being; that God knows whatever is knowable; and that God wills that every rational agent do what practical reason requires. But what these theological truths imply depends on the sense in which God is the first necessary being.

As many philosophers and theologians have understood it, the greatest being Leibniz, the proposition that God is a necessary being means that God is of such a nature that the sentence "God does not exist" can, in principle at least, be shown to be the contradictory of a law of logic—to be analytically false in Frege's sense. If this were the case, and if the other two propositions I have offered as truths of theology really are so, then it will be a *logical* truth that if the proposition p is knowable, then it is true both that *p* and that God knows that *p*. And in that case, it will be a logical truth that for every knowable nontheological truth there is a corresponding theological truth. By a parallel argument, it will also be a logical truth that for every deliverance of practical reason there is a corresponding truth about the divine will.

This, in my opinion, goes too far. I agree with Frege that any logical system according to which a sentence of the form "God does not exist" can be shown to contradict a truth of logic will turn out to be defective as a logical system. The theological principle that God is the first necessary being should be interpreted as metaphysical, not logical: that is, as being equivalent to the proposition that nothing that can happen in the world at any time can bring it about that God does not exist; and that, whereas God's existence depends on nothing else whatever, even the other necessary beings depend for their existence on him. As I understand them, that was how Maimonides and Aquinas understood the principle.[8] So understood, if the three propositions I offered as truths of theology really are so, it will also be true that if a proposition is knowable then God knows it, and that if a precept is required by practical reason then God wills that it be obeyed. But these will not be logical truths: to deny them will be error, but it will be theological error, not logical. Those who accept the truths of theology will not be able to sever their scientific beliefs from their beliefs about what God knows, or their commitments about what practical reason requires from their beliefs about what God wills. Holding one, they will consider themselves theologically constrained to hold the other. But this constraint will be wholly theological.

The law conception of ethics could survive loss of belief in a divine lawgiver, because it was part of both the Stoic and the Christian conception of the divine lawgiver that the divinely sanctioned law was a deliverance of practical reason, intelligible to human beings. The cultural possibility that the traditional Stoic, Jewish, and Christian views of what practical reason requires might persist, while belief in the existence of a divine lawgiver who sanctions those requirements might decay, has been actual for a long time now. The beginning of the process is observable in the philosophical writings of Kant, who saw better than most of his successors what the traditional law conception of ethics was. The later stages of it can be studied in the neo-Kantians and in nonphilosophical writers like Orwell. This cultural separation does not ignore any *logical* connection. Propositions about what practical reason requires are not logically connected with theological propositions about what God wills. However, if Christian theology is true, there are true propositions about God's knowledge and will in virtue of which, given a scientific truth, or a requirement of practical reason, a corresponding truth about what God knows or wills will be derivable. It is a pity that this connection within theology has, among Christians, been so widely mistaken for a cultural, or even for a logical one.

Long before this point, I am afraid, many of you will have formed an objection to what I have been saying that would run something like this. "In all you have been saying, you have presupposed something fundamental to your argument which you have not even begun to prove: namely, that our practical reason does furnish us with a rule of conduct with respect to human beings. Until you have shown that this is so—shown, and not merely cited authorities—your concept of the moral law as a law of practical reason may for all we know be chimerical, a concept of what cannot be. You yourself have urged that St. Paul's declaration that the things that are made suffice to show us that God made them was culturally conditioned; may not his doctrine that all men can work out the moral law for themselves likewise be culturally conditioned, even if, as you have maintained, it holds for a wider range of cultures?"

This objection is perfectly reasonable. So I shall now try to state, as simply as I can, how the traditional Hebrew-Stoic-Christian morality is required by our practical reason. The bare and simple statement that is all I can here attempt will neither say all that ultimately must be said, nor meet objections; but neither of those desirable things could have been done in this lecture, even if I had found a way of dispensing with all that has brought us to this point.

Most philosophers in the Western world, who have set out to construct a system of ethics on purely rational foundations, independently of religion, have taken practical reason to have to do with the attainment of attainable ends. It is exercised, other things being equal, in choosing the means found to be most efficient for attaining the end sought. As for ends, they have taken human beings to be naturally so constituted as to seek happiness, which, despite a certain amount of high-minded chat to the effect that it was better to be Socrates dissatisfied than a pig satisfied, was in practice taken to consist in as much as possible of the things on Freud's immortal list: honor, power, riches, fame, and the love of women. The natural completion of this theory, as Sidgwick saw, is egoistic; but most philosophers who have espoused it have preferred to assert (the grounds they have offered vary) that if each human being naturally desires his or her own happiness, then practical reason requires everybody to try to produce as much happiness as possible, no matter whose. As early as the beginning of the eighteenth century, there were moral theologians who argued that this utilitarian principle is the foundation of Hebrew-Christian ethics, Archdeacon William Paley, in his *Principles of Moral and Political Philosophy* of 1785, being its most notorious advocate.[9]

I mention utilitarianism because you will need to know why I dismiss it. Whether as a theory by which individual human beings are to decide what to do in individual cases, or as one by which societies are to agree upon complete moral codes, it seems to me hopeless. Neither individuals nor societies possess anything approaching the information they would need for the necessary calculations. What we are offered in utilitarian writings on any seriously disputed moral question is a variety of opinions that are strictly correlated with the authors' known prejudices, and rhetoric.

What is much more disturbing, however, is that in almost no writings sympathetic to utilitarianism (some of W. K. Frankena's are the only exceptions I can think of) can you find a statement of what the traditional position of Christian ethics on utilitarianism is, even as one to be repudiated. The entire Hebrew-Christian tradition agrees that happiness (interpreted as including the Freudian ingredients already mentioned) is naturally sought by human beings. But, instead of proceeding at once to construct an egoist or a utilitarian ethical system, moralists in the Hebrew-Christian tradition first insist on asking a plainly reasonable question: "Offhand, we are most of us inclined to agree that, since human beings naturally seek happiness, practical reason requires them to seek it, unless there should turn out to be some overriding reason for forgoing it—well, are most of us right in so agreeing? And if we are, why are we?"

Since the answer to this question that is given within the Hebrew-Christian tradition is neither difficult nor unfamiliar once mentioned, it is surprising that it is so little discussed by philosophers. It is this: practical reason requires human beings to seek what they naturally seek because it regards rational beings—beings whose actions depend on choice made after deliberation—as the only beings for whose sake it is ultimately rational to act. The happiness of a human being matters because human beings matter; if they did not matter, the fact that they naturally seek happiness would not, even for them, be a *reason* for seeking it. Only one major philosopher of the modern era has, to my knowledge, stated this in terms; but, since he is the greatest of all moral philosophers—I mean, of course, Immanuel Kant—perhaps there is no cause for complaint.

The formula in which Kant expressed this fundamental idea is "Rational nature exists as an end in itself [*die vernünftige Natur existiert als Zweck an sich selbst*]."[10] This has been dismissed by the father of modern moral philosophy in the English-speaking world, Henry Sidgwick, with false pedantry, on the ground that "by an end we commonly mean something to be realized, whereas 'humanity' [he should have written 'rational nature'] is, as Kant says, a self-subsistent end."[11] This is pedantic, because, in appealing to what "we commonly mean" by an end, Sidgwick leaves little doubt that he perfectly well understood what Kant meant; and it is false pedantry, because, as the *Oxford English Dictionary* instructs us, the word "end" can mean the object for which something exists, quoting from Golding as long ago as 1587: "And as Man is the end of the World, so is God the end of Man." Who can seriously say that he does not understand that sentence?

It would be foolish, in this lecture, to attempt to do justice to the subtle considerations in virtue of which Kant's fundamental idea can be asserted to be true. Since it is fundamental, it cannot be demonstrated by deriving it from some more ultimate moral truth. Some philosophers whose work I respect have recently tried to show that it is practically absurd to deny it, or something very like it. Thus my colleague Alan Gewirth, in his book *Reason and Morality*, with which, as its readers will have had no difficulty in perceiving, I am in considerable sympathy, has argued that to reject something very like it would contradict a principle about all rational agents which we necessarily accept in setting out to act at all. And Thomas Nagel has argued that something very like it can only be denied on pain of adopting, in practice, a solipsistic attitude to others. Reaching an intelligent verdict on arguments as complex as those of Gewirth and Nagel is delicate; and we cannot yet speak of a verdict of informed opinion on either. But it does not follow that we cannot reach an informed opinion on the foundation of morality.

The curious error that every fundamental principle of a pure science must be immediately self-evident to anybody who can grasp the sense of a sentence expressing it, and who considers the question of its truth impartially, has had a long life since Descartes revealed his new scientific method; but the history of set theory in the past century should have put an end to it. As Aristotle long ago remarked, what is necessarily true in itself is not necessarily self-evident to us. The human intellect resembles an owl's eye: too much light blinds it. Whether an alleged axiom of set theory is true, such as Frege's fifth basic law or Russell's axiom of reducibility, is settled not by asking whether or not it is self-evident, but what difference its acceptance or rejection makes to set theory as a system. And that, I hope I need not add, is not the same as what difference its acceptance or rejection would make to the acceptance or rejection of this or that derivative proposition.

Let me sketch one consideration—it is by no means the only one—which supports the truth of Kant's fundamental idea. This consideration presupposes our capacity to distinguish between those historical codes of conduct which might plausibly be considered as binding on rational beings as such from those which might not. It is intelligible, for example, that the codes of human conduct taught within Islam, or Christianity, or Stoicism, or Judaism, or Confucianism, or Buddhism, or some form of Hinduism, should be so considered; it is not plausible that a code prescribing ritual cannibalism should be, or the Marquis de Sade's doctrine (which he lived by) that human beings are at liberty to do, if they can, what their natures prompt them to do. Of these, every code according to which human beings really are rational animals inhabiting a world of nature (that is, every code according to which human life is not an illusion) both allows that the maximizing of happiness (of which there are different conceptions) is a rational end, and forbids certain means of pursuing that end. To the best of my knowledge, only one kind of fundamental principle will generate a system of this twofold character, namely, one that unconditionally prescribes that beings who are capable of happiness be respected. Such a principle plainly endorses the pursuit of happiness as a rational end; for happiness is, by definition, something which those capable of it naturally pursue, and respect for beings capable of happiness necessarily entails goodwill for their pursuit of what they naturally pursue. But equally, such a principle forbids expressing that goodwill by means, if there be such, which violate the respect from which that goodwill derives. Now, if it be conceded that beings capable of happiness are to be unconditionally respected, what beings are of that kind? I do not see, in the end, how the conclusion can be escaped that only rational beings fill the bill. Brute animals are perhaps capable of happiness in a secondary sense; but happiness in the full sense is impossible without awareness of oneself and one's world to a degree that requires rationality. On the other hand, nonhuman rational beings, whether terrestrial (perhaps whales or dolphins—though I do not believe it) or nonterrestrial (there do not appear to be any Martians or Venusians, but there are other planets in the galaxy) would seem to be as fully capable of happiness as human beings.

I do not pretend that this is a proof. Nor are Russell's arguments for the axiom of reducibility proofs. But, unless it be denied that what the high civilizations of the past have recognized as rationally binding codes of conduct even approximate to being so, some explanation of the resemblance between the structures of those codes is called for. Such an explanation is possible according to Kant's fundamental idea. I do not think it is on any other idea that is not more or less equivalent to his.

Yet Kant's doctrine that rational nature is an end in itself cannot be elicited from the various codes in question by what used to be called intuitive induction. It explains why those codes resemble one another in structure, but it cannot be reconciled with any of them in detail. Now is that not exactly what we want? Even those who hold, as I do, that the moral systems of Judaism and Christianity are sound in principle, do not for the most part imagine either that now those principles are in all respects correctly applied to specific questions, or that they have been at any time in the past. We may not be better men and women than our great-grandparents; but our opinions on the legitimate treatment of Indians, Africans, and Chinese, on the legitimate exercise of parental authority, and on the nature of cruelty, will more probably than not be nearer the truth than theirs. Yet who would dream of endorsing all of the views prevalent at any given time in human history on decent relations between women and men? Here I contend that rational criticism of the moral opinions actually held at any time can be made sense of only in terms of Kant's doctrine, or of one more or less equivalent to it.

Let me sum up what I am contending for: (i) what we need, as a foundation for morals, is a fundamental principle that *both* makes sense of the *structure* of all high moralities in which human life is not dismissed as an illusion, *and* makes sense of the kinds of criticism to which particular systems having that structure are held to be susceptible, and (ii) the Kantian principle of respect for rational nature has this character. I further contend that Christianity (and before it Judaism) does not claim that that principle can be known only by revelation, but that it can be known in its own right to be a fundamental principle of practical reason. God, as the author of our being, and of reason, is the author of our discovery of the moral law in ourselves, and God has independently declared that law <in revelation.> But these facts are irrelevant to me, in the sense that <my commitments about what practical reason requires are logically (though not theologically) independent of my beliefs about the existence of a creator God and what He wills.>

II. The Relevance of Theology to Ethics

Let me begin by repeating the main theme of my first lecture. It was this. Ethics, considered as the study of what a good life is for a rational being, and in particular for a human being, has many parts. One of them is morality, which may be simply described as that part of ethics that has to do with fundamental human decency.

What fundamental human decency is can be determined rationally, by considering what human beings are, and what is the general nature of the universe they inhabit. Philosophically speaking, it is not necessary to mention any theological considerations at all in working out a theory of morality.[12] This calls for elaboration. In what I said about the difference between the philosophical status of St. Paul's remarks about our knowledge of God and that of his remarks about morality, I hoped to have given reasons, although sketchy reasons, for two propositions:

> (1) that while the grounds on which St. Paul presumably asserted that human beings without revelation can ascertain what the moral law is are substantially the grounds on which we today—and Kant and various others before us—assert it, the grounds on which he asserted that human beings without revelation can assert that God exists were grounds that are not acceptable outside the cultures he knew—*even though some of those cultures accepted the propositions about man and the world that are presupposed in his ethics* (e.g., the Chinese, and some forms of the post-Christian western worldview), <and>
> (2) I do not think that the existence of God can be philosophically or metaphysically established. It can be shown to be *possible*; but it cannot be proved to be true. For my own part, I should not have believed it at all, except for believing that God has revealed himself in the world—especially to Moses, and finally in Jesus. For this reason, I do not think that morality is helped out by philosophical theism. The facts of metaphysics that are pertinent to it have to do with man and the natural universe.

Of course, those who accept some form of theism according to which God has revealed a code of conduct binding on mankind must hold that code of conduct to be compatible with a rationally determined moral system, and will presumably consider that compatibility, if they find it to obtain, to confirm both their moral philosophy and their revealed theology. If they find it not to obtain in any respect, then both their moral philosophy and their revealed theology will be to some extent in question until that incompatibility is removed. To give an up-to-date example: any Roman Catholic moralist who has convinced himself, as a majority reputedly have, that certain forms of contraception are morally licit, but who also holds that the teachings of the magisterium of the Roman Catholic Church are to be accepted, must change his mind either on the moral issue or on the extent of the authority of the magisterium. Until he does, both must, for him, be under suspicion.

It is with respect to morality that I have maintained that theology is irrelevant to ethics. Not, of course, in the sense that they have nothing to do with one another: that they can, in practice, come into conflict shows that. But in the sense that, when a moral philosopher goes about his business of rationally ascertaining what the moral law is—what fundamental human decency is—he is not to wander into the province of theology in search of premises.

If theology is irrelevant to ethics in this crucial respect, it is relevant in many others. What are they?

I have already mentioned one. Genuine truths of moral philosophy, as distinct from what are believed to be such, must be compatible with genuine truths of divine revelation, as distinct from what are believed to be such. If we find that our beliefs about morality and our beliefs about divine revelation are incompatible, one or the other must give—and perhaps both. To the philosophically minded, this is apt to seem irrational, and to the theologically minded impious; but it is neither. I take it that no moral philosopher considers all his conclusions about what is morally permissible to be beyond doubt. Well, then, a theistic moral philosopher does not abandon reason when a conflict between some moral conclusion of his and a teaching of his Church makes him wonder whether he has made a philosophical mistake. On the other side, I take it that few believers imagine that all their beliefs about revealed truth really are so. I profess to believe all that the Church teaches, but I know that those who know more about what the Church teaches than I honestly differ about various points in what it teaches. Am I then impious in wondering whether a belief of mine about what the Church teaches is false, when I find it to contradict a moral conclusion about which I am reasonably confident?

To take a historical case: the moral impermissibility of persecuting anybody for professing his honest beliefs, or for worshiping in accordance with them, when that worship does not itself consist in committing crimes upon others (e.g., human sacrifice, ritual murder, temple prostitution, and the like), is philosophically well established. Yet virtually every branch of the Christian Church between 400 A.D. and 1600 A.D. has regarded the persecution of unbelievers particularly obnoxious to it (e.g., atheists, Jews, unitarians) as a religious duty. Since the second Vatican Council (for the Roman Catholic Church the official pronouncement was as late as that) every branch of the Christian Church now teaches that religious persecution is not a religious duty, and is to be condemned as immoral. A moral teaching once confined to a minority of unbelievers is thus now confessed by believers to have been right, and what believers taught as revealed to have been wrong. It is true that this change of heart is also a return to the Church's primitive teaching—but that strengthens the point that matters: even if revelation cannot err, beliefs about it can.

There is a second, and related, respect in which theology is relevant not merely to ethics but to morality. It was an important part of St. Paul's teaching, which I accept as far as I understand it. I mention it here because I think it has given rise to some unfortunate misunderstandings.

In his *Epistle to the Romans* St. Paul asserted that all men break the moral law they acknowledge, because the principle of the moral law is spiritual, whereas the principle of the actions of natural man is what he called "flesh." Thus he went on to say (I use Knox's lucid version here): "To live the life of nature is to think the thoughts of nature; to live the life of the spirit is to think the thoughts of the spirit; and natural wisdom brings only death, whereas the wisdom of the spirit brings life and peace" (8:5–6).

I suppose this to correspond to something in the life of every believer, although I do not consider myself a proper person to expound what it is. For my purpose it is more important to say what it is not. St. Paul does say that a new principle is at work in the life of a believer, and that it is only by that principle that the life of anybody can satisfy the demands of the moral law—not to speak of other and higher demands. But in saying that only by the spirit can the demands of the law be satisfied, he does not imply that everybody in whom there is a rudimentary life of the spirit will satisfy them. Putting it as coarsely as I can, he is saying that, because of the life of the spirit in them, believers will do better with regard to the demands of the moral law than they would otherwise do. He is not saying that they will satisfy those demands. And he emphatically is not saying that believers as a class will behave better, morally speaking, than unbelievers.

In a biography of the novelist Evelyn Waugh, Christopher Sykes records that, when asked why his religious faith had to all appearances made so little difference to a character he himself acknowledged to be appalling (in fact, as far as I can tell, it was better than most), Waugh replied that, without his faith, he would have been scarcely human.

With regard to morality, as distinct from ethics as a whole, I have been arguing that the relevance of theology is limited. In principle, the content of morality can be ascertained without recourse to theology at all. However, it is true that our philosophical conclusions about morality can be confirmed or disconfirmed by our theological conclusions about permissible ways of life—but the converse is also true. And, finally, if Christianity is true, human beings can satisfy the demands of morality only by an inner life of the spirit that is a gift of grace; but that inner life, as it is found in most Christians, is no guarantee of moral virtue. The ordinary Christian is not necessarily the moral superior of his unbelieving neighbors.

All this has, I hope, brought us to a point at which my central thesis may seem at least discussable. That thesis is *theology is relevant to ethics not principally with regard to morality, but with regard to the question of what life is for.* In both the Jewish and the Christian religious traditions, and in what I have maintained is the major philosophical tradition, morality is a matter of respect for rational beings as subsisting ends, not as ends to be produced. But morality, so understood, is not a complete way of life. If we should imagine somebody to whom it was granted to observe in spirit and letter the entire Jewish-Christian moral code—all its precepts of justice, benevolence, and self-cultivation—we should not have imagined what his conception of happiness was or what he chose to live for. To mention only an Aristotelian question: from the fact that a human being is just, benevolent, and develops his or her capacities harmoniously, it follows neither that he leads a contemplative life nor that he leads a politically active one, yet contemplation and political action are Aristotle's two principal candidates for the correct answer to the question "what is life for?"

The answer of traditional Christianity to this question bypasses all those considered by Aristotle. The most succinct statement of it I know is from what the *Oxford English Dictionary* refers to as the *Shorter Catechism* of 1648, presumably a Calvinist work. It runs "Man's chief end is to glorify God and to enjoy him forever." As the epistles of the New Testament show, "forever" did not, in the early Church, refer to a state attainable in this life. In this life, as St. Paul remarked in his first *Epistle to the Corinthians*, we see in a glass darkly; after death, we shall see face to face: we "shall . . . know even as also [we are] known" (13:12).

In the past century and a half numerous biblical scholars and theologians have labored to show that such statements as St. Paul's (not to speak of their counterparts in promises attributed to Jesus in the Gospels) had a sense in the life of the early Church that was expressed, in the manner of the period, mythologically; and that our task is to recover that sense for our own time by demythologizing the scriptural statements and expressing them in the nonmythological language of today. Obviously, such major issues of biblical scholarship cannot be settled in a few brief remarks, even had I the requisite scholarly credentials.

However, if I am to say what I think about the bearing of revealed theology on ethics, I cannot avoid saying what I take the scriptural basis of revealed theology to be. Modern textual scholarship as applied to the New Testament texts has the same credentials as applied to any other texts of the same period. And here, from a Christian point of view, the results are reassuring. Most, if not all, of the New Testament was composed between about twenty and eighty years after Jesus' death; and the writings that make it up were received in the second century as embodying apostolic teaching. If we approach these writings with the conviction that some form of naturalism or materialism is true, then we shall be compelled to treat them pretty much as a first-century Epicurean would have: as superstitious mythology. The efforts of the nineteenth and twentieth centuries to provide a demythologized version of the apostolic faith seem to me misdirected. My reason is not that, given the naturalist assumptions, the effort was not intellectually respectable, but that, both from an ethical and from a religious point of view, its results have been worthless. Take the Christian gospel according to any demythologizer you like—it would be invidious to single one out—and ask two questions about it: first, is there anything distinctively Christian about it, that cannot be more directly obtained from secular philosophers and moralists? And second, if there is, is it acceptable? To the best of my knowledge, in all cases, the answer to one question or the other is "No."

The late C. S. Lewis put the point very well, when he remarked that an ordinary uneducated man simply will not recognize as Christianity "a theology which denies the historicity of nearly everything in the Gospels to which Christian life and affections and thought have been fastened for nearly two millennia." When offered such a theology, "if he holds to what he calls Christianity he will leave a Church in which it is no longer taught and look for one where it is"; and if he agrees with what he is offered, "he will no longer call himself a Christian and no longer come to church." And Lewis unkindly adds, "in his crude, coarse way, he would respect [the preacher who offers him a 'demythologized' theology] much more if [he] did the same."[13] Of course Professor Lewis, who was not a biblical scholar, but was a medievalist and a philosopher, shared the opinions he ascribed to ordinary uneducated men. I must confess that I do too. But I hope you have noticed that Lewis has, in his vivid characterization, enforced the consideration implicit in my questions. Nobody has any difficulty in saying what traditional Christianity held about what life is for, or what was distinctive about it. Well, when you have elicited a plain statement of the answer demythologized Christianity offers, ask yourself what accepting such an answer has to do with anything recognizable as religious practice.

If the philosophical assumption which all demythologizing scholarship brings to its interpretations of the New Testament is not made—the assumption that the natural universe is all there is, and that Christianity is to be understood as a phenomenon occurring in the natural universe—then the way is open for accepting the teachings of the Gospels and Epistles as they stand: that *what life is for* is something that *begins here and now*, but will not be attained until, after death or at the return of Christ, we have been radically transformed, both in soul and in body.

It is difficult to talk about this, for several reasons. First, we know *almost nothing* about what we are promised: a few descriptions of the resurrected Jesus, a few mysterious utterances by St. Paul, and the obviously symbolic visions of the Apocalypse. Saying a lot about what we know little is as unprofitable as it is presumptuous. Second, ethics, as it applies to our conduct, applies to our conduct here and now. No doubt there will be *human action* after the general resurrection, but we know even less about it than we do about *the state* of the resurrected. It follows that *the nature of our life* when we (if we ever) live the life we were created to live, cannot be the subject of serious philosophical conclusions. We know it will be *better than anything we can ask or think*, that is about all. Third, talking about it in most circumstances is scandalous— that is, it is apt to impair people's faith, not to confirm it. (I remember as a teenager, when at a family gathering an uncle of mine, who was a Baptist of some eminence, said something in conversation which showed that he really took seriously Jesus' promise to return, a sort of freezing silence fell on the adults present—all professing Christians. To talk as I am talking now at most philosophical or scientific gatherings—and many theological ones, incidentally—is regarded as bordering on insanity, if not across the border. This despite cheerful readiness to introduce into discussions of abortion speculations about what we should say about the rights of offspring if human mothers began giving birth to cats.)

Although difficult, we cannot avoid investigating *what Christian teaching that the end of man is a transformed life of knowledge and enjoyment of God implies for ethics in this life*, which we know all too well.

The first thing to be said is that *this transformed life begins in this world*, in the *life of membership in the Christian Church*, the Church described in the parable of the vine, and also in the parables of the sheep and goats, of the tares and wheat. Unfortunately, something has gone wrong even here: Christians differ about what the Church, the mystical body of Christ, is; and there are now almost *no* Christians who do not think that all parts of the body were to blame—although perhaps not in the same degree.

This leaves us with the question: *What is the relation of life in the body of Christ* (however damaged and diseased our particular part of that great vine may be) *to the moral life?* I venture to offer the following theses:

(1) It is a life to which a new and overriding *motive* has been added: the motive of expressing our love of God, and our enjoyment of him, so far as we have become capable of it.

(2) This motive does not destroy in us the motivation—let us call it the Aristotelian motivation—of earthly human happiness, but it overrides it (whether or not we always act on it).

(3) To the extent that it takes possession of us, this new motive *makes it unnecessary* for us to consider *either* natural motives as such *or* the moral law as such (i.e., the constraints of human decency on our pursuit of natural happiness). Somebody who is filled with the love of God will behave, for that alone, as St. Paul described a believer <possessed of charity behaving>[14] in *1 Cor.* 13. And I believe that he will enjoy, in season, the good things of natural life, as Jesus is described to have done while he was on earth.

(4) *To the extent*—but of whom has the love of God taken possession *to that extent?* I do not say of none. But *I do observe that the greatest saints*—such as those Apostles the sight of whom in heaven I believe Dante describes as like seeing mountains—in their lives tend to go out of their way to deny that it is true of them. And when not—well, we can try to improve. But what does that imply?

(5) (i) Living the life of the Church, by the means made available in it.

   (ii) *Obeying the moral law*, for which the life of the Church supplies grace.

   (iii) <<Seeking properly>> for natural happiness. The life of the Church will help us to that.

   (iv) Standing ready to give up (iii). <However,> we are even authorized by our Lord to pray that we never be put to the test.

What is the relevance of Christian theology to ethics? The answer is contained in <the question>: What is the difference between an ethical life, as philosophy unenlightened by revelation would describe it, and a Christian life? <An> ethical life <unenlightened by revelation is> a decent life (we must not cheat anybody, <etc.>), with <good> luck a happy one, with bad luck, not a happy one, and even the lucky have to live with the undeserved unhappiness of many (it is a lot easier than living with your own).

> None can usurp this height…
> But those to whom the miseries of the world
> Are misery, and will not let them rest.[15]

A Christian life, <on the other hand, is not only> a decent life, <but also> one in which the reasons for living are not in the world at all.

Notes

1. G. E. M. Anscombe, "Modern Moral Philosophy," in J. J. Thomson and Gerald Dworkin, eds., *Ethics* (New York: Harper and Row, 1968), pp. 192–93. (This paper originally appeared in *Philosophy* 33 [1958]: 1–19.)

2. Ibid., p. 202.

3. Ibid.; cf. pp. 187–88—"The concept of legislation requires superior power in the legislator."

4. Ibid., p. 204.

5. Christopher Dawson, *Progress and Religion, An Historical Enquiry* (New York: Sheed and Ward, 1938), pp. 243–44.

6. Anscombe, "Modern Moral Philosophy," p. 188.

7. George Orwell, *Collected Essays, Journalism, and Letters*, ed. Sonia Orwell and Ian Angus (London: Secker and Warburg, 1968), vol. 3, p. 7 (from *The English People*, London, 1947).

8. See Maimonides, *The Guide of the Perplexed*, trans. S. Pines (Chicago: University of Chicago Press, 1963), pp. 247–49 (II, 1, 8a–9a); Aquinas, *Summa contra gentiles* I, 15, 5; cf. *Summa theologiae* I, 10, 2–3.

9. For a summary of Paley's position, see Sidgwick, *Outlines of the History of Ethics*, 6th ed. (Boston: Beacon Press, 1931), pp. 238–39.

10. Kant, *Grundlegung zur Metaphysik der Sitten* 2d ed. (Riga: J. F. Hartnoch, 1786), p. 66 (Akad. ed., p. 429) [*Groundwork of the Metaphysic of Morals*, trans. H. J. Paton (New York: Harper and Row, 1964; originally published in 1948 by the Hutchinson University Library under the title *The Moral Law, or Kant's Groundwork of the Metaphysic of Morals*), p. 96.]

11. Henry Sidgwick, *The Methods of Ethics*, 7th ed. (London: Macmillan, 1907), p. 300.

12. The remainder of this paragraph represents a response to an objection made by Professor Richard Purtill that the preceding lecture had "waffled" by failing to mark the distinction between revealed theology and philosophical or metaphysical theology, thereby permitting the reply that, even if what was said about the irrelevance of revealed theology to ethics were true, it would not follow that it applied to philosophical or metaphysical theology, a consequence granted by Donagan. Ed.

13. C. S. Lewis, *Christian Reflections*, ed. Walter Hooper (Grand Rapids, Michigan: William B. Eerdmans Publishing Company, 1967), p. 153. The essay quoted, "Modern Theology and Biblical Criticism," was delivered as a lecture at Westcott House, Cambridge, in 1959. Ed.

14. The word or words immediately before "believer" are indecipherable in the manuscript. Ed.

15. John Keats, "The Fall of Hyperion," Canto I, lines 147–49. Ed.

Index